Modern Islamic Thinking and Activism
Dynamics in the West and in the Middle East

Modern Islamic Thinking and Activism
Dynamics in the West and in the Middle East

CURRENT ISSUES IN ISLAM

Editorial board

Baderin, Mashood, *SOAS, University of London*
Fadil, Nadia, *KU Leuven*
Goddeeris, Idesbald, *KU Leuven*
Hashemi, Nader, *University of Denver*
Leman, Johan, *GCIS, emeritus, KU Leuven*
Nicaise, Ides, *KU Leuven*
Pang, Chinglin, *University of Antwerp, and KU Leuven*
Platti, Emilio, *emeritus, KU Leuven*
Schallenbergh, Gino, *KU Leuven*
Tayob, Abdulkader, *University of Cape Town*
Stallaert, Christiane, *University of Antwerp, and KU Leuven*
Toğuşlu, Erkan, *GCIS, KU Leuven*
Zemni, Sami, *Universiteit Gent*

Modern Islamic Thinking and Activism

Dynamics in the West and in the Middle East

Edited by

Erkan Toğuşlu & Johan Leman

LEUVEN UNIVERSITY PRESS

ISBN 978 90 5867 999 4
D / 2014 / 1869 / 28
NUR: 741/717

Layout: CO2 Premedia
Cover design: Paul Verrept

Table of Contents

Part III: Contemporary Islamic Social Activism

Conclusion

Introduction

CHAPTER I

Contemporary Islamic Activism and Muslims

Erkan Toğuşlu and Johan Leman

In this book we invited some authors to look at the basic issues that Islam faces today, touching political, cultural, spiritual and economic dimensions in which Muslims are involved to develop their understanding and strategies in different geographical and national contexts. We asked them to do that by focusing on some very precise situations. Such an approach cannot be a complete one. We are very conscious that such analysis has its weaknesses. But it surely also has some very strong points. It avoids analyses that are so general that they become quite abstract and can never be found in the reality of social and cultural praxis at grassroots level.

So, the chapters in the book focus on some areas of applied Islamic principles and understandings including welfare organizations, educational institutions, political implications in civil society and spiritual authority. Confronted with modernity and a Western form of secularism, Muslim socio-religious activism develops a Muslim-self at various dimensions and intersection points. The exploration of Muslim implications in these socio-economic and political domains enables us to analyse the new salient identity of Muslims.

The recent debates on current issues in Islam emphasize the question of the Muslim adaptability-compatibility in a global civil society and how to contribute to it. In this regard, the different aspects of Muslims living in Britain, France, Egypt, Turkey and so on show how they engage with modernity and pluralism. The chapters offer an analysis of a contextualized and localized Islam in the modern world while having different ideological, identical positions. The chapters look at various types of Islamic groups and identities in different frames. Inside the confines of one volume we will try to be attentive to a variety of interpretations in the Islamic tradition, i.e. also looking at Sunni and some new Sufi dynamics. The multidisciplinary view of certain Islamic figures, organizations, ideologies and thinking provides some elements to figure out Islamic socio-religious activities.

The chapters investigate the characteristics and dynamics of Islamic activism in politics, social work and intellectual thought. They pose the question whether the change and transformation of this activism offers new points for the development of civil society and democratization at the social-political and intellectual level. It also analyses how this Islamic-Muslim activism can be comprehended in terms of democracy, modernity, and also in social work.

A loose definition of Islamic activism

The term Islamic activism refers to Muslim engagement in different socio-economic problems, not just in terms of politics. Thus, Islam is not taken as a political factor. This indicates the endeavours of ordinary Muslims who are inspired in their activities by an Islamic framework (Fuller 2004). According to Fuller, political Islam conveys a body of ideas that emphasizes certain political thinking derived from religion to suggest how society should be ordered (Fuller 2004: xi). This framework includes discourses, public actors, organizations, symbols, idioms and rhetoric as well as religion (Eickelman and Piscatori 1996). Islamization refers to the organization of politics, state, law and society according to Islamic principles and religious rules. Researchers use this concept widely to analyse the political activism of Muslims (Roy 2004 and 1994; Kepel 2003). Salwa Ismail defines the terms Islamism and islamization (or re-islamization) interchangeably to signify a process of changing the nature of the social sphere through religious symbols, signs and actions. In her formula, all ordinary Muslims who believe and follow Islamic practices are actors in the islamization project. She gives the examples of Muslim entrepreneurs and veiled female Muslims who promote the principles and values of Islam. This personal engagement is ascribed in the identity politics of Islamism (Ismail 2004: 616). This sort of misleading account that Islamism is everywhere is often countered by the complex analysis of religious activities such as Muslim agency and particular practices of piety (Mahmood 2005; Deeb 2006), possible ways to modernity (Göle, 2000; 2005) and the emergence of a pious bourgeoisie (Haenni 2005; White 2012; Yankaya 2013). The new public-private practices (Göle 2006; 2002; Deeb 2006) cannot be purely reformulated in the Islamist lens and picture. However in the following pages Ismail notes that the new forms of religious sociability cannot be reduced to the label of post-Islamism, new age Islamism. For her, these labels obscure the differentiated situations and complex realities of Muslim identifications in relation to globalization and post-modernity (Ismail 2004: 626). However, Islamic activism in this formula is ambiguous, since this meaning can be applied to every ordinary Muslim. Thus the view that Islam as politic is the blueprint of Muslims does not encompass what is going on at the social level to understand the aspiration of young Muslims who do not refer to Islamist utopia or Islamist politics (Haenni 2005; Nasr 2009). Islamic activism is manifested as an orientation of praxis through different orientations that emphasize several sources of Islam. Then the question is whether Islamic movements and groups maintain their Islamist ideology or over time change their politics, their understanding of society. Many studies treat Islamic activism in terms of religious revivalism and a manifestation of loyalty-authority; however this phenomenon can be analysed in different categories of social sciences such as social movement theories (Bayat 2010). How can a large population be defined in terms of social-religious activism referring to different understandings of Islam, from a very conservative, essentialist one to the very tolerant, modern and pragmatic? What is the actual emergence among Muslim activists and intellectuals in politics, charity and education? What constructive role does religion play in stabilizing and strengthening civil society today?

In the aftermath of the Arab revolutions, more complex modern forces of demographic shifts, economic disparity, cultural transformation, political turmoil and social crises should be considered as the key factors to explain the socio-religious activism happening among Muslims. The disruptive change in and transformation of societies where Muslims live describes a malaise of modernity (Taylor 1998). The social transformation, economic crises and experience with modernity deepen and extend this malaise in various ways from ambiguity to strengthening a revival of religion and religious particularities in public spheres as a result of this malaise. In a secular worldview, Islam is always questioned and interrogated, as it can be adjustable and flexible to change. In other words, individualization, pluralism, democracy, human rights and gender issues are the main challenges that Muslims encounter in the western world (Bayat 2007; Bilgin 2011; Hashemi 2009). How can Islam take care of and respond all these issues? Islamic actors witness these challenges as a replacement of old identities and practices with new ones and patterns. This replacement has sometimes happened in a brutal way, creating violence, rupture and failure. To understand these changes and ruptures, this book looks at different aspects of Muslims' presence and experience with this malaise of modernity which is manifested in similar debates on secularism, democracy, human rights, and social cohesion.

Islamic social movements working in different areas and emphasizing new cultural-religious identities contribute to the extending of public space and civil society. They do not want to turn from it (Yavuz 2003: 21), but the civic side is embedded in the socio-religious activities to actualize their politics, strategies and practices. Islamic activity is conceptualized as "signifying agents of engaged in the social construction of meaning" (Wictorowicz 2004:15). It creates collective action through Islamic frameworks and notions. The social mobilization of Muslims via different Muslim thinkers, organizations and movements brings with it the idea that multiple modernities (Eisenstadt 2000; Göle 2000) are emerging from this social construction of meaning. Muslim scholars have influenced this emergence of Islamic modernity and Muslim politics as explained by Eickelman and Piscatori (1996).

Islamic scholars: making Islamic reasoning in secular coding

Muslim thinkers and activists cannot be reduced to a single pattern of Islamic behaviour or religious orientation, simply using Islamist-Islamic intellectuals and *ulema* (Abu-Rabi 1996; Zaman 2002). Islamic scholars vary politically and ideologically (Mandaville 2007). The first part of this volume looks at these particular differences and variations to describe autonomous labels of Islamic scholars, often described using the references taken from Islam. Islamic scholars can be understood as part of the religious-cultural contexts; in each their respective roles and influences are diverse. Thus, among Islamic scholars, intellectuals and thinkers, they have actively committed to a modern, secular and democratic debate. They support discursive elaboration of democratic Islamic thought. Toğuşlu's and Limpens' chapters examine how Islamic scholars use Islamic reasoning to deal with contemporary issues. Some notions such as *maslaha* and *nasiha* have gained importance for understanding the circulation of Islamic idioms and narratives which has become a tool implying the role of Muslim scholars in the new socio-political debates. Toğuşlu reflects on how

Gülen, Ramadan and Qaradawi apply the classical concepts and how they consider these concepts in the articulation of Islamic reasoning referring to secular language. These conceptions formulated by these contemporary scholars shape Islamic knowledge faced with secular knowledge. Making Islamic reasoning in secular coding fits well to describe and categorize Muslim scholars' engagement with modernity and pluralism (Esack 1997; Hefner 2005). This approach manifests the rational-comprehensive engagement of Muslim scholars and places them at the centre of Islamic thinking. Limpens' formulation in this volume on conservative-liberal and reformist Muslim thinkers analyses Ramadan's and an-Naim's influence on Muslim women living in Brussels. The emancipation of women constitutes one of the emblematic issues in Europe to categorize Muslim thinkers. The case of LGBT has become more interesting to discuss how young female Muslims adopt the liberation discourses of Ramadan and an-Naim in a small-scale area in Brussels.

It is interesting to see that these scholars do not develop an opposition to "Western ideas". Instead, we argue that many elements come into play, such as citizenship, entrepreneurial sensitiveness and secularism issues, when Islamic scholars discuss a question. The fear of Muslim terrorism has spread and been manipulated in public opinion (for an example of the effects of it see Leman 2012). It thus becomes a common comment and argument that assumes Islamic scholars nourish these sectarian, fundamentalist religious values and strategies of militant Muslims that foster anti-modernism, secularism and the West. They have been suspected of harbouring anti-modernism, misogyny and hatred messages. In this vein, Metcalf underlines how Deobandi *madrasas* and *ulama* are accused of always being part of terrorism (Metcalf 2002). This sentiment against Muslims is widely present in all strata in Europe among different ideological positions. Parekh highlights the European liberal anxiety about Muslims concerning their non-integration and their particular situation (Parekh 2006). To tackle this anxiety, Muslim scholars' role has primarily become important in suggesting and discussing new possibilities and ways to construct a meaningful dialogue and understanding between Muslims and non-Muslims. In this context of misunderstanding and suspicion, the new interpretations of Islamic knowledge and Islamic training have gained importance. A reasonable and workable Islam in Europe depends, on this argument, on the intellectual side of Islam, and training of imams who can put into practice a change in Muslim theology adaptable to European values such as democracy, human rights, gender equality and secularism (Toğuşlu 2012).

The Sufi path is another important element in this workable Islam in Europe. Along with the first two chapters, islamologist Eric Geoffroy draws on a reading of Sufi thought and its influence in Europe, especially among French contexts and converts. His analysis seeks to show how Sufi terminology spread out in Europe and attracted non-Muslims. The notion of spiritual taste (*zhahwk*) is recognized as a part of this contribution to the spread of Islamic knowledge (Geoffroy 2010). For Geoffroy, young Muslims in Europe look forward to more open and non-strict use of Islamic knowledge and practices. The Sufi terminology, idioms and symbols endorse this demand in some circles by contributing to whole debates and current issues in Islam. It is explained that Sufis deal with the internal side (*batin*) of Islam that is approved by many Islamic scholars (Hodgson 1974: 219).

Indeed, Sufi and traditional brotherhood networks are effective in the dissemination of Islamic knowledge as practice. They help people to preserve continuity with the corpus of socio-religious practices (Eickelman and Piscatori 1996). Many scholars examine the influence of Sufism as an alternative to political Islam in the dissemination of knowledge (van Bruinessen 2009).

Although some Islamic scholars are politically active and engage in politics in radical ways, the chapters in this book look at traditional, modern and reformist Muslim thinkers. Their primary focus is on religious renovation in secular and democratic contexts. Their message influences distinctive political thought, not as a political party as they have not directly participated in politics. In fact, these scholars have never played a leadership role among Muslim political activists. In the next part, Yılmaz, Meijer and Platti call attention to the great variations in state-religion-society relations that constitute the multiple ways of practising the politics of Muslims.

Islamic activities as Muslim politics

Debates on Islamic activism have been focused on politics since the 1960s and since the Arab revolutions. Islamic activism is directly linked to the political area and power relations (Eickelman and Piscatori 1996). In the so-called Muslim world, the political participation of Islamic movements has been considered as the end of democracy, because in line with this argument, when they arrive and control power, they end democratic secular regimes. In the immediate aftermath of the fall of the Berlin Wall and the Twin Towers, this perception is widely accepted and circulated in academia. Islam is considered as an emerging threat to the liberal democracies. The al-Qaeda attacks on 11 September 2001 resurfaced this debate.

Many Islamist activists think sovereignty is not divisible and reject the idea of democracy and human rights, because it is a contradiction of God's sovereignty. According to these political islamists, an Islamic society based on sharia rules and a theocratic regime can work with the rules of God and not humans' values and norms. The objective of the political Islamist is the creation of an Islamic state in which politics serves only the sharia rules.

However, Islamic activists do not form a homogenic and monolithic structure. An apparent question is to place Muslim politics into the wider multiple and shifting contexts, in this sense, Muslim politics is not unique (Eickelman and Piscatori 1996: 20-21). The various varieties of political Islamists now use different discourses and implement several politics from democracy to fundamentalism. They participate in democratic rules in the existing political system. They now see democracy as a non-vulnerable element of the political regime, which can be a basis of the Islamic system and Islamic values (Brusse and Schoonenboom 2006). They do not oppose human rights and do not consider them as a product of western models. They try to connect Islamic ideas with democracy and human rights to reconcile secular thought with Islamic thinking by formulating political programmes, joining in coalitions, producing policies on different socio-economic problems and issues (Yilmaz 2012). All of these processes push Islamist activists to re-think in secular worlds, because they are facing secular problems. They are now fighting against fundamentalist, not secular ideologies. The younger generation, often nourished by Islamist ideas and political thinking, coming from the grassroots level, have become more familiar with human rights, democracy, and liberty issues through participation in socio-economic life. They develop ideas against political oppression, social injustice, fraud and corruption. They do not use the same dialectic, Islamic utopia, top-down organizational model (Haenni 2005), do not admire apologetic, non-reasonable Islamist discourses. In this vein, the examples of the Muslim Brotherhood in Egypt and the Justice and Development Party (Adalet ve Kalkınma Partisi) in Turkey are very keen to observe this change and evolution in a broader sense.

The young generation in the party and movement want to transform the Brotherhood into a political party. In this process, they are looking at the Turkish model, the AK Party experience. They want to separate the movement from the political party (Meijer in this volume). However, for Meijer, the biggest problem of the Brotherhood is its insufficient embracing of politics, which results in a duality between acceptance and rejection of a parliamentary democracy and a constitution. The social transformation of and cultural change in Arab society contributed to the change in the Brotherhood. It had become embarrassed by the Islamist populist rhetoric of "Islam is the solution". Indeed, the paradoxes still emerge in the politics of the Brotherhood and between different streams in the party. Initially, following the example of the Muslim Brotherhood in Egypt, Islamist movements abandoned their initial radical standpoint against democratic rules. They adopted pragmatic solutions which drove these groups towards accepting the constitutional system. One of these examples is the shift seen in the Muslim Brotherhood in Egypt. Under the Mubarak regime, they ceased to use violence and renounced armed Islamic struggle saying that using violence delegitimized their Islamic cause and principles. They created the Freedom and Justice Party to compete in the political debates and elections. Mohammed Morsi was elected in the summer 2012 from this party. This engagement and creation of a political party during the last elections can be understood as a sign of the acceptance of secular rules of the political process. This decision can be regarded as a strategic adaptation and acceptance of the Brotherhood's leaders; at the same time the old Islamic elites have been pressed to distance themselves from fundamentalist political ideology. This enables them to open up to the general public and to gain the support of Egyptians. This pragmatic turn resulted in a discursive and epistemological change appearing in theological discussions on the sovereignty of God, engaging in politics, democracy and pluralism. Despite this evolution and moderation, some members kept their political Islamist identity forging dichotomist ideological positions on Islam, democracy and liberalism. The development of new notions embracing liberalism in terms of economy opens up new spaces for new actors, new elites and a young generation frustrated with Islamic slogans and Islamic utopia. The other aim is to encourage economic liberalization that provides new opportunities for the middle class to overcome the authoritarian and corrupted elite's control over the political and economic system (Perthes 2004).

This is why in a country such as Egypt, a sharp contrast remains between old elites and new elites who negotiate between them the possible future scenarios on democracy and Islam, pluralism. There are still major problems in representing all parts of society, including minority groups and non-Muslims, in the coming constitution. The struggle about the essence and substance of the political regime, whether Egypt is to be a pluralist Islamic democracy or an authoritarian regime, is on the table. Two chapters (Yılmaz and Platti) echo the familiar problem of interiorization of the democratization and secular ideals in the coming constitutional processes in Turkey and in Egypt. The proposed chapters in the new constitution guarantee freedom of speech and in some cases (prohibiting blasphemy) limiting this freedom; the state is considered the primary means of protecting religion and religious values.

Why is there a resistance to democratic change in the so-called Muslim world? What went wrong, as Bernard Lewis asked in his book? (Lewis 2002). The core problem is political; however; the uprising of the middle class in Egyptian economic life has much more to do with the new society adopting new values and shrinking into a kind of authoritarian politics. Some scholars argue that the lack of civil society and democracy in Muslim societies is the result of Islamic fundamentalism, a unique problem linked with Islam (Lewis 1990). The perception of the Middle East and, more generally, Muslim exceptionalism argued that Muslim societies tend to be static and resistant to change (Bayat 2010; Lakoff 2004). Thus, Muslim activists have trouble with adopting human values, liberalism and human rights, and there is always a gap between modern western values and Islamic countries (Bielefeldt 2000).

Another explanation focuses on the forced, top-down modernization in Muslim societies. Different processes of modernization initiated by Western or westernized elites in Muslim societies are considered to be colonialism, instead of innovation, a quick imitation, a catch up process to close the gap between the west and Islam. This policy undertaken by modernized elites creates a discrepancy between elites and wider society. Political and social changes are top down, not to be internalized by the public. These reforms and political measures did not engage and incorporate civil society. Turkey and Iran are the best examples, as both countries exercised a forced modernization.

In the case of Egypt, the military and the new business elites are the key elements and allies of Morsi before the election of 2012. Their concern is to maintain the stability of the regime after Mubarak; thus they do not target the promotion of Sharia law in the country. Within this transition process, one should acknowledge the continuation of the military's role in politics. This is similar to the Turkish situation where military force has played a major role in every dimension to guarantee the secular regime. Political power does not allow a free space for civil society and civil actors. It is very important how political power, including Islamist and *Salafi* groups, shapes the public sphere and civil society. In fact, the authoritarian character remains even in the revolutionary change which ended the Mubarak regime. In order to protect the regime and the hegemony of the state over civil society, the military is the determinant. The biggest mistake of the Muslim Brotherhood in Egypt is that in some cases it is found to be very opportunist in its thirst for power. The Muslim Brotherhood (MB) thinks and develops its policies at state level. This strategy does not let it go back to its non-state social mission in support of the change coming from society, continuing its efforts in education and supporting the middle class. Thus, the middle class and the young generation in the Brotherhood take the initiative to change their state oriented politics. In Mubarek's times, its supporters already experienced the failure of its strategy. Some members of the MB noticed the growing discrepancy between real politics and high Islamic ideals, political Islam. In this vein, MB goes in different directions having various factions, some of which follow a more liberal economic programme and model and do not believe in an Islamist utopia; others probably become more radical and concerned more with state oriented politics. Whatever does happen in the MB, Egyptian society will rise against any kind of authoritarianism, corruption and social injustice. The major dilemma is to understand the new socio-economic direction that society wants to go in. Social justice and economic development will be key elements in the new process of politicization in the Arab regimes. According to the optimistic evolution among young educated Arabs, new elites emphasize practising new models. In recent years, a "Turkish model" has spread in the media to give an example in which democracy and Islam live side by side, an educated middle class grows and becomes the transporter of Muslim democracy and Muslim politics. However, an anomaly has appeared in Turkish politics during the Justice and Development Party's (AKP-Adalet ve Kalkınma Partisi) reign. When the Arab spring spread out into the Middle East, many democrats and intellectuals sought for a model and experience among Muslim countries, and they turned to the AKP's experience. At that time, Turkey seemed to combine Islamic values with economic prosperity, democracy and secularism. The Gezi protests in Taksim square and the corruption investigations in 2013 have changed this hopeful image of the 'Turkish model'. The last corruption investigation seriously damaged the image of the AKP that made meaningful constitutional reforms between 2003 and 2011. The AKP has become more authoritarian and tries to control civil society, religious groups and the economy by creating big companies that support the AKP's policies. Reference to the religious values, prohibition of alcohol in certain public areas and the abortion debate signifies a return to the old Islamist discourses. İhsan Yılmaz's chapter gives an insight into the dilemma of being secular and religious in politics. The AKP's example characterizes this dilemma after the 2011 elections. Meijer follows this dilemma in the pragmatism of the Muslim Brotherhood in Egypt whose candidate, Mohammed Morsi, won the presidential election in 2012 before being deposed by the military. It did not respect the balance between different groups in the country. As many ask, has the Arab Spring turned into an Arab Winter? The rise of Islamist parties after the toppling of longstanding dictators in Tunisia, Libya and Egypt seems to suggest so. How can we begin to make sense of these events? The second part of this volume answers these questions, drawing upon lessons from the early phases of the Arab revolutions.

Charity and social welfare networks

The third part focuses on faith-based NGOs among Muslim activists in order to understand their missions and activities that are based on Islamic concepts, discourses and sense. Are there any specific differences between Muslim-Islamic aid organizations and non-Muslim ones? How do humanitarian principles go hand in hand with Islamic values? What are the changes and challenges for Islamic aid organizations? In these three chapters, we follow some fault lines to demonstrate their identity, their mobilization channels and local-transnational networks.

Charity and almsgiving have been transformed from family-individual care and beneficence to the social welfare system (Singer 2008: 176). This transition was accompanied by the development of secular-religious philanthropy[1] and voluntary associations who deal with the question of poverty and development. However, the traditional forms of charity and individual efforts still continue as the modern welfare state system progresses well. Organizations and foundations linked with faith-based communities and movements participate and involve themselves in charity activities. Over time, charity is mixed with various actors, individuals, organizations, professionals, religious movements, states and governments. Each of these new actors expands the borders and the meaning of charity and humanitarian aid in Islamic terms. The increasing of a "mixed economy of charity" raises the question of how Islamic charity is defined. Is it a social welfare net, a humanitarian programme, an Islamic missionary activity? In the coming chapters, the discussion focuses largely on the charitable organization, network, discourses and objectives of NGOs which participate in the work of social-educational services, public works and economic projects. In the classical time before modern times, the most visible charitable individuals were rulers, dynastic families and wealthy people (Singer 2008). After the modernization in the nineteenth century, the growing middle class took the initiative in implementing new charity institutions and activities, and individuals en masse joined in charitable giving thanks to religious belief which is the fundamental part and impetus of the social safety networks. The month of Ramadan and religious holidays are the occasions and times when Muslims are more sensible and attracted by NGOs and states. The shifting point of the traditional charity is the contribution coming from contemporary governments in the form of social welfare assistance, public service and international aid (Singer 2008: 179). The Turkish *Kızılay*, supported directly by the state, is one of the examples that classify this social welfare system as charity. However, the connection between the state's social welfare responsibility-duty and charity is not apparent voluntarily, because it is the state's obligation towards its citizens. This connection is another complex debate on charity and the social welfare system (Ostrower 1996). As Singer puts it, the state's motivations and obligations are somehow different from individuals' and NGOs'. Spiritual and religious considerations have strong influence on the individual's decisions. The welfare system's connection with charity has been analysed in connection with public-private relief and rehabilitation efforts, to provide minimum living conditions for the citizens. However, after the 80s, an economic liberalism re-opened the doors to local actors and religious organizations which regained the social work arena. It is noted that the role of religion in social service is increased and highlighted in the recent studies (Cnaan 1999). Sometimes, the line between government politics and faith-based initiatives is blurred. The *zakat* (obligatory almsgiving) and *sadaqa* (voluntary almsgiving) are two examples of the blurred areas of Islamic charity. There is state-organized collection of *zakat* in many Muslim countries (Clark 2003; Benthall and Bellion-Jourdan 2003; Singer 2009). The idea of social justice would be achieved by major non-economic means, which is *zakat*. In this regard, *zakat* is not a part of charity, but it is a fulfilment of the Islamic mission and Islamic economic thought. *Zakat* takes a central place in the moral economy.

In the contemporary application of *zakat,* or more generally in Islamic safety nets, there is an extention of the traditional use of *zakat* in new conditions and contexts. The classic regulation on *zakat, sadaqa* has been reinterpreted and adopted to take into account the changing of boundaries between Muslims and non-Muslims, certain issues such as gender, poverty and mass education, as we follow in different examples in this book. In opposition to the idea of state oriented charity organization and *zakat* distribution which envisages the state as the agent of the aid, *Kimse Yok mu* and *Islamic Relief* provide such examples of the civil society organizations that have been stimulated, created by individuals, social movements and religious groups. The funds collected by these civil organizations and NGOs have been used in the creation of schools, clinics, water wheels, the distribution of food, and helping poor people. In some cases, Muslims choose to donate to civil organizations rather than a state institution (Scott 1987; Scott 2013).[2]

It is also important to note that contemporary governments do not act only by their own means and institutions; they collaborate with the growing number of associations, networks, civil society organizations and partners using different motivations, aims and methods. All of those constitute the welfare networks composed by families, religious movements, professional groups, *tariqats*, friends, people coming from same country-city-village. Each welfare network is more or less formalized and institutionalized. As discussed in different chapters of this book, the charity ethos and social responsibility are the main ideas rooted from Islamic notions at large. One might point to these networks as the output of civil society's implementation and realization of (de)centralized institutions which are working with different agglomeration of nodes, peoples and centres.

In all of these faith-based initiatives, one of the major socio-cultural changes is the secularization of social work among Muslim aid projects and programmes at discursive and organizational level after the liberalization turning point in the 80s. Muslim social welfare associations have emerged in this era also for different reasons (Adama 2005; Yavuz 2003). The relative disengagement of the state from certain social domains opened up new opportunities to religious civil organizations. It is noteworthy to observe how religion is implemented or a humanitarian motivation inputted into the religious sense of charity and philanthropy. The ambivalent existences of secular social works and religious based social activities interchangeably replace each other, and this replacement surprisingly creates spaces for religio-secular (Marty 2003) habitations.

Islamic relief organizations are active in different areas and domains, such as in education, health, social welfare and employment. They achieve these activities in various geographies, including non-Muslim societies. The concerns of these NGOs are clearly drawn up as a remedy and struggle against the poverty problem; in fact, they tackle relatively different issues: human rights, gender and environment crises are discovered in the humanitarian field that Islamic

NGOs encounter. The Islamic NGOs face different problematic issues in various domains, and this makes complex the social aid. The studies on Muslim NGOs (Benthall and Bellion-Jourdan 2003; Clark 2004; Harmsen 2008), give some insights into these complexities between Islamic and humanitarian. They work and collaborate with other non-Muslim NGOs, including western development agencies. This collaboration and working with other western NGOs drives Islamic NGOs to modify their engagement in the Islamic framework against the poverty and developing humanitarian aid to needy people. The historical studies on the Islamic charity and aid system give some points on the continuity and new interpretations of Islamic notions on almsgiving (*zakat* and *sadaqa*). Studying the charity from a historical point of view enables valuable insights to be drawn (Singer 2008). Where do they stand and for what purpose? In these transnational complexities and multiple localities, the NGOs' work exemplifies the blurring areas of belonging and participating, especially when they do work with other non-Muslim NGOs. Such Islamic NGOs use an Islamic notion and discourse in their practices and motivations. The discourses used by Muslim actors are cherished by an Islamic sense and values. The new orientation as opening to humanitarian discourse and sensibility reduces the Islamic tonality of the mission. Stemming from Islamic political ideology to moderate humanitarian discourse is not necessarily a break from Islamic piety and devoted religious attitude. *Kimse yok mu*, a humanitarian faith-inspired association, is working for different causes: delivering hot meals, medical treatments, waterwheels projects and vocational training. In these projects, a kind of hybridization between Islamic devotional practice and global development approach takes place (Harmsen 2007).

Doing humanitarian work in a locality where the population is Muslim or not, no matter to whom the aid is conveyed, has the effect of changing the nature and identity of the Islamic NGO. There is a continual transformation and strengthening of Islamic identity and reference to a Muslim organization: from faith-based initiatives to more humanitarian activity. Michel's chapter deals with the question of this border between Muslim and non-Muslim communities.

The Islamic and Muslim NGOs deal with educational, environmental and religious issues in different part of the so-called Muslim world. One of the largest Islamic NGOs in Europe, Islamic Relief, is providing aid, food, materials in different countries. At the grass roots level, their efforts are appreciated and very welcome. They open Quranic schools which offer religious courses and Arabic language classes. In these religious spaces, the chapter demonstrates how Islamic solidarity is maintained by social projects and institutions. Harmsen, whose PhD is on Muslim NGOs in Jordan, discusses the practices and strategies of Al-Afaf Society. Harmsen points out that much of Islamic voluntary activism is linked to the political question and Islamic NGOs are analysed under the political science framework, such as Islamic solidarity, revivalism, realizing *umma* and Islamist movements (Harmsen 2007). For him, the emphasis on the political and ideological function of Islamic associations reveals the empowerment of the Muslim middle class. Islamic voluntary activism strengthens underprivileged Muslims by offering them education, health service. In this case, Islamic welfare associations avoid political aims and address social-economical purposes and questions of the people. Harmsen's chapter reviews the empowerment of the orphans and families struggling suffering from poverty.

There is a strong emphasis on the importance of education and developing the educational skills of young Muslims, as Michel and Harmsen indicate in this book. Supporting the achievement of educational projects and tutoring schoolboys and girls during their education by opening learning centres, private schools are targeting the embodiment of the religious duty with humanitarian responsibility. Social welfare organizations give priority to some values such as hard work, doing good deeds, being useful to society. The examples and various programmes in Muslim NGOs illustrate how an empowerment process is operated in civil welfare organizations. Building on ethnographic studies from Jordan, Harmsen argues that a combination between a paternalistic approach and empowerment designates the orientation of the NGOs' activities. Such paternalistic and empowerment orientation has been nuanced in different contexts and associations. In the Jordanian case, the paternalistic view encapsulates the Islamic notion of religious duty; in *Kimse Yok mu* from Turkey the philosophy is derived from Islamic concepts, targeting not only Muslims and operating in different areas and geographies. In this case, the paternalistic view of solidarity is weakened, however, by using the humanistic discourse, the organizers' aim is to focus on poverty and development. They call for businessmen to invest in the region, opening new economic opportunities, schools, building houses after earthquakes.

Contents of the book

Islamic activism and thinking are not simply the political project of some Muslims reflecting on questions relating to contemporary issues. The chapters in this book are intended to respond to the demand of the current play of Islam and Muslims in an ongoing discussion about Muslim scholars' authority, Muslim politics and Islamic social welfare systems. The chapters are based on papers of which most were first presented at the Lecture series in KU Leuven Gülen Chair on "Current issues in Islam", held at the KU Leuven University in 2012. This book opens with a chapter by Erkan Toğuşlu on Muslim scholars and Islamic knowledge. This chapter reveals the paradoxes and dynamics of Islamic public reasoning used by Muslim public intellectuals among Muslims in Europe. This public reasoning is much more fragmented due to the secularism and individualization effect on the pluralization and functionalization of Islamic knowledge in Fethullah Gülen, Tariq Ramadan and al-Qaradawi's views.

A critical rethinking of reformative-conservative framework and labelization requires, argues Thierry Limpens in the second chapter, a deconstructive reading of Muslim scholars. Limpens brings an ethnographic study of the gender reformative theories, networking and programmes of the Islamic scholars Abdullahi An-Na'im and Tariq Ramadan. It concludes from the 2007-2013 field data that were collected in a Moroccan dominant Muslim area of so-called 'core Islamic Brussels' in Belgium that the Muslim community shows an elevated level of what is called in the text 'categorical ethnicity'. This refers to the building of relationships that are 'remote' or not so 'directly' defined for reasons that they are clearly 'differential' as gathered around 'higher values' that come under the idea of justice.

A chapter by Eric Geoffroy shifts the discussion of the reformulation of Islamic knowledge in sufi circles and among Muslim scholars. It is necessary also to look at how some Islamic notions are re-circulated by French Sufi scholars in Europe. Drawing from the imaginable world (*âlam al-khayâl*), or the world of spiritual imagination, Sufism knows how to apply its creativity to remove religious and cultural blocks. Being grounded in the vertical axis of Unicity (*tawhîd*), the Sufi should be able to contemplate multiplicity around him serenely; thus Islamic knowledge encapsulates plural thinking.

Ihsan Yılmaz discusses the post-islamist shift to see if and to what extent Islam and secularism could accommodate each other. What is more, revival of Islam and deprivatization of Islam are more observable phenomena compared to the other religions; especially after the Arab revolutions, we look at the return of Islamism in political sphere. Yılmaz argues that a post-Islamist understanding of religion-state-society relations is more compatible with this Habermasian post-secularist condition with regard to religion in the public sphere. Following the same line, in the next chapter Emilio Platti focuses attention on the apparent contradiction in the term of "Islamic citizenship" in the draft constitution in Egypt. At Tahrir Square, people used the complex term of "*muwâtana islâmiyya*", "Islamic citizenship", meaning a civil Nation-State (*dawla madaniyya*) with an Islamic reference or background; few want the Islamic character of Egypt completely to be erased from the new Constitution. For Platti, these terms mean that there is no contradiction between a democratic system and Islamic Law. Platti went to Tahrir Square many times and observed the Egyptian revolution and counter-revolution. Roel Meijer is asking one of the crucial questions of this book: aside from the continuous struggle with the Egyptian military and the tactics of the Brotherhood, what will the Muslim Brotherhood do in the coming years? Is there a line in the policy of the Brotherhood or is it simple political opportunism? The argument developed by Meijer is that one of the problems with the Brotherhood is not that it mingles religion with politics but that in the past it has not embraced the political sufficiently. It is still to a large extent a religious movement that has included politics as one option. Meijer also analyses the effects of the Muslim Brotherhood's evolution in politics for Europe in terms of politics and ideology. In this regard, this chapter focuses especially on the attitude towards politics and development of political thought in the Brotherhood.

Tracing how the categories of the islamist, post-islamist and salafis in politics work to produce assumptions about the nature of Muslim politics, in the last part the secular, the humanitarian and the religious categories of social safety nets are examined. Benthall, Michel and Harmsen look at the activities of religious humanitarian organizations and workers in the context of globalization and transnationalism. Benthall says that voluntary welfare provision by Muslims has much in common with other charitable traditions, though with some differences relating especially to the Quranic doctrine of *zakat*, the Islamic tithe (deemed to be obligatory), as well as the concepts of *sadaqa* (charity over and above what is obligatory) and *waqf* (the Islamic charitable trust). Harmsen's chapter deals with a particular form of Muslim social activism, namely the activity of Muslim voluntary welfare organizations delivering services of a varied nature (financial and in-kind support, counsel, employment, education etcetera) to socially vulnerable target groups such as the poor, orphans, single parent families, children at risk and the disabled. It analyses this activity from the perspective of the respective roles of tradition and modernity, especially in relation to civil society theory. In the final chapter of this book, Thomas Michel reflects on the realization of Islamic humanitarian networks. Using the example of the *Kimse*

Yok Mu? aid organization, Michel depicts the circulation of Islamic motivation in the humanitarian-secular works to show the complexity of purely 'Islamic activism'.

In closing this introduction, the editors would like to end with some personal thanks to Veerle De Laet (Acquisitions Editor) for her help and support in the range of practical issues which arose. The editors would like also to thank the two reviewers for their inputs. All the editors would also like to express their thanks for what they acknowledge as the continued patient support of their families and friends throughout their work on this book.

Notes

1 Philantrophy is always interconnected with charity, even if there are some differences between them. Charity is directed towards the needy poor people by organizing relief services, while the concept of philantrophy is broader than charity, and includes many private donations, contributions and social service institutions. These activities do not directly target the poor. For more discussion see Ostrower (1995).

2 Scott analyses the Muslim peasant in Malaysia to see how he resists a central bureaucracy in the state *zakat* fund. He minimizes his obligatory payments to the state. He does not just resist the state *zakat* system, but he develops another way in which he can fullfill his religious duty to return to local needs.

References

Abu-Rabi, İ.M. (1996). *Intellectual Origins of Islamic Resurgence in the Modern Arab World*, Albany: SUNY.

Adama, Hamadou. (2005). Islamic Associations in Cameroon: Between the Umma and the State, in *Islam and Muslim Politics in Africa*, Benjamin F. Soares and Rene Otayek (eds.), London, Palgrave Macmillian.

Bayat, A. (2007). *Making Islam Democratic: Social Movements and the Post-Islamist Turn.* Palo Alto, California: Stanford University Press.

Bayat, A. (2010). *Life as Politics: How Ordinary People Change the Middle East*, Stanford: Stanford University Press.

Benthall, J., Bellion-Jourdan, J. (2003). *The Charitable Crescent: Politics of Aid in the Muslim World*, London: I. B. Tauris.

Bielefeldt, H. (2000). ''Western' versus 'Islamic' Human Right Conceptions? A Critique of Cultural Essentialism in the Discussion on Human Rights', *Political Theory*, 28, 1: 90-121.

Bilgin, F. (2011). *Political Liberalism in Muslim Societies*, Routledge: Taylor & Francis.

Bowen, R., (2009). *Can Islam be French? Pluralism and Pragmatism in a Secularist State*, Princeton: Princeton University Press.

Brusse, W. A., Schoonenboom, J. (2006) Islamic Activism and Democratization, *ISIM Review* 18: 8-9.

Clark, Janine A. (2004). *Islam, Charity, and Activism: Middle-Class Networks and Social Welfare in Egypt, Jordan, and Yemen*, Bloomington: Indiana University Press.

Cnaan, Ram A., Wineburg, Robert J. and Boddie, Stephanie C. (1999). *The Newer Deal Social Work and Religion in Partnership*, New York, Columbia University Press.

Deeb, L., (2006). *An Enchanted Modern: Gender and Public Piety in Shi'i Lebanon*, Princeton University Press.

Dijkzeul, D. (2008). 'Transnational Humanitarian NGO's, A progress report', in *Rethinking Transnationalism, The Meso-link of organisations*, Ludger Pries (ed.), London, Routledge.

Eickelman, Dale F., Piscatori J. (1996). Muslim Politics, Princeton: New Jersey, Princeton University Press.

Eisenstadt, S. (2000). 'Multiple Modernities', *Daedalus*, 129, 3, pp. 14-31.

Fuller, G., (2004). *The Future of Political Islam*, Palgrave/MacMillan.

Geoffroy, E. (2010). *Introduction to Sufism: The Inner Path of Islam*, Bloomignton, World Wisdom.

Göle, N., Ammann, L. (eds) (2006). *Islam in public. Turkey, Iran and Europe*, Istanbul, Bilgi University press.

Göle, N. (2000). 'Snapshots of Islamic Modernities', *Daedalus*, 129, 1: 91-117.

Göle, N. (2002). 'Islam in Public: New Visibilities and New Imaginaries', *Public Culture*, 1.

Göle, N. (2005). *Interpenetrations. L'Islam et l'Europe*, Paris, Galaade Editions.

Haenni, P. (2005). *L'islam de marché: l'autre révolution conservatrice*, Paris, Seuil.

Hashemi, N. (2009). *Islam, Secularism and Liberal Democracy: Toward a Democratic Theory for Muslim Societies*, Oxford University Press.

Harmsen, E. (2007). 'Between Empoverment and Patternalism', *ISIM Review* 20: 10-11.

Hodgson, M.G.S. (1974). *The Venture of Islam Conscience and History in a World Civilization*, (3 vols); v. 2: *The expansion of Islam in the Middle Periods Chicago*, The University of Chicago Press.

Ismail, S. (2004). 'Being Muslim: Islam, Islamism and Identity Politics', *Government and Opposition*, 39 (4). pp. 614-31.

Kepel, G. (2002). *Jihad: The Trail of Political Islam*, London, I.B. Tauris.

Lakoff, S. (2004). 'The Reality of Muslim Exceptionalism', *Journal of Democracy*, 15, 4, 133-139.

Laurence, J. (2012). *The Emancipation of Europe's Muslims: The State's Role in Minority Integration*, Princeton, Princeton University Press.

Leman, J. (2012) "Flemish Interest' (VB) and Islamophobia: Political, legal and judicial dealings,' in Ansari, H. and F. Hafez (eds). *From the Far Right to the Mainstream. Islamophobia in Party Politics and the Media*. Frankfurt/New York: Campus Verlag, 69-90.

Lewis, B. (1990). 'The Roots of Muslim Rage', *Atlantic Monthly*, 266, 3: 47-60.

Mahmood, S. (2005). *Politics of Piety: The Islamic Revival and the Feminist Subject*, Princeton: Princeton University Press.

Mandaville, P. (2007). *Global Political Islam*, Oxon, Routledge.

Marty, Martin E. (2003). 'Our Religio-Secular World', *Daedalus*, vol. 32, n. 3: 42-48.

Meijer, R. (2005). 'Jihadi Opposition in Saudi Arabia', *ISIM Review*, 15.

Meijer, R. (ed.) (2009). *Global Salafism: Islam's New Religious Movement*, Hurst: Columbia University Press.

Metcalf, B. D. (2002). *Traditionalist, Islamic Activism: Deoband, Tablighis and Talibs*, Leiden, ISIM.

Nasr, V. (2009). *Forces of Fortune: The rise of New Middle Muslim Class and What it will Mean for Our World*, New York, Free Press.

Ostrower, F. (1995). *Why the Wealthy Give: The Culture of Elite Philanthropy*, Princeton, Princeton University Press.

Parekh, B. (2006). 'Europe, liberalism and the 'Muslim question'', in *Multiculturalism, Muslims And Citizenship: A European Approach*, (eds) T. Modood, A. Triandafyllidou, R. Zapata Barrero, New York, Routledge.

Perthes, V. (ed.) (2004). *Arab elites. Negotiating the politics of change*, Boulder: Lynne Riener.

Platti, E. (2008). *Islam, friend or foe?*, Leuven, Peeters.

Qutb, S. (2000). *Social Justice in Islam*, Islamic Publications International.

Roy, O. (2004). *Globalized Islam: The Search for a new Ummah*, New York, Columbia University Press.

Roy., O. (1994). *The Failure of Political Islam*, Cambridge: Harvard University Press.

Roy, O., Haenni, P. (eds) (1999). 'Le post-islamisme', *Revue des mondes musulmans et de la Méditerranée*, n°s 85-86 Aix-en-Provence, Edisud.

Sadouni, S. (2005). 'New Religious Actors in South Africa: The Example of Islamic Humanitarianism,' in *Islam and Muslim Politics in Africa*, B.F. Soares and R. Otayek (eds), London, Palgrave Macmillian.

Scott, James C. (1987). 'Resistance without Protest and without Organization: Peasent Opposition to the Islamic Zakat and the Christian Tithe,' in *Comparative Studies in Society and History*, Cambridge University Press, V. 29, No. 3, pp. 417-452.

Scott, James C. (2013). *Decoding Subaltern Politics, Ideology, disguise, and resistance in agrarian politics*, New York, Routledge.

Singer, A. (2008). *Charity in Islamic Societies*, Cambridge: Cambridge University Press.

Taylor, C. (1998). *The Malaise of Modernity*, House of Anansi Press.

Toğuşlu, E. (2012). 'European Public Sphere, Islam and Islamic authority: Tariq Ramadan and Fethullah Gülen,' in Weller P., Yilmaz I. (eds), *European Muslims, Civility and Public Life Perspectives On and From the Gülen Movement*, Continuum, 65-79.

Van Bruinessen, M. (2009). 'Popular Islam and the Encounter with Modernity,' in *Islam and Modernity: key issues and debates*, Masud, Salvatore and van Bruinessen (eds), Edinburg: Edinburg University Press.

Van den Boss, M. (2012). 'European Shiisme? Counterpoints from Shiites' organization in Britain and the Netherlands,' *Ethnicities*, vol. 12 (5): 556-580.

Wiktorowicz, Quintan (2002). 'Embedded Authoritarianism, Bureaucratic Obstacles and Limits to Non-Governmental Organizations in Jordan,' in *Jordan in Transition*, G. Joff (ed.), London: Hurst and Company, 115-122.

Wiktorowicz, Q. (ed.) (2004). *Islamic Activism. A Social Movement Theory Approach*, Bloomington: Indiana University Press.

Yankaya, D. (2013). *La nouvelle bourgeoisie islamique: le modèle turc*, Paris, PUF.

Yavuz, M. (2003). *Islamic Political Identity in Turkey*, Oxford: Oxford University Press.

Yılmaz, İ. (2012). 'Towards a Muslim Secularism? An Islamic Twin Tolerations Understanding of Religion in the Public Sphere,' *Turkish Journal of Politics*, v.3, n.2.

White, J. (2012). *Muslim Nationalism and New Turks*, Princeton: Princeton University Press.

Zaman, M.Q. (2002). *The Ulama in Contemporary Islam: custodians of change*, Princeton, Princeton University Press.

Part I:
Modern Islamic Thinking

Fethullah Gülen, Tariq Ramadan and Yusuf al-Qaradawi: The Pluralisation of Islamic Knowledge

Erkan Toğuşlu

It is difficult to attribute to Islamic public intellectuals and actors the classical Islamic vocabulary of *muftis*, *alims*, *cheikhs* (van Bruinessen and Allievi 2011). They exist in theory, but in reality different types of Islamic actors have legitimacy and a specific social-religious authority in Islamic settings such as educational institutions, mosques and associations has emerged (Bowen 2011:24). Bowen notes that the roles of teachers, *imams* and leaders of local associations are equally important in discussing the traditional (dis)continuity of Islamic scholars in France. One may simplify this list into Islamic public intellectuals and actors who speak for Islam and in the name of Islam.

This chapter reveals the paradoxes and dynamics in Islamic public reasoning used by Muslim public intellectuals among Muslims in Europe. This public reasoning is much more fragmented due to the secularism and individualization effect on the pluralization and functionalization of Islamic knowledge in Islamic settings such as schools, mosques and associations. Secularism signifies the decline of religious influence and its role in society in many areas. In the secularization processes, Muslims' presence and their individuality in secular Europe may be seen as an automatic decline in religious practice and religious authority. In other words, Islamic intellectual authority loses its orthodoxy and power to channel the main Islamic debates.

The rise in educational opportunities and the global effect of mass media on the formation of Islamic discourse do not mean the breakdown of the monopoly of the traditional *ulama* over religious interpretation, as some scholars say they do. They are not autodidacts and practise and teach the theology in a classical way. Engaged in secular matters and issues, they do not do as classical traditional *ulama* did. They attempted to reconcile the modern values and challenges they faced with the ethics and morality of Islam. These intellectuals are more acceptable than the classical *ulama*. They provide adequate economic, social and cultural solutions and alternatives to the needs of Muslims in Europe. Preoccupied with a variety of Islamic disciplines such as Islamic philosophical theology (*kalam*), exegesis (*tafsir*), jurisprudence (*fiqh*) and prophetic tradition (*hadith*), their ideas bring together diverse networks of knowledge. Their ideas are formulated in mosques, cafes, through the pulpit, books and media.

This chapter highlights what kind of arguments and justifications Islamic scholars use and pursue, and how these arguments are circulated, accepted, refused and received by local Muslims. Through these questions this chapter problematizes the question of Islamic reasoning and authority following three Muslim scholars: Fethullah Gülen, Tariq Ramadan and Yusuf al-Qaradawi. When I use authority here, I mean people who speak about Islam and have been endowed with legitimacy coming from their talents and ability to interpret Islam. This authority is attributed to the new pioneers of Islam by Muslim followers and local and national institutions. Public reasoning reveals the justification positions on different policy issues. Bowen talks about repertoires of evaluation (Bowen, 2010:6). He says, "repertoires, therefore, can be mapped onto particular territories" (Bowen 2010: 6). The particular question is how Muslims engage in deliberating about Islamic practices, the issue always being whether they are pure Muslim or becoming something other than just Muslim. Particular political territories play a significant role in determining and forming these deliberations and justification processes.

The first dimension and instrument analysed in this chapter consists of the discussion of their work as Muslim scholars, re-activating the classical Islamic terminology in secular coding and time. In the second dimension, we will try to analyse the discursive and pragmatic change which has occurred during the last decade. This shift has become an important element in seeing the new articulation of Islamic reasoning among young Muslims. The last aspect of this chapter looks at how Islamic reasoning is produced alongside the question of *ijtihad*.

Muslim public intellectuals

A brief look at the educational journey of these Islamic scholars according to what we say about the new faces of Islam shows how Muslim intellectuals, Muslim authority and its transformation came about.

Fethullah Gülen

Fethullah Gülen completed his three primary years in a state school. He continued his traditional Islamic education in eastern *medreses* (traditional Islamic education institutions) and in a mosque school. He became an official preacher and *imam* in the Turkish Directorate of Religious Affairs in Turkey in various cities during the 1970s and 1980s. In those years, Gülen became very influential among young university students and middle class people. He organized lectures, preaching in several mosques. His sermons focused on morality, education, social cohesion and civility. His ideas were followed by a younger generation to establish a system of modern secular educational institutions in Turkey and abroad after the 1990s. Known as the Gülen movement or *Hizmet* (service), the movement became transnational and active in education, dialogue, media and charity (Ebaugh, 2010).

A heuristic glance at Gülen's works and speeches enables us to define him as *arif-alim* who gathers together two poles which are called *zahiri* (exoteric) and *batini* (esoteric). Gülen plays this double role and figure between *arif* and *alim*; spiritual and rational. On this point, Gaborieau and Zeghal (2004:7) propose the *alim-arif* framework that indicates a combination of *ulama* and *sufi*'s understanding of Islam. Through this framework related to an esoteric style of interpretation of the Qur'an, in various subjects, Gülen refers to spiritual knowledge (*marifa*). He emphasizes this *sufi* way of interpretation, while Ramadan's discourse, which we will discuss farther in the text, will be outlined by a critical position in *academia*. Gülen develops a language shaped by *sufi* idioms and narrations.

Elizabeth Özdalga notes, "[Gülen] adopts a solid, conventional Hanafi/Sunni understanding of the religious traditions. So it does not seem to be the content of the religious interpretation as such, but the very existence of a new relatively strong group, filled with religious fervor and claiming a place in the public arena that annoys the establishment in Turkey radical margins who see this as a threat to their ideology" (Özdalga, 2005:441).

Tariq Ramadan

Our second Muslim intellectual is Tariq Ramadan, a Swiss-born Muslim. His grandfather, Hasan al-Banna (1906-49), was the founder of the Muslim Brotherhood in Egypt. He studied philosophy, French literature, social sciences and Islamic studies. He is professor of contemporary Islamic studies at Oxford University, in the Oriental Institute. His works emphasize Islamic studies, theology and European Muslims, and he endeavours to reinterpret Islam on many issues according to contemporary developments. Ramadan's use of fluent English and French is very influential on young Muslims, especially among France's suburban young Muslims.

Ramadan's career is considerable, putting him among the emerging new Islamic authorities. Basically new Islamic intellectuals almost always come from the secular education institutions and have access to a modern type of knowledge (Göle 1996). Ramadan however studied the *Qur'an* and *Hadith* for many years, and he refers to classical Muslim scholars on different issues in his books and speeches. At the same time, he uses the same language and vocabulary with secular thinkers, even participating in debates with leftist and far leftist intellectuals.[1] He circulates this Islamic knowledge in connection with contemporary issues such as globalization and women's emancipation (Limpens 2013).

Al-Qaradawi

Al-Qaradawi, an Egyptian Muslim scholar, is considered a 'global mufti' due to his fatwas on broadcasts on Al-Jazeera and Islamonline, a popular website. He was born in Egypt in 1926. He has published more than 120 books. He has long been a prominent intellectual leader among the Muslim Brotherhood. He obtained his PhD at Al-Azhar University on Islamic almsgiving (*zakat*) and its modern usage. His expertise on *zakat* provided him with a position in the emergence of Islamic finance and banking (Benthall 2013). He is the founder of many Islamic centres at different universities. He himself is actually at Qatar University. He is also an important figure in the establishment of the religious education system in Qatar (Graf and Skovgaard-Petersen, 3). He is closely linked to the al-Jazeera TV station. Al-Qaradawi is the head of the European Council for Fatwa and Research, a Dublin-based private foundation established by the Federation of Islamic Organizations in Europe. In the Council they try to re-establish the role of *ulama* for European Muslims to refer to.

Al-Qaradawi's profile corresponds to that of the traditional *ulama* who deals with daily questions. He illustrates the relative importance of the role of *ulama* in

Europe having an intellectual capacity, recognized as having authority to answer many crucial questions linked to contemporary problems such as the example of Islamic banking, insurance. In the main, Qaradawi's pragmatic approach to Islamic jurisprudence as a response to urgent questions is followed by young Muslims. A brief look at *fatwas* shows a concentration on issues for the Muslim minority living in Europe. Skovgaard-Petersen finds Qaradawi's scholarship ambiguous. He resumes his understanding: "…skeptical questioning of established knowledge and dogma … is clearly an evil to be avoided" (Skovgaard-Petersen and Graf, 2009: 43).

His popular book *The Lawful and the Prohibited* in Islam (1960) is an often translated book providing guidance on the daily life of Muslims. In his famous broadcast programme, *Shari'a and Life*, a programme of TV channel, al-Qaradawi develops a discourse based on argument and on educational aspects of life which is not contradictory to Islamic beliefs.

These three Muslim scholars are involved as activist, preacher and intellectual in various areas that transcend the limits of national borders. Through their homepages, translated into many languages, their ideas are transmitted globally. These three people are impressively 'gifted orators'. Among these Muslim intellectuals, Qaradawi has received the label of 'global mufti' (Skovgaard-Petersen, 2004). Al-Qaradawi addresses a Muslim World from an Arabic Muslim context.[2] Using the Arabic language, he is currently working in Qatar on Islamic theology. Meanwhile, Gülen and Ramadan live in a country with a Muslim minority. They directly face issues relating to Muslims in the West, being aware of the post-secularity of Western societies. They try to reformulate new social and political issues comfortable with an original and 'authentic' way.

The origin of modern intellectual pluralization in Islam

The three Islamic public intellectuals studied in this chapter issue Islamic discourses to suggest how best to create a workable Islamic reality in the contemporary world. As Islamic public actors, they exercise an influence and impact on Muslims living in Europe. Their writings in blogs and on websites and their books are translated into different languages and their views channel debates on Islam. Each of those Muslim scholars has his own type of legitimacy and justification based on Islamic tradition: a professor at a European university, a scholar who gives *fatwas* and interprets scriptural texts, an inspirational leader of a transnational movement living in the US. These figures' messages are circulated in the transnational public sphere. They formulate their own judgements and commentaries on current issues such as gender equality, secularity, democracy and modernity. Those transnational public authorities develop their opinions to answer different questions: Tariq Ramadan's writings emphasize how Muslims live their faith in secular societies such as marrying and worshipping. Fethullah Gülen highlights the establishment of a common moral language between different peoples and beliefs. Yusuf al-Qaradawi looks for a possible restoration of Islamic formulations on contemporary problems that face Muslims.

Promoting a moderate Islamic view arguing for the limitation of the expansion of militant islamists is one of the ideas that one obtains from this new discourse and from this change of authority (Bayat 2007, 2010). A quick outline of this new authority, which is based on both the traditional and modern role of Islamic intellectuals, seems to support a non-state oriented Islam (Yılmaz 2005). It is not a product of official Islam under strict control of the state, but is becoming a transborder and transnational phenomenon.

In the last century, the media, the Internet and communication technologies have played a significant role in the production and expansion of Islamic knowledge. The nature of the traditional mode of Islamic knowledge adapted to these new technologies – blogs, web pages, facebook, youtube forums – have become new channels and mediums in the spreading of Islamic idioms, narratives and information. Mass media and education also influence the fragmentation of Islamic knowledge (Eickelman 1992; Mandaville 2001). A modern discourse of textuality has emerged among Muslim scholars in recent years. Including this textuality, the hermeneutical-historical approach is underlined by Islamic scholars (Roussillion 2005; Filaly-Ansari 2003). As a result of this new discursive and methodological approach to and interpretation of Islam, the pluralization of knowledge has been noted (Mandaville 2007). In numerous ways, we can observe a meaningful shift in the production of knowledge from a traditional one to a more modern complex of contextual interpretations. In our case, all of the three Islamic intellectuals we have presented use the new media and communication technologies to expand their views and ideas.

Classical Islamic reasoning and modernity

The three Islamic scholars continue the classical *nasiha* tradition in Islam. Asad discusses in his work the practice of *nasiha* in Saudi Arabia as an example of public reasoning (Asad 1993: 200-238). According to him, this public reasoning is different from liberal criticism. It has its own authority, logical arguments and set of moral principles. Another notion that we use for understanding the modern articulation of Islamic reasoning of these three scholars is the term *maslaha*. I use *maslaha* with broader reference to the conventional juristic sense. My aim is to understand the contemporary use of this notion to scrutinize the salience and limits of flexibility in Islamic discussions. As suggested Armando Salvatore,

> "…the principal focus here is not the specifically juridical articulation of this key concept of Islamic jurisprudence. Rather, it is *maslaha's* capacity to open up specific discursive alleys to publicly engaged *ulama*, so as to allow them to articulate positions of some political relevance, yet distinct from the discourse of "political Islam" proper. In this sense, *maslaha* has become….a privileged tool for the insertion of *ulama* into modern public spheres" (Salvatore 2009:240).

Compared to Ramadan, Gülen accentuates the question of the coexistence of differences and shared human values. In Ramadan's and Gülen's teachings one discovers a kind of social-religious pragmatism seeking the general Muslim interest and public good (*maslaha*), which is founded on the quest to give space for Muslims in different contexts. Qaradawi focuses on Muslims' daily questions relating to the licite-illicite issue. Salvatore argues that Qaradawi's use of the term public good (*maslaha*) gives rise to debates on social questions and activism (Salvatore 2009). *Maslaha*, a general term, is understood as a practical solution "for devising solutions to new, and in this sense modern, social problems" (Masud et al. 2009: 241). For Salvatore, this engagement around that term signifies a concrete contribution to social economic problems that face Muslims. Responding to a question about the duty of Muslims living in Europe, Qaradawi underlines firstly the religious responsibilities and obligations of Muslims being in a Muslim community. Calling and inviting non-Muslims to Islam is another duty and responsibility. Qaradawi's focus is on the whole of the Muslim community and the individual Muslim believer's role in this community. He has written more than 100 books on different subjects such as Islamic jurisprudence and Islamic education. Graf and Skovgaard-Petersen argue that an independent civilization (*hadara*) and a comprehensive way of life (*shumiliyya*) are two essential terms that Qaradawi emphasizes in the Islamic awakening (*al-sahwa al-islamiyya*) (2009:5). The main themes developed in his works and writings are: Islamic finance, the Muslim family, Muslim women and minority rights. He sees secularization and pluralism as a danger and threat to Islamic civilization and the Muslim community.

Discursive changes and the double agenda issue

Asef Bayat (2002) remarks on the shift from the discourse of politicization of Islam to personal piety and ethics. This pluralization of Islamic knowledge and attitude has an effect in the public sphere involving social and political debates in Europe. Islamic issues are taken as a discursive practice, and in this approach we forget to look to daily practices that give rise to new debates about the implementation of Islam. The encounter with the West and the secular meaning of life force Muslim authorities to rethink traditional settings and corpus of text.

The new Islamic public intellectuals question the very strict and limited views on Islam, and on Europe and non-Muslims. They criticize the fact that these views look only at the scriptures and their literal meaning, not at their interpretative meaning. They contextualize the Islamic past, but do not touch the essential question: what are the new ways of reasoning and teaching for today's Muslims? However, there are complexities of Islamic knowledge within the tradition that can extend this knowledge into new domains such as social responsibility, citizenship and secularism, as we see in the modern discourse of Muslim intellectuals. Masud states that studying Islamic modernism is quite problematic, because no Muslim thinker calls himself or herself a modernist (Masud, 2009). For Masud, Islamic modernism takes into consideration the challenges posed by modernism to the classical Islamic theology. For this reason, modernist Muslim thinkers seek a new theology (Masud, 2009: 238). Defending a modernist way, but without calling them modernist, is symptomatic of our three Muslim public intellectuals. Ramadan is quite open to defining himself as a reformist, but not a modernist. The relationship with the idea of the West, westernization and western modernity is still contentious. This ambivalence is seen in the argument that modernity is compatible with Islam and there is no contradiction with human values and Islam.

The teachings of these three Muslim scholars highlight what we found from the Islamic tradition. What do the *ulama say?* To decrypt the complexities between today and the past, they try to understand what are the aim, the context and the environment. And finally, these three Islamic scholars propose alternatives and judgements based on general framing of Islamic knowledge, to find coherence in Islam with today. There is no abandonment of the past, of tradition, of a legal school of Islamic thought; indeed, there is a deeper and conscious understanding to renew the Islamic thinking in the contemporary world. The past was very different from today's societies, and there is a need for a general, comprehensive and complete view on socio-economic problems that Muslims face today.

The confrontation with the West was a challenge in the 19th century for Muslim thinkers and reformists who were tackling the question of why the Muslim world was undeveloped and backward. In effect, the question of reform was debated among those Islamic scholars and intellectuals. Today we are not speaking about simply a confrontation between the West and Islam, because Muslim visibility is a part of the Western side of the debate (Göle 2005). In recent years, at a time when an "Islamic threat" (Esposito 1999) has emerged as the dominant categorization of Muslims in Europe, some influential discourses and initiatives have been highly articulated around the Islamic scholars whose ideas are inspired by a cumulative traditional Islamic language. These intellectuals have pluralistic discourses giving rebirth to an Islamic knowledge facing modernity. These voices are mistrusted and have all too frequently been accused of having a double agenda and language. The reality however is much more complex and not all three intellectuals we discuss in this chapter correspond to a similar pathway in their internal developments. The way Fethullah Gülen has elaborated his thinking has become quite different from Qardawi's path.

Before examining the internal division among the Islamic scholars and intellectuals, referring to the political Islam whereby religion becomes a means and a way for the expression and politics of Islam, their discourse and writing can be associated with political Islamic discourses as far back as the middle of the 19th century. The young ottomans expressed some notions imported from Europe through the prism of Islam. For them, Islam was not a belief, but was taken as a social and political system which is accountable to foster the creation of independent, modern nations based on rationality, development and free thinking. Addressing *ijtihad* and giving a new interpretation of Islamic issues as a result of confrontation with modernity, Muslim thinkers focused on minimizing the gap between the West and the Muslim world. The Muslim world experienced the entry of modernity mostly as a shock like military and political intrusion into their lands.

The early years of the 1900s met the emergence of political voices and establishments which put political activism into action by means of religion in public areas. The foundation of Hassan Al-Banna's Muslim Brotherhood in Egypt, Maududi's Jamaat-e-Islami, the Islamic revivalist party in British India, Sayyid Qutb's effectiveness and influence in increasing the Islamic activities and efforts to delegitimize the existing states expanded the Islamist movements. In fact, many of the followers and militants joined some fundamentalist organizations to overthrow power. By the failure of political Islam (Roy 1996), the islamist organizations and groups are losing their influence among the young generation which is open to and seeking an individual quest and salvation. Called market Islam (Haenni 2005) the breakup and separation from the Islamist top down ideology leaves the non-hierarchical and pyramidal organization of Islam (Ibid.). Suffering from the dialectic of "Islam is the solution for all ills", such organizations prefer to use a multi-layered language, and previous discourses no longer fit into a single profile and etiquette.

In this regard, we should try to analyse our three Islamic scholars' views and their typology in a way that gives them a quite different place in their discursive changes. We should portray them as new pioneers of Islam in a secular context, inside a process of variegating shifting Islamic thinking in today's Europe. Our aim is to understand the emergence of these new personalities in the changing context of evaluating the West, nationalization, *ijtihad* and the coexistence of Muslims and non-Muslims. While the first generation's views and ideas, like Mawdudi's and Al-Banna's, emphasized anti-imperialism and were against westernization, our second group of Islamic intellectuals speaks about the coexistence between East and West, pluralism, democracy and human rights, but their options for answering these challenges may be different. Familiarizing themselves with these notions, Muslims in Europe who are following new Islamic scholars' ideas seek to accommodate them in their public-private life, to adjust religious principles in social and economic fields, but in line also with these differences in thinking, Muslims in Europe will also become a highly pluralist cluster of communities.

Some authors will claim that all these Muslim intellectuals emphasize democracy, human rights, rule of law, but do it as a departure from an Islamist strategy going to new doctrinal strategies, in other words turning from Islamism to post-islamism. The term post-islamism has been used to refer to the shift in attitudes and strategies of Islamist movements and militants in the Muslim world

(Roy 1999; Kepel 2000). Post-islamism is a term used for the metamorphosis of Islamism in structural, ideological and practical ways.[3] Before identifying these intellectuals as post-islamist, we should note that some Muslim intellectuals, such as Fethullah Gülen, have just defended fundamental rights as universal values which are compatible with Islamic ones.

What all three intellectuals have in common is that they do not believe in the ideologization of religion. In their writings, the attempt to reconcile between faith and secular, sacred and profane, liberty and submission to God is obviously made to rediscover the Islamic texts in new circumstances. They endeavour to find possible links between the West and Islam, to intensify the interaction between Muslims and the whole of society. It can be seen in the emergence of the new Muslim actors in Europe who refuse Muslim exceptionalism, a discourse of victimization. They promote an inclusive attitude, a "positive constructive dialogue"[4]. But they do it in different ways and gradations. The case of Qaradawi, who abandoned his traditional ideas about an exclusivist Islamist discourse which is biased in favour of the Islamic state, may be seen indeed as a post-islamist adaptation. For Al-Qaradawi, the rule of God or Shariah is valid for all time and there are some contradictions between so-called modern society's requirements and Islam; thus he rejected values of the modern world (Al-Qaradawi 1983: 121). Salvatore argues that the emphasis on *maslaha* allows Qaradawi to accept moderation and inclusivism in Islam. Thus, for Salvatore, Qaradawi applies *ijtihad* and free reasoning to modern social problems (Salvatore 2009: 241).

However, he has a binary concept of the world between religious and secular in which religion loses its role and capacity. His close ties with the Muslim Brotherhood, even if he rejects it, and his explicit support for suicide terrorist attacks in Iraq and Israel, have as a consequence that he is considered a fundamentalist preacher and *ulema* representing a militant Islam.

Between openness and exclusivism

Along with a disapproval of secular society and political regimes, the islamists' conception of the organization of society is based on re-establishing the *Sharia,* as some small radical groups advocate. In the case of interpretation of the Qur'an and *hadiths*, contrarily to a literalist approach, as if the sacred text remains frozen in time and place, the new *ijtihad* approach of Muslim intellectuals such as Gülen and Ramadan seeks to revive and reconceptualize the Islamic notions and vocabulary in today's' context. The question of *ijtihad* is not only a renewal of Islamic tradition and past, but it also signifies an openness and inclusivism. Muslim scholars who oppose a literalist-frozen version of Islam as a misguided interpretation embrace a dynamic and context-driven multiple regards approach that enables Muslims and non-Muslims to co-habit.

According to them, the Qur'an invites humans to think, to discover rather than to imitate unconsciously the religious texts which are to be known only through reasoning and deliberation. Free thinking is the first phase in being faithful and understanding the Qur'anic message and prophetic tradition. Their efforts and discourses are comprehended as a continuum of revitalization of Islamic concepts and notions. These efforts are identified as "...a continuation of the radical *tajdid* tradition in Islam. In practice, they built on the accomplishments of the early Islamic modernists and the new-style Muslim associations. ...but at the same time, went far beyond the traditionalism of the remaining conservative *ulama* establishment" (Esposito and O.Voll, 2001: 20).

In the former exclusivist Qur'anic interpretation, the capacity and faculty of understanding of new changing and evolving circumstances is absent. For the literalist tradition, the gates of *ijtihad* are closed because all things are examined. The duty is only to understand what has been said before; in other words simple imitation is sufficient for Muslims. For the new voices of Islam, the *ijtihad* is an "élan vital" of religion. By the way, the religion is readapted to modern circumstances respecting the traditional jurisprudence. To present viable solutions to the complex social and economic problems arising, our three Islamic scholars look to *ijtihad* to renew some issues. On the contrary to call believers to regress into an *umma* (great community) and mythical past, Gülen and Ramadan offer ideas for breaking stereotypes and advocate investing in social economic life. In this sense, Gülen says, "We are in search of an awakening of reason, as well as of heart, spirit and mind. Yet, if it possible to assume a harvest fruits of efforts and works resulting from this" (Gülen 2005: 458). In parallel to these lines, Ramadan argues, "a new, positive and constructive posture which relies on a fine comprehension of Islam's priorities, a clear vision of what is absolute definitively fixed and what is subject to change and adopting..." (Ramadan, 1999: 132-134). For him, Muslims strive for change and adaptation "to avoid reactive and overcautious attitudes and to develop a feeling of self-confidence, based on a deep sense of responsibility" (Ramadan 1999: 150).

In this vein, the concept of what Ramadan uses, *shahada* (testimony), appears interesting, and significantly for him it becomes more applicable in a global period, which permits Muslims to participate in and be involved in their society. "This *shahada* is not only a matter of speech. A Muslim is the one who believes and acts consequently and consistently. *"Those who attain to Faith and do good works"*, as we read in the Qur'an, stress the fact that the *shahada* has an inevitable impact on the actions of the Muslim whatever society he/she lives in. To observe the *shahada* signifies being involved in the society in all fields where need requires it: unemployment, marginalization, delinquency, etc. This also means being engaged in those processes which could lead to a positive reform of both the institutions and the legal, economic, social and political system in order to bring about more justice and a real popular participation at grassroots level" (Ramadan 1999: 147).

Qaradawi most of the time does not go as far as Ramadan, but he also uses the traditional Islamic concept of "*taysir*," translated as "facility," to argue that Muslims in the West are feeble and are not equivalent to Muslims living in Islamic countries. One of the principal terminologies is *wasatiyah* (middle way), aiming to reconcile the renewal of Islamic thought (in other term tajdid) and religious orthodoxy (Benthall 2013). This tendency is seen in his book *al-Halal wa-al-haram fi al-islam* (*The Lawful and the Prohibited in Islam*). Qaradawi, for instance, promulgated a decision permitting a European woman to remain married to her non-Muslim husband after she converted to Islam. A second example is about taking mortgages on houses and business. For western Muslims, mortgages to buy houses or invest in business are permitted, but these were forbidden in traditional interpretations of Islamic law. For European Muslims, Qaradawi has developed various interpretations from Islamic jurisprudence called *fiqh al-aqalliyyat* that apply legal theory to a Muslim minority that lives in the West. But he continues to use the binary position between *dar-ul islam* and *dar-ul harb,* which means, in his thinking, that the needs of Muslims living in a non-Muslim country, as well as their conditions and circumstances, may differ from those in other countries where Muslims live as a majority. But in the case of Muslims living in the West, the rules can be adjusted in accordance with the rule of their country. And that makes him again different from some more traditionalist thinkers.

Conclusion: in search of authority

An analysis of these three Muslim scholars shows how religious tradition is reproduced and transformed in new contexts. The production of Islamic knowledge and authority is seen as fragmented and diluted. Due to this enlargement it becomes clearly more problematic and questionable among the Muslim young generation raised in Europe. Their religious life is influenced by individualism, privacy, autonomy, eclecticism and ethnicity. These factors are influential on the practices and deliberating processes. Bowen argues that Muslims took two possible ways to justify this: first, a transnational one based on norms and traditions of Islam; and, second, a national local one based on local norms and values (Bowen, 2004). These two ways of carrying out practices do not require a diametrical opposition one to other, but each one uses a different repertory which explains and justifies actions. In our case, three Muslim scholars, encountering issues at transnational level, each in their own way, try to produce arguments which are workable in national contexts. To fit Islam into national contexts, values and norms, these scholars revisit and renew the Islamic history, practices and identity.

The problems that the Muslim generation encounters are to find an authoritative Islamic tradition that challenges the fragmented character of their identity. The difficulty of referring publicly to an Islamic identity without withdrawing into the Muslim community, shaping their moral and ethical views based on Islamic principles pushes young Muslims to follow new figures.

Politically, Qaradawi has a classical Islamist tendency stemming from the Muslim Brotherhood background. He divides the world between Muslims and non-muslims and takes his position along this formulation. In his book, *Sharia and Life*, he continues to follow this mainstream interpretation in Islam. This political stand is significantly manifested in several Muslim campaigns, such as the calling for a boycott of Danish products after the cartoons affair published by the Danish Jyllands-Posten newspaper. As Husam Tammam argues, Qaradawi has positioned himself not only as an activist of Egyptian Muslim Brothers, but also as a mentor of the political language of Muslims (Tammam, 2009). One may describe Qaradawi as a 'religiopolitical activist'. The term is used by Muhammad Qasim Zaman to identify the political reference intermingled with religious discourse. He employs the language of *fiqh* to address the modern political questions.

Notes

1 See his book *L'Islam en questions* (Actes-Sud/Sindbad, 2000) with Alain Gresh, a far leftist columnist in Le monde diplomatique.

2 Muslim World does not express an entity covering all Muslims. It signifies the cultural, theological and social divergence and variety of Muslims who live in different countries. The term should not evoke some essentialistic view which inadequately describes the whole of the Muslim people.

3 First used by Bayat. For him, post-islamism represents a condition and project. It attempts to reconcile faith and democracy, Islam and liberty. It is a result of inadequacies and contradictions that persuade Islamist militants to change their discourse and strategies (Bayat, 2007, p. 10-11).

4 This motto appears mainly in many Gülen-inspired dialogue centres such as the Dialogue Society in London and Intercultural Dialogue Platform in Brussels. For more see www.dialoguesociety.org and www.idp-pdi.be

References

Agai Bekim (2003). 'The Gülen Movement's Islamic Ethic of Education', in Esposito, John L. and Yavuz, M. Hakan (ed.), *Turkish Islam and The Secular State, The Gülen Movement*, New York, Syracuse University Pres, 48-68.

Alkan, A. T. (1996). Entellektüel ile arifin kesişme noktası. *Fethullah Gülen Hocaefendi ile Ufuk Turu*, Eyüp can, İstanbul: Milliyet Yayınları, 202.203.

Asad, T. (2003). *Formation of the Secular, Christianity, Islam, Modernity*, Stanford: Stanford University Press.

Ayoob, M. (2005). 'The future of political Islam: the importance of external variables', International Affairs 81: 951-961.

Babes, L. (1997). *L'islam positif. La religion des jeunes musulmans de France*, Editions de l'Atelier, Paris.

Bayat, A. (2007). *Making Islam democratic: social movements and post-Islamist turn*, Stanford, California, Stanford University Press.

Bayat, A. (2002). 'Piety, Privilege and Egyptian Youths', *ISIM Newsletter*, 10.

Bulut, F. (1998). *Kim Bu Fethullah Gülen: Dünü, Bugünü, Hedefi (Who is Fethullah Gülen? His Past, Today and Target)*, Istanbul, Ozan Yayıncılık.

Çetinkaya, H. (2004). *Fethullah Gülen'in Kırk Yıllık Serüveni (The 40 years adventure of Fethullah Gülen)*, Istanbul, Günizi Yayıncılık.

Davie, G. (1994). *Religion in Britain since 1945: Believing without Belonging*, Oxford.

Demir E. (2007). *Les nouvelles sociabilités religieuses, Les logiques organisationnelles et discursives du mouvement néo-communautaire de Fethullah Gülen en France*, Master Thesis l'Institut Politique de Strasbourg.

Ebaugh, H.R. (2010). *The Gülen Movement: A sociological analysis of a civic movement rooted in moderate Islam*, New York, Springer.

Esposito, John L., Yavuz, M. Hakan (eds) (2003). *Turkish Islam and The Secular State, The Gülen Movement*, New York, Syracuse University Press.

Esposito, J.L. and Voll, J.O. (2001). *Makers of contemporary Islam*, New York, Oxford University Press.

Esposito, J.L. (1999). *The Islamic threat: Myth or reality?*, New York, Oxford University Press.

Favrot L. (2004). *Tariq Ramadan dévoilé*, Lyon, Lyon Mag.

Filali-Ansari, A. (2002). *Reformer l'Islam? Une introduction aux débats contemporains*, Paris, La Découverte.

Fourest C. (2004). *Frère Tariq: discours, stratégie et méthode de Tariq Ramadan*, Paris, Grasset.

Fraser, N. (1992). 'Rethinking the Public Sphere: A Contribution to the Critique of Actually Existing Democracy' in Craig Calhoun (ed.), *Habermas and the Public Sphere*, Cambridge, MA: MIT Press, 109-142.

Gaborieau, M. and Zeghal, M. (2004). 'Autorités religieuses en islam', *Archives de sciences sociales des religions,* 125.

Graf, B. (2007). 'Sheikh Yusuf al-Qaradawi in cyberspace', *Die Welt des Islams,* 47 (3-4), 403-421.

Graf, B. and Skovgaard-Petersen, J. (eds.) (2009). *Global Mufti: The phenomenon of Yusuf Al-Qaradawi*, London, Hurst.

Göle, N. (1996). *The Forbidden Modern: Civilization and Veiling*, The University of Michigan Press.

Göle, N. (2005). *Interpénétrations. L'Islam et l'Europe*, Paris, Galaade Editions.

Gülen, F. (2005). 'An Interview with Fethullah Gülen', in 'Islam in Contemporary Turkey: the Contributions of Fethullah Gülen', *Muslim World*, v. 95, n. 3.

Kepel, G. (2005). *The Roots of Radical Islam*, Saqi Books.

Kepel, G. (2003). *Jihad: The trail of political Islam*, Harvard University Press.

Koningsveld, V.P.S. and Shadid, W. (2002). 'The Negative Image of Islam and Muslims in the West: Causes and Solution,' in Shadid, W and van Koningsveld, P.S (eds), *Religious Freedom and the Neutrality of the State: The Position of Islam in the European Union*, Leuven.

Lamine, A.S. (2004). *La coexistence des Dieux, Pluralité religieuse et laïcité*, Paris, Puf, 2004.

Mandaville, P. (2007). 'Globalization and the Politics of Religious Knowledge: Pluralizing Authority in the Muslim World,' *Theory, Culture and Society*, Vol. 24, No. 2.

Mandaville, P. (2001). *Transnational Muslim Politics: Reimagining the Umma*, London: Routledge.

Masud, M.H., Salvatore, A., van Bruinessen, M (eds). (2009). *Islam and Modernity, Key Issues and Debates*, Edinburgh, Edinburgh University Press.

Michel, T. (2003). 'Fethullah Gülen as Educator', in Esposito and Yavuz (eds).

Özdalga, E. (2000). 'Worldly ascetism in islamic casting Fethullah Gulen's inspired piety and activisms', *Critique: Journal for critical studies of the Middle East*, n. 17.

Özdalga E. (2005). 'Redeemer or Outsider? The Gülen Community in the Civilizing Process', *Islam in Contemporary Turkey: The Contributions of Fethullah Gülen, The Muslim World*, V. 95, N. 3: 441.

Pauly, R.J. (2004). *Islam in Europe: Integration or Marginalization?*, Burlington, VT Ashgate Publishing.

Al-Qaradawi, Y. (1994). *Al-ijtihad al-moâsir bayna al-indibat wa al-infiraat*, Cairo, Dar attawziâ wa an-nachr al-islamiya.

'The Qaradawi Fatwas', *Middle East Quarterly*, Summer 2004.

Al-Qaradawi, Y. (1985). *Al-ijtihâd fi achariâ al-islamiya maâ nadharat tahliliya fi al-ijtihad al-moâsir*, Dar al-Qalam, Koweït.

Al-Qaradawi, Y. (2010). *Introduction to Islam*, Malaysia, Islamic Book Trust.

Al-Qaradawi, Y. (1983). *Al-Hulul al-mustavradah wa kayfa janaat 'alaa ummatina*, Beirut, Mussa al-risal.

Ramadan, T. (1999). *To Be a European Muslim*, Leicester, The Islamic Foundation.

Ramadan, T. (2003). *Western Muslims and the Future of Islam*, New York: Oxford University Press USA.

Roussillon, A. (2005). *La pensée islamique contemporaine, acteurs et enjeux*, Paris, Teraedre.

Roy, O. et Haenni, P. (eds.) (1999). 'Le post-islamisme', special issue of *Revue des mondes musulmans et de la Méditerranée*, n° 85-86, Aix-en-Provence, Edisud.

Roy, O. (1996). *The Failure of Political Islam*, Harvard University Press.

Tammam, H. (2009). 'Yusuf Qaradawi and the Muslim Brothers: The Nature of a Special Relationship', in B. Graf and J. Skovgaard-Petersen (eds), *The Global Mufti: The Phenomenon of Yusuf al-Qaradawi* (Columbia/Hurst).

Salvatore, A. (2009). 'Qaradawi's Maslaha' in Graff, B. and Skovgaard-Petersen J. (eds.) *Global Mufti: The Phenomenon of Yusuf Al-Qaradawi*, New York: Columbia University Press.

Skovgaard-Petersen, J. (2004). 'The Global Mufti', in B. Schaebler and L. Stenberg (eds), *Globalization and Muslim World: Culture, Religion and Modernity*, New York, NY: Syracuse University Press, 153-165.

Van Bruinessen, M. and S. Allievi (ed.) (2011). *Producing Islamic Knowledge, Transmission and Dissemination in Western Europe*, Oxon, Routledge.

Voll, J.O. (1983). 'Renewal and Reform in Islamic History: Tajdid and Islah,' in John L. Esposito (ed.), *Voices of Resurgent Islam*, New York, Oxford University Press.

Yılmaz, I. (2003). 'Ijtihad and Tajdid by Conduct', in M. Hakan Yavuz, John L. Esposito (eds), *Turkish Islam and Secular State, The Gülen Movement*, New York, Syracuse University Press.

Yılmaz, I. (2005). 'State, Law, Civil Society and Islam in Contemporary Turkey', *The Muslim World*, v.95, n.3.

Watt, W.M. (1971). *Muslim Intellectual, A study of al-Ghazali*, Edinburg, Edinburg University Press, 1971, 128; www.muslimphilosophy.com/gz/articles/watt-p1.htm.

Zaman, M. Q. (2002). *The Ulama in Contemporary Islam: custodians of change*, Princeton, Princeton University Press.

Zaman, M.Q. (2004). 'The Ulama of Contemporary Islam and their Conception of the Common Good,' in A. Salvatore, D. Eickelman (eds.), *Public Islam and the Common Good*, Leiden: Brill, 129-156.

CHAPTER 3

Tariq Ramadan and Abdullahi An-Na'im's Islamic Gender Reform in the Brussels Moroccan Community

Thierry Limpens

Scholarship and followership: a different 'liberalizing'

Over the past decades, grassroots emancipatory groups in Belgium have succeeded in setting the promotion of gender equality as an express state agenda. Liberal laws protecting women's rights were the first in the country to be voted (Ouali 2012: 101 ff.), and in 2003 same-sex marriage became legal.[1] This change confronts state recognized religions, resulting in Muslim scholars calling for reflection on the position of the Islamic community in the more and more secularized, non-religious Belgian society. The answers given by these scholars echo among both Muslims and non-Muslims. To the latter group Muslims' position is not clear, as it has issued out of three to four generations of peasant migrants since the 1950s, mainly Moroccans and Turks, who form an urbanized ethnic minority with a religion that is conceived in the Belgian non-Muslim mentality as 'imported', or even 'imposed'. Non-Muslims feel overwhelmed by the incoming Muslim culture that over the past decades has rapidly expanded in the major cities where Muslims constitute perhaps over 80 or 90 per cent of the population living together in concentrated zones, particularly in parts of a few central Brussels boroughs. These zones in the state capital are densely populated and young, implanted in 'Muslim halves' of districts of 100,000 habitants each that are known for their poverty, particularly of women (cf. Ouali 2012: 107-108; H'Madoun 2011; Bendadi 26-04-2010; www.observatbru.be).

For many of the secularized majority of Belgians, including the small remaining number of Christians in these districts who over the past few decades have themselves become liberal-moderate, Muslims, and Moroccans in particular, are perceived as stagnating in religious conservatism, not least on gender norms. This opinion is often deduced from the number of Islamic projects that are set up, usually in mosques. For example, more than half of the mosques in the 19 Brussels districts are in three highly multicultural central boroughs with significant Moroccan dominated zones (cf. Manço & Kanmaz 2009: 36; Kanmaz e.a. 09-2004: 16). This evolution is seen by some non-Muslims as 'scary' and likely to 'Islamize' the whole of the Belgian state capital.[2]

This chapter is witness to another situation. The 2007-2013 'emic', or 'Muslim inside', data we collected through participant observations and through nearly 90 interviews and talks in one of the Moroccan dominant zones in Brussels conclude about Muslims' developing an almost invisible, natural and not so profiled 'intermixing', in Eriksen's (2002: 40-44) terms 'ethnic categorical' networking, resulting in a varying 'liberalizing' of religious identities, which is easily overlooked by outsiders, such as whereas they call for more women's rights and gay-friendliness in the Muslim community. This complex, highly diffuse process is characterized by a series of combined aspects that go beyond knowing whether liberal Muslims on the research side form a minority or not. Practically speaking we can presume that from a religious point of view the conservative line is more against gay rights (LGBTQ) than against women's rights. Though, whatever the issue of rates, the utility of our qualitative research study lies in bringing into the picture in what settings 'liberalization' finds place.

A first 'categorical' aspect brings us to the intersection theory defining gender as about the totality of 'sections' composing our social relations, such as race, sexuality, social class, etc. (cf. Ferguson 2013). In other words, religion is just one aspect contributing to liberalization, even if it seemingly dominates in certain places. What is more, people can subscribe conservative religious ideas, but when it comes to putting them into practice in daily life, in order to remain in balance with other 'sections' in their lives, they re-translate them into liberal ones in such 'smart' ways that their conservative status is visibly never endangered.

A second feature has to do with the gradual and competition based mediation of change in the Islamic community with its impact on Muslim society. This facet makes us look at Clifford Geertz's (2001 [1966]: 62-68; 1979) standard conclusion about Moroccans functioning with Islam as a cultural complex of rules and ideas that are transmitted over generations and thought over by influential personalities.

In this context, we have on the research site observed a rivalry between, on the one side, patriarchal women-unfriendly norms and anti-gay machismo and, on the other side, women's and homosexuals' (LGBTQs)[3] emancipation wishes. These are ethnic belongings in which Islam has for many on both sides of the 'liberals-vs.-conservatives' dichotomy a mediatory role, but not only preaching in local mosques, and in recent years also by Youtube/Dailymotion, where important and other kinds of scholars upload their teachings. This mechanism can be called 'religious ethnicity' (Greeley, 1971: 42), referring to some Muslims' seeking from Islam answers to enable them to position themselves in society. In this context, on the research site we have observed Moroccan women talking about their evolution from conservative to more liberal and their looking after the liberalizing Islamic stances of the 'moderate' Tariq Ramadan, though these references tend to be overlooked by mainstream opinion if they are not reported in the media.[4] They are put in even more of a bad light if the scholar himself is pictured as a 'double-speaker', nicely hiding from the non-Muslim world his 'real fundamentalist' objectives (Fourest 2008; s.d., 'The doublespeak'; Favrot 2004).

Gilles Deleuze's (cf. 1990, 1986) observations on 'bodily affection' bring in a third, last aspect of liberal Muslims' categorical ethnicity. This refers to people's experience-based ability, through their affections of the 'body' (in its broadest sense), to find or not find the means to create daily wellbeing. In Deleuze's analysis, for the religious Muslim this searching for meaning is 'transcendentally immanent', or: one's longing for something 'more', 'higher' or 'central', while being unquestionably anchored in the proper contingent iterative context. In this setting, our data reveal that Islamic liberalism finds its way from inside Muslims' sometimes contradictory and often complex contexts. This is observed differently for scholarship and for followership, as we learn in this chapter from our analysis of the journeying of two gender reformative, liberalizing Islamic scholars, Tariq Ramadan and Abdullahi An-Na'im. Both reformers' scholarship has in common the idea that theories become more 'iterative' once they search for applications in often competitive fields. Agent followers, on their part, often yet more seek to reconcile local oppositions and collaborate with 'de-essentializing' Islamic bridging figures. In sum, 'bodily affection' is about the iterativeness of both an engaged scholarship and an agency followership, about people's relation to pluralism, to the possibilities that are created and the challenges that are met. This aspect of liberalism reveals a process of 'un-decidability', or not "... paralysis in the face of the power to decide ..." (Derrida 1999: 66), but our responsibility towards two or more valuable options. Often without that we find support in procedures and programmes.

A first type of this 'un-decidable' liberalizing scholarship brings us to the worldwide influential Swiss-born Islamic scholar (cf. Esposito 2009: 85, 97), Tariq Ramadan (b. 1962). This scholar can be counted among the 'liberal-conservative' voices pleading for gender change in the Muslim community. Ramadan is liberal whereas he calls himself a 'radical reformer' (2008b), or a 'deconstructionist' (2008a: 67-68, 92-93), referring to his hermeneutics (2008b: 14, 111 ff., 173 ff., 279 ff.) that plead for iterative, time-bound translations of Qur'anic/traditional 'higher objectives' into more gender-friendly cultural principles. In his eyes, this is a 'Muslim internal' operation for which he provides the support of intercultural dialogue (2009, 2002b) and the help of modern science (2008b: 278), such as anthropology and other social sciences for a reinterpretation of society. In practice, these liberal hermeneutics make the 'gender reformist' scholar (2008a: 94 ff.; 2008b: 10, 201-203, 267-301) not only call for letting women make their own independent decisions and even developing Islamic leadership. As is less evident in today's Islam, he (2008a: 30-32) calls for more tolerance towards homosexuals (LGBTQs).

Ramadan is also a conservative thinker, calling himself (2008b: 7-15; 2004: 24-30; 2002: 19-30) a 'reformed Salafi'5, meaning that he does not shrink from centering his 'liberal un-decidability' back on 'classical' Islamic norms, such as that religiously devoted Muslim women are supposed to wear an Islamic veil ('*hijab*') (2004b: 72-73) and that LGBTQs must not have gay sex (2008a: 30-32). For the scholar (LCP, 'Audition', 02-05-2012), this conservatism has its 'Muslim internal' justification as he believes that the theological debates in Islam must have their own autonomy as long as they broadly respect state law. In sum, Ramadan is 'liberal-conservative', whereas he pleads for letting Muslim internal/external 'un-decidability' result in liberal practical/theoretical tolerance and change in combination with a 'centering back' on conservative Islamic ideals.

According to some (cf. Zemni 2009: 89; Salvatore 2006: 99; Sunier 24-10-2001), Ramadan overlooks 'Muslim meaning in the plural', whereas he concentrates Islamic reform around his idealizing stances, this with the public he finds for it. This chapter builds on this critique while completing it by observing the scholar's iterativeness when he exposes himself on TV and other platforms to oppositional debates, making him, for instance, slightly revise former opinions about the fact that women are supposed not to lead mixed-gender prayers (Ramadan, Interview by Mende 2009b; Neirynck & Ramadan 1999: 118). What is more, the data reveal an agency followership of the scholar that is even more than himself engaged into 'un-decidability'. This we conclude from both the 'liberal-conservative' mosque 'pole' and the 'liberal' women's and gay rights associations 'pole'.

The liberal-conservative Ramadan 'pole' of the research site, which we have observed in a Brussels district since May 2007, is described in the last section of this chapter. It is represented by a few 'Ramadan-inspired' mosques, and particularly by one 'mega-mosque' in which rivalry among Islamic currents makes agents engage in the 'pragmatic un-decidability' of working together on joint projects. This is that these initiatives cannot incorporate the identity of this or that current in particular, though they create space for Ramadan's call to have female Muslim leadership implemented. At this point, the 'mega-mosque' that also calls itself the Islamic centre is, in the light of its expansion as among the biggest in its kind in Belgium, the place par excellence for Muslim difference. Today (January 2014) it has prayer floors for up to 4,000 women and men, classes for its educational projects that every week attract almost 1,000 youngsters, and it regularly invites Ramadan among other scholars to give public talks.

Within walking distance from the observed 'mega-mosque', there are a series of women's emancipation centres, and a bit further on a Muslim LGBTQ rights association that is also active. These form the 'liberal pole' in which Ramadan finds another, specific gender reformative agency and public. This pole was followed for the study from February 2011 through participant observations in the gender emancipatory programmes that annually reach up to several hundred participants, mainly local Muslim women. Agents there are inspired not only by Ramadan, but also by a few leading scholars within the so-called international 'liberal Muslim movement' (cf. Moosa 2007: 115-118). They believe that Islamic scholars from different liberalizing ideological backgrounds must be put forward with the aim of letting them form a bridge between the liberal and conservative adherents in the local community. In this position, as liberals they show themselves to be close also to the type of far driven 'un-decidability' scholarship we find represented by the U.S. based Sudanese born human rights scholar, Abdullahi An-Na'im (b. 1946).[6] This reformer (2008, 1996) pleads for women's rights in Islam, for coming up for freedom of opinion and for a deconstructionist, or a de-essentializing and democratizing (Baderin 2010: xxxvii-xxxviii), declaring that as long as Muslims submit to the principle of international human rights standards, none of them, whether liberal or conservative, must be discriminated against, in either the Islamic community or society at large. An-Na'im (idem; 2010, 1999, 1990) is 'Muslim un-decidable' in a protagonistic way, calling himself 'visionary heretical'[7], as he considers that Muslims actually do not and principally cannot take the lead in the higher international human rights ideal, though at the same time he declares that Islamic fundaments are not at all strangers to it. These highly 'un-decidable' stances are taken over by local gender agents, though they are able to soften them down in order to reconcile the differences of their target public.

The 'liberal pole': creating separated Islamic free-zones

A first 'pole' of gender reformation brings us to the so-called 'liberal Muslim movement'. This movement has in recent years been known for endeavouring, mainly from outside the U.S., to create separate gay-friendly, mixed-gender and women-imam mosques (cf. Taylor 23-06-2007; Safi 02-05-2006) and, also in Europe, of other 'free-zones' such as women's emancipatory centres and gay-rights associations. On our Brussels research site there has so far been no network of these new mosques, but what we see developing are (i) ad hoc, very occasional and discrete liberal Muslim prayer gatherings, (ii) pro-gay Muslim associations, and (iii) women's emancipatory groups. These are the sites that we will discuss in this chapter. The evolution in these sites is highly iterative and close to the type of An-Na'im's de-centrist 'un-decidability'.

A new promoting of 'de-centrist un-decidability' – In August 2007, 'Muslims for Progressive Values' (MPV) was created by Ani Zonneveld and Pamela Taylor to build a network of new-style mosques based on gay and women imams, on gender-mixing, as well as to call for socio-economic justice. This is an expanding movement in which imam Daayiee Abdullah of the Washington D.C. chapter is internationally one of the leading personalities, but also in which, just before its creation, the well-known Northern American Islamic scholar, Amina Wadud, played a crucial role with her public support and protagonism (Taylor 23-06-2007, 18-03-2006). In 2005-2006, Wadud 'shocked' half of the Muslim world when she led mixed-gender prayers and preached at the same occasion, first inside a church and later in a mosque. Many mainstream Muslim intellectuals, also on the research site, were critical of the act. The liberal An-Na'im (Bartlett, 08-08-2005) considered it sensational instead of persuasive and a possible hindrance to the defenders of women's rights in Muslim majority countries.

Since this episode, an evolution in networking has been observed. Giving a few examples relating to An-Na'im, we stay first with 'Muslims for Progressive Values'. Looking at the group's website, it can be noted that on the 2011 version An-Na'im's works and also those of Ramadan were largely recommended (retrieved 02-02-2011). More recently, greater space has been given to An-Na'im and less to Ramadan, but the latter is referred to as an important Islamic reformer and as a militant against the death penalty.[8] In the context of MPV's gay rights position, this explicit reference to Ramadan may look strange, particularly after the scholar was criticized by some in the movement. The scholar's (2008a: 30-32) call for a kind of tolerance towards homosexuals (LGBTQs), whom he considers Islamically sinful, and his plea not to create 'separate gay mosques'[9] are conceived by some as too passive and not de-stigmatizing enough ('Response', s.d.). Others believe that the scholar's position is a step in the right direction.

A second liberal 'un-decidable' network to which An-Na'im's name is formally linked is the 'American Islamic Fellowship' (AIF) of which the scholar is an advisory member. AIF was created in October 2007 in Atlanta in the U.S., where An-Na'im is based at Emory University, as a 'spiritual awakening movement' open to all, Muslims and non-Muslims, connected with a liberal Islam[10], as is explained on its website:

"The fellowship believes that all people regardless of age, race, disability, sexual orientation, gender, ethnicity, culture, language, social status, religious or philosophical affiliation, or education have the ability to be valuable contributory members to the fellowship".[11]

Since 2011, AIF has become 'Muslims for Progressive Values Atlanta' and is centered more on Muslims' longing to find a place and modality of gathering that can stand for a 'liberal mosque'. This 'Muslim centering' may be misleading, as MPV's approach enabling it to attract participating non-Muslims must not be ignored. Comparing our field data in contrast to this expanding U.S. network of 'visible mosques', the Brussels 'liberal Muslim movement' shows a much more discrete and ad hoc approach to endeavouring to use inclusive Muslim prayers. Nonetheless, the two movements are otherwise similar in 'un-decidability' as far as the gender 'liberationist' objectives they foster towards their target group are concerned.

Thirdly, An-Na'in says, in a 2008 interview (cf. Jones 2008: 136), that he has set up in his home town a de-centrist 'alternative religious Muslim network' outside the traditional Islamic associations that he considers 'superficial', 'partisan' and 'narrow'. About this network he remains vague in that one is not sure whether he is talking of AIF or either of the local poles of the 'Republican movement' that was founded decades ago in Khartoum by the late Sudanese sheikh, Mahmoud Taha (1909-1985), or whether he sees in Atlanta these two groups linked to each other. The fact is that the 'Republicans', of whom An-Na'im is a notable life member, met in January 2009 round the '100 years of progressive Islam conference' that was organized at Ohio State University in the U.S. by the scholar and by other academics in the movement[12]. In January 2010, they gathered in Khartoum in Sudan for the inauguration of the Mahmoud Taha Cultural Centre in the sheik's family house under the direction of his daughter, Asma Taha. This happened after 25 years of Diaspora since the reformer's hanging for 'heresy'. Taha told us on that occasion (Interview 18-01-2010), at which we were present in Khartoum, that the Republican movement is an informal network that is open to all, Muslims and others, who share her father's message of peace. We had the chance to attend the inaugural meetings and discovered the 'Republicans' operating by way of platforms for open discussions on Muslims' need to liberalize (Islamic) practices. During the sessions, all who wanted to address the delegates on either spiritual or societal-cultural topics relating to the discussion were free to come forward and to speak, for as long as they wished, about their chosen angle. To compare, in Brussels, in the observed emancipation centre, we have found similar kinds of platforms, for instance, at women-only tea gatherings that regularly take place. These create moments of free exchange of opinion around a chosen topic, while the 'liberal', 'non-centered' place that is given to Islam – to the extent that religion enters into the discussion – creates margins for reform-minded religious and for secular Muslims feeling at ease together.

In the same context of setting up platforms for open discussion, but more at an intellectual level, a fourth, ad hoc and scholarly de-centrist, 'un-decidable' networking in which An-Na'im is involved as one of the initiative takers is linked to the 2008 'Muslim Heretics Conference' in Atlanta in the U.S., also known as 'A Celebration of Heresy Conference: Critical Thinking for Islamic Reform'. The conference gathered, beyond divergences of opinion, liberal intellectuals and scholars[13], Muslims and non-Muslims, some of whom An-Na'im has closer academic contact with[14]. It believed that "... it is the Muslims that need reform not Islam ...", and, hence, pleaded for having more 'un-decidable', de-centrist debates.[15] In this model, we recognize the observed emancipation centre's organization of

Local women like to be informed on societal issues. Here, they are returning from a group visit to the bank.
© *Bouabbane Lahcene 2012*

debate evenings with keynote speakers from different ideological backgrounds, as this approach corresponds to the Belgian socio-cultural state-funding requiring a sufficient level of discursive pluralism. This setting is not perfect, as the observed centre coordinator points out that in Belgium 'openness towards different directions' after all remains a wishful ideal. She experiences secularism being too much state imposed and hindering Muslims' internal and external reflections from going hand in hand. Whereas Islam is discussed, secularized Westerners are less likely to join the debates, except where the 'Muslim organizers' choose the card of religious liberalization for which state funds can easily be found. Meanwhile, in the latter case, the dominantly conservative Muslim public of the research site remains visibly more absent.

'Un-decidable' free-zones in 'core-Islamic' Brussels – For some years, the de-centrist 'un-decidability' approach of women's emancipation centres on the research site has attracted the attention of a local Muslim gay rights association trying to mediate a wider 'liberalization' there. This objective is not evident towards the often highly 'conservative' attenders at the women's centres on the site. Witness

of it gives a state subsidised meeting on gender justice that was organized by the end of 2011 with the support of the Moroccan female coordinator of the centre who was closely observed for the study.

Discussions we had with both organizers of the meeting made clear that the LGBTQ coordinator, herself a woman, was encouraged to come to the emancipation centre as she believed that it could positively change the opinions of the women there. Despite this conviction, in the centre it was only the coordinator who explicitly engaged in the debate. This has reasons beyond a good part of these women's personal 'not so open' ideology, relating to the fact that in the eyes of many local 'conservative' Muslims, particularly of men, gay rights activists are conceived as being like 'heretics'. As a consequence, for the women it is clear that endeavouring to attain their own so far delicate rights must not be endangered by their willingly or unwillingly joining the homosexuals battle. Their situation is today not at the level of the past evolution in Belgium of women emancipating first from the society's dominant catholic patriarchalism and then, openly or not, supporting the LGBTQs' liberation wishes.

With the 2011 meeting it was LGBTQ Muslims who sought 'ethnic incorporation' in Brussels by means of a local women's emancipating centre. The latter's coordinator felt that it would have been better to work with the more moderate Ramadan instead of with the so-called 'pink Imam' from South Africa, Mushin Hendricks, who was invited to the meeting. In the group of women, Hendricks was perceived as too 'centrist' because of his wanting to prove what is not necessarily accepted by all Muslim LGBTQ activists (cf. interview 21-11-2010); this is that the Qur'an and the Islamic tradition must be seen as 'gay neutral'.

The women of the centre did not join Hendricks' lessons that were open to a larger public attracting many non-Muslims. They gathered around Amina Wadud, who was also invited. This scholar showed understanding as she did not confront the women with her support of the day before on her Belgian tour, in more 'internal liberal circles', for the creation of 'gay-friendly mosques'. Instead, she shared her experiences with Malaysian Muslim women, with whom she organizes discussions about gender-friendly interpretations in Islam. This general topic was supposed to be recognizable by the Moroccan women because of its 'un-decidability', giving space to reflection and open discussion. Nevertheless, the women's quasi silence contrasted with their eagerness to seek advice from a Moroccan female keynote speaker some months later in a meeting in the local 'mega-mosque'. According to the coordinator, the interventions of the day were

Islamically too ideological and they did not advise mothers on what to do when they themselves had an LGBTQ daughter or son.

Wadud's presentation was attended by a male representative of the local 'Ramadan-friendly' 'mega-mosque'. He pointed out that what the scholar proposed had already been achieved in his institute. His remark led to a discussion afterwards between him and the centre coordinator. The latter was of the opinion that mosques, even those inspired by Ramadan, still have a long way to go before becoming fully gay- and women-friendly. On the other hand, she complained about the difficulty in her association of obtaining state subsidies for 'liberal-conservative' Islamic thinkers like Ramadan. She argued that in this setting conservative local Muslim women attending her centre did not feel sufficiently state supported to create the emancipatory 'free zones' they wished for. They viewed the inviting of liberal scholars with the use of state money as an external interference from the dominant non-Muslim society. Other women in the group themselves evolved from conservative to liberal. Or they were just liberal 'by nature' and they had sympathy for Ramadan and for other reformative thinkers, but in the context of the tense religious environment in which they lived they preferred not to be associated with the most liberal ones. Because of these feelings in the women's group, the coordinator suggested in the end that there should be a 'counter' reconciliatory meeting. She hoped to be able to invite Ramadan for that occasion.

The 'liberal-conservative' pole: inculturalizing reformed Salafism

The 'liberal-conservative' Ramadan (2008b: 7-15; 2004: 24-30; 2002: 19-30) calls himself a 'reformed Salafi' as regards his belief in a constant 'opening' reinterpreting, or 'liberalizing', of classical 'conservative-centrist' Islamic sources. His promoting of these legacies has its greatest impact in mainstream Muslim circles. As is observed by Dassetto (2011: 229, 257-259) in the Brussels context and pointed out by Ramadan himself (2008a: 11, 14-15, 38-39), the scholar stands opposed to the 'hermetic centrism' of those whom he calls 'literalist Salafis' wanting to apply textually 7th century Islamic prescriptions. We will see in this section that over and above this binary rivalry there is room for competition among a wider variety of Salafi currents that end up in 'pragmatic un-decidability' once they engage in joint projects and mediate or even give occasion to common Muslims' higher level of iterativeness. In this sense, our data reveal that

Ramadan's definition of 'Salafi literalists' is best adjusted to draw a distinction, among other possible nuances, between moderate or 'harmonizing literalists' and radical or 'conflicting' ones. Finally, the 'classical pole' is, apart from the agency of Ramadan's own created civil society organizations, not so much involved in the scholar's call for more gay-friendliness. The pole's Ramadan-friendly agency must be sought in the scholar's plea for giving women a better place in the Muslim community.

'Open centrism': connecting gender reformative Islam to civil society – Ramadan is a brilliant networker in both 'Islamic' and 'secular' civil society, setting up direct collaborations everywhere and reaching out to large numbers of people. His agency is 'open to the Western condition', a fact which has in the past few years given him assignments as an advisor to the European Union, to the British Government, to the Rotterdam municipality in the Netherlands and to the French parliament, all relating to Muslims', in the scholar's (2008a, 96-104) own words, 'post- integration' of which, in the end, he says that the theological debates are 'Muslim internal' matters (Shavit 2014: 166; LCP, 'Audition' 02-05-2012; Baum 2009: 16; Ramadan 30-04-2008). In Belgium, Ramadan is not connected to politics, but some of his public talks attract nationwide media attention (cf. 'Foire musulmane' 29-09-2012; Vanlommel 03-02-2012). On the research site, he mainly joins the 'Muslim-internal' settings in which his 'liberal-conservative' reform proposals find a public. In this position, he happens to express critiques on 'classical' Islamic institutions (interview by Widmann 2008), as he (2002: 14 ff.) observes them competing with each other and not seeking to understand Muslims' modern life condition.

Ramadan's first international organization, the collective 'Muslim Presence' (MP), was set up by the end of the 1990s positively to incorporate reformative Muslims' position inside the faith community and society at large. MP's aim is to network towards 'Muslim citizenship', or the idea of Muslims contributing to the larger society and their reflecting about what Islamic spirituality encourages them to do to that end. This it does by creating 'small sized platforms for dialogue and exchange', leading to gender advocacy against forced marriage and honour killing, against discrimination against LGBTQs' and their punishment by the state (Seniguer & Sambe 21-07-2013), as well as in defence of women's rights to make decisions for themselves, such as on whether or not to wear an Islamic headscarf (Diallo 12-03-2013).[16]

In the past few years, MP's expansion looks as though it has slowed down. Whereas in 2011 the movement still mentioned on its website local poles in Belgium, France and Canada, today it seems to have limited its activities to the last country, more particularly to Montréal and Ottawa, and to CIMEF or its biannual African colloquium[17]. The Belgian (Brussels) branch that was active on the research site succeeded for almost a decade in gathering young Muslim women and men from different social and educational backgrounds. Since about 2008, the group has stopped its activities after most of its leading members themselves became busy personalities, some still in new projects in collaboration with Ramadan, or, more independently, in Ramadan-inspired initiatives inside the local 'mega-mosque' or elsewhere. Others suffered from external pressure to stop or reduce their advocacy for marginalized Muslims.

Another event that may explain the disappearance of a 'Muslim Presence' in Belgium is that in 2007-2008 Ramadan, together with some of MP's key members, created the 'European Muslim Network' (EMN). EMN is a Muslim advocatory think thank having its seat in Brussels and Muslim spokespersons in 15 European countries. On its website, Malika Hamida, the EMN director, is the main author of opinion texts discussing issues of gender justice. The network is militant against female genital mutilation and against the stigmatization of homosexuals[18], for which, in its Brussels agency, it works together with Ramadan-friendly Muslim civil society organizations, with some of them being active on the research site.

The mosque: centrist competitions, 'pragmatic un-decidability' – Ramadan is regularly present in a few of the Belgian 'mega-mosques', and, on the research site, in a particular one that calls itself 'Islamic centre'. These are 'Muslim only', highly 'internal' places where we find different 'Salafi currents' competing over having space and Islamic influence. Specific in this rivalry is that while these groups each have their own theoretical centrism, they become 'un-decidable' once they engage in joint projects in which their divergences are never really defined openly and in which they cannot one-sidedly impose their own Islamic current.

In the 'Ramadan-inspired' Islamic centre mosque where we made our participant observations, the daily direction does not judge specific currents, except extreme liberal and fundamentalist ones. Like when its highly influential sheikh preached on a Friday at the beginning of 2011 to a public of up to 4,000 women and men against

Women and men after Eid pray together for a street feast in front of the 'mega-mosque'. Social media photo.

"... separated Salafis who think to know Islam better than their parents and even their imam, after they have read only a few Islamic works".

In the sheikh's 'mega-mosque', two 'Salafi currents' are most represented: (i) the 'liberalizing', or 'reformed' 'Ramadan-type', and (ii) the one slightly more 'conservative', or 'moderate, harmonizing literalist', as e.g. linked to the scholar's brother, Hani Ramadan.[19] If compared to the criticized 'separatists', the two groups are 'mainstream Salafis'. Inside the mosque, they can easily be distinguished. For instance, the 'Ramadan-liberal' women, who do not hide their admiration for the scholar, are dressed in fancy, 'blinkingly coloured' head covers (*'hijab'*), and, a few of them are even without. The latter are more usually present on the scholar's 500,000 fan-rich Facebook pages and on his personal website[20], but it is clear that women need courage to appear without a *'hijab'* in the mosque, where this dress is highly recommended. These 'Ramadan-Salafi' women also shake hands with men and they are easily found working in mixed-gender mosque offices, often together with their fellow male 'Ramadan followers' in the institute. In contrast to them, the more 'conservative Salafi' women are dressed in dark coloured veils covering the whole body. They stay only on the side of the separate 'women's mosque' and do not shake hands with men to whom they avoid or even refuse to address themselves verbally.

It is not clear which group of these two 'mainstream Salafi' women is more present and active in the Islamic centre mosque, but both are certainly not always involved in the same projects. The degree holding women of the 'Ramadan type' do not often attend the prayers and activities of the so-called 'women's mosque', separated from men, where the less educated and even analphabets are more represented and where at times alphabetization courses are organized. In projects in which the 'Ramadan liberal-conservatives' are involved, women like putting themselves at the same level as men. This challenges the official line of the exclusively *male* general direction board of the Islamic centre mosque, despite the fact that we have observed in recent years the projects of that institute also following Ramadan's call for letting mainstream Islam be more gender equal. For instance, its school for compulsory state education that was opened in 2007 is today directed by the only woman to whom is given a significant leadership position inside the institute. She is one of Ramadan's Islamic feminist fans in the place. Among the teachers working for her, who are mostly women, there are different Ramadan followers, but also others who are ideologically closer to the conservative 'moderate-literalists'. Because of this divergence, this civil society project, just like others in the Islamic centre mosque, finds it difficult to develop a fixed Islamic identity, though once it becomes state subsidized, as this is part of the Belgian agreement with religion, the secular contracts in which it is engaged will have occasion to develop wider gender reformative standards that appear to be closer to the 'liberal-conservative' 'Ramadan line'.

'Anti-hudûd' agency: practical and theoretical 'un-decidability' – Ramadan's gender reformation echoes in the 'liberal-conservative pole' of the research site through his setting up of field campaigns, such as that relating to what the scholar (2008a, 92-93) defines as cultural deconstruction, or the release of Islam from unauthentic, patriarchal malpractices. As such, there is his (2008a: 93; cf. 2008b: 294 n.1) international 2007-2008 campaign against forced marriage, against female excision and honour crimes. This campaign was supported by

the 'European Muslim Network' (EMN) and by some other connected Muslim organizations, also on the research site. It found large support, as according to our data, today there is the practically 'centrist' opinion that these customs have no place in Islam. Forced marriage seems to have disappeared and female excision is not really a Belgian-Moroccan practice. Only common Muslims are more 'un-decidable', whereas they often do not find theological arguments to defend this customary change. This brings in new 'practical un-decidability'. For instance, in the choice of a marriage partner the parents' interference is still significant, and even more dramatic can be the case of a Muslim Moroccan woman wanting to marry a non-Muslim man. We have ourselves witnessed a young single mother who was a divorcee from her first, Moroccan husband. When she started dating a non-Muslim Belgian, her brothers got to know about it, and before her father was informed, one of them decided to threaten to kill her boyfriend. She then hid herself for a while in the house of one of her sisters while her boyfriend thought about converting to Islam. Other quite common issues of genderized 'honour pressure' among Moroccans we find are that girls must be virgins on the day of marriage and that their husbands may ask them to start wearing an Islamic headscarf.

A similar theoretical/practical 'un-decidability' we find when looking at the field relevance of Ramadan's earlier 2005 campaign entitled 'An International call for Moratorium on corporal punishment, stoning and the death penalty in the Islamic World'. The official text of this call (05-04-2005) challenges Muslims in favour of 'classical' Islamic corporal punishments ('*hudûd*') like stoning to death. The initiative touches Ramadan's (2008a, 92-93) prediction of 'scriptural deconstruction' or critically looking at normative religious traditions. According to the scholar (idem), this deconstruction cannot be isolated from the cultural debate in which Islamic norms find their translation into state laws.

Ramadan (2008b: 356 ff.) does not agree with '*hudûd*' in Muslim dominant countries being imposed almost exclusively on women and on the poor. Nonetheless, he (28-04-2005) believes (i) that their Qur'anic tradition must be somehow respected, for instance with regard to the 'higher objective' of the necessity of 'Divine forgiveness' (cf. Neyrinck & Ramadan 1999: 109), but also (ii) that their interpretation is difficult, and above all (iii) that there are no fulfilled conditions to apply to them today. As regards this combined 'un-decidability', Ramadan (2008b: 356 ff.) defends himself against Western critiques that he is not as clear as liberal reformists, like Abdullahi An-Na'im (2005), calling for a complete abolition and not for 'only' a moratorium. The scholar replies preferring the 'pragmatic-centrist', steadfast position of wanting to save lives while Islamic legal scholars can take their 'un-decidable' time to resolve the issue at a decisive judicial level. Ramadan compares the issue to what happens in the U.S., where calling for the abolition of the death penalty so far has never been successful. Finally, it is clear that his most *personal* opinion is outspokenly 'anti-*hudûd*' whereas he calls the punishments 'un-Islamic', as he did in following interview:

> "I consider stoning, the death penalty and corporal punishment un-Islamic. There are a number of prominent Muslims who see that the same way" (Interview by Widmann 2008).

Unlike Islamic critiques of the campaign in Muslim dominant countries, particularly Egypt (cf. Ramadan 29-04-2005b, 29-04-2005a, 28-04-2005, 10-05-2005), on the research site 'common' Muslims, not at least Ramadan followers, are clear that a harsh penalizing state has no *practical* place in today's (Western) society. In contrast, some remain *theoretically* 'un-decidable' effectively calling for the abolition or even a moratorium of '*hudûd*' punishments that help them remember about 'higher' Islamic objectives relating to the idea of the ' just society'. This leads to conservative idiomatic interpretations among (but not uniquely) impoverished Muslims and among first generation migrant ones. For instance, as regards the rule of stoning to death for adultery and for fornication, the ideal can mean that chastity and respect for each other's sexual dignity must be promoted and that adultery and 'public sex' ('cheap one') are to be considered damaging to one's 'purity of the soul'. This is sometimes interpreted differently by men and women. Some men, not so much the Ramadan followers, use the idea of '*hudûd*' as a patriarchal threat against women, fostering female seclusion and other mobility restrictions, as explained by one of our female informants:

> "If a woman, not a man, has sex outside marriage, the result is a figurative death sentence. No wonder that there are so many abortions among Moroccan Muslim girls here. Many young girls leave, in a manner of speaking, their father's house for the first time on the day of their marriage, and, after that, without the accompaniment of their husband, they will never travel outside their village or town (Interview 27-09-2010).".

Women, particularly those who are 'Ramadan-inspired', have their own idiomatic interpretations insisting on gender equality, on men being prohibited from sexually abusing women in both a wide and a strict sense; if not 'divine forgiveness' through 'punishment' must be sought. This does not literally mean 'stoning', but the cruelty of this ancient punishment must make the faith seeker remember about the holiness of Islamic prescriptions and seek correction of behaviour. This feminine gender standard is today co-promoted by the male Ramadan entourage of the site. The more classical sheikh in the Ramadan-inspired 'mega-mosque' is likely to follow this position, though with this difference: that he is tempted to propose male polygamy as a solution for some men's difficulties in meeting the ideal of chastity. Another leading imam in this mosque follows Ramadan's line (cf. Neirynck & Ramadan 1999: 87, 99), and one of the scholar's female followers, when he pleads for not speaking today in favour of male polygamy, this based on the idea that Islam promotes monogamy in the first place.

Some women in the observed 'liberalizing' emancipation centre complain about a few very 'hostile' male 'literalist *hudûd* promoters' in their neighbourhood. Because of their emancipation wishes they are pictured by the latter as 'weak', as 'easily influenced' ('unguided', or: heretical) and as sensitive to accepting men's seduction. The centre coordinator says that on occasions she is herself personally intimidated by women and men who sometimes come to create disorder in the centre's gatherings or who aggressively address her when they pass in the street. This is the work of those whom Ramadan (2008a: 11, 14-15, 38-39) calls 'radical Salafi literalists', the ones who are also hostile to him. They consider '*hudûd*' a fundamental part of 'Shari`a' that must be applied once the Muslim community reaches out to the level of 'Islamic society'. They feel themselves obliged to prepare the Muslim community for this. As a reason they give for this highly 'centrist' position, they refer to their belief in the classical idea that, for instance, it is through stoning that the sinner is forgiven by God and, hence, again allowed to enter the after-life paradise. In this conception, for these 'radical Salafi literalists', God's mercy as a 'higher objective' depends on the state application of 'eternal' (unchangeable) and 'divine laws'. In sum, as 'non-deconstructionists' they call for not making a distinction between state law and religious norms.

Conclusion

In the highly multicultural Belgian state capital, Brussels, Moroccan gender agents on women's and gay rights find conditions and modalities enabling them to mediate Islamic liberalization. From inside their ethnic community they are directly or indirectly connected with the reformative legacies of both the 'liberal-conservative' scholar, Tariq Ramadan, and the liberal one, Abdullahi An-Na'im. This does not just bring them closer to the Belgian gender liberal state agenda. From inside mosques and state subsidised centres, they also respond to the emancipatory wishes of local Muslims. Agents in such centres are close to An-Na'im's outspoken iterative and open gender model calling for more women's and gay rights. They are also directly inspired by Ramadan whom they see as a bridging figure between the more conservative belongings of the local environment. Ramadan is more for women's rights and less for LGBTQs' ones, though he calls for tolerance towards the latter. This line fits the 'liberal-conservative' Ramadan-inspired mosques.

Both engaged scholars and agents understand through the projects they set up or coordinate that local Muslims seek guidance to the plurality of their environment and society at large. This condition is not evident as it demands mutual adaptation in which all parties try to find their own ways, try to work out their own answers and take positions. Despite this common perception, in this setting agents and local Muslims are slightly more than engaged scholars in their discursiveness, and in their self-styled projects hold by the need to mediate local differences.

Notes

1   Belgium legalized same-sex marriage on 01-06-2003 as the second country worldwide after the Netherlands did the same on 01-04- 2001 (Lee, 2010: 18-20).

2   See the following popularizing writings about the so-called Islamic fundamentalism of the Belgian Muslim community and particularly the Moroccan one that was observed for this study: Benyaich 2013, Calluy 2012; van Rooy & van Rooy 2010; Dedecker 2009; Dewinter 2009; Van Amerongen 2008; Fraihi 2006).

3   LGBTQ meaning: Lesbian, Gay, Bisexual, Transgender, Queer; or extended to LGBTQIA: adding Intersex and Asexual.

4   On the rise of 'Islamophobia' see Zemni's (2011) critique denouncing the negative role of the Belgian regular media.

5   Many definitions exist about 'conservative' Islamic currents that are linked to Salafism, such as relating to their connection or not to modernity (cf. Zemni 2006). In this chapter we do not go further in this academic debate, but we build on our Muslim-internal ('emic') data that we have centered around Ramadan's defining of Salafism as a sometimes more 'liberal-conservative', or 'reformative' (for himself), and sometimes more dominantly 'conservative', or the 'classical' current, the latter what in its extreme form is called 'Salafi literalism' by the scholar (Ramadan 2008a: 11, 14-15, 38-39) (cf. infra).

6   During our observations we did not find Moroccan agents referring to An-Na'im, in what may be due to the language difference (An-Na'im not publishing in French). Nevertheless, some of them collaborate with 'liberal' Islamic scholars who are part of An-Na'im's circle. Apart from this, in Belgium 'the scholar's 'direct followers' are found among the handful of Belgian-Sudanese Muslims who belong, just like him, to the Sufi inspired so-called 'Republican movement' of the late sheikh Mahmoud Taha (1909-1985) (cf. Mahmoud 2007; An-Na'im 2008: 108-109 ff.). An-Na'im also has contacts in a group of militants of the Altermondialist movement, like e.g. Samir Amin (cf. 2000), who are linked with the World Social Forum founder and Taha admirer, the Belgian François Houtart (cf. 2002). Finally, his theories are internationally reflected on among academic human rights defenders, such as the promoters of his 2009 honorary doctorate at the universities of Leuven and Louvain-la-Neuve in Belgium (cf. Flobets 2010).

7   See: http://www.youtube.com/user/muslimheretics (retrieved 13-02-2013).

8   See: http://mpvusa.org/portfolio/ijtihad (retrieved 27-03-2013).

9   See Ramadan's intervention in the TV debate 'Hondelatte Dimanche «Homosexuel et bon musulman»' (16/05/2013) (http://www.youtube.com/watch?v=2O2J6DtKhU8, uploaded by Tariq Ramadan on 03-06-2013; retrieved 20-06-2013).

10 See: http//www.americanislamicfellowship.org (retrieved 13-04-2011).

11 See: http://mpvatlanta.org/faq (retrieved 06-04-2011).

12 See: http://www.african.ohio.edu/Conferences/index.html (retrieved 19-05-2011).

13 See: http://www.youtube.com/user/muslimheretics (retrieved 13-02-2013).

14 See An-Na'im's academic websites at Emory University: http://www.law.emory.edu/aannaim and some other places (retrieved 02-03-2013).

15 See: http://tabari.com/blog1/about (retrieved 05-05-2011).

16 See: http://muslimpresence.com (retrieved 01-04-2011, 02-03-2013).

17 See: http://www.cimef.net (retrieved 12-09-2013).

18 See: http///www.euro-muslims.eu (retrieved 16-02-2013).

19 Of Hani Ramadan it is reported his defending, 'on Western ground', Islamic corporal punishments (cf. Widmann 2008). Whatever the truth of the case, our data reveal that the

scholar stands today in the observed mosque/Islamic centre for a less 'liberal' and a more 'literalist' Salafi line, as the two brothers are often compared to each other there.

20 See: http://www.tariqramadan.com (retrieved 15-02-2013).

References

Amin, S. (2000). 'Vers une théologie islamique de la libération? L'oeuvre de Mahmoud Mohamed Taha,' in Centre-tricontinental, *Théologies de la libération*, 209-214, (Alternatives Sud, 7 (1): point de vue du Sud). Paris, Montréal: l'Harmattan.

An-Na'im, A. A. (2005). 'Globalization and jurisprudenc: an Islamic law perspective,' *Emory Law Journal*, 54, 25-51.

An-Na'im, A. A. (1990). 'Human rights in the Muslim world: socio-political conditions and scriptural imperatives,' *Harvard Human Rights Journal* (3), 13-52.

An-Na'im, A. A. (2008). *Islam and the secular state: Negotiating the future of Shari'a.* Cambridge, MA: Harvard University Press.

An-Na'im, A. A. (2010). 'The Compatibility Dialectic: Mediating the Legitimate Coexistence of Islamic Law and State Law,' *Modern Law Review*, 73 (1), 1-29.

An-Na'im, A. A. (1996). *Toward an Islamic reformation: Civil liberties, human rights, and international law* (Contemporary Issues in the Middle East). Syracuse, NY: Syracuse University Press.

An-Na'im, A. A. (1999).'Universality of human rights: an Islamic law perspective,' in Ando, N. (ed.), *Japan and international law: past, present and future* (pp. 311-325), The Hague, London, Boston: Kluwer Law International.

Baderin, M. A. (2010). 'Introduction: Abdullahi An-Na'im's philosophy on Islam and human rights,' in Baderin, M.A. (ed.), *Islam and human rights: Selected essays of Abdullahi An-Na'im*, i-xxxix), (Series: Collected Essays in Law). Farnham / Burlington (VT): Ashgate.

Bartlett, T. (08-08-2005). 'The quiet heretic [on Amina Wadud, professor of Islamic studies at Virginia Commonwealth University],' *Chronicle of Higher Education* (Retrieved 03-05-2011 from http://www.campus-watch.org/article/id/2128).

Baum, G. (2009). *The theology of Tariq Ramadan: a Catholic perspective.* Notre Dame (IN): University of Notre Dame Press.

Bendadi, S. (26-04-2010). 'Vrouwen van Molenbeek staan hun mannetje,' *MO Magazine, online* (Retrieved 02-03-2012 from http://www.mo.be/artikel/vrouwen-van-molenbeek-staan-hun-mannetje).

Benyaich, B. (2013). *Islam en radicalisme bij Marokkanen in Brussel*, (i.s.m. Zibar Omar) Leuven: Van Halewyck.

Calluy, P. (2010). *Kroniek van een aangekondigd onheil: Radicale islam in Vlaanderen.* Brussel: ASP Editions.

Dassetto, F. (2011). *L'iris et le croissant: Bruxelles et l'islam au défi de la co-inclusion.* Louvain-la-Neuve: Presses universitaires de Louvain.

Dedecker, J.-M. (2009). *Hoofddoek of blinddoek? De migratie ontsluierd.* Leuven: Van Halewyck.

Deleuze, G. (1986). *Cinema 1: The movement-image,* Minneapolis (MN): University of Minnesota.

Deleuze, G. (1990). *The logic of sense,* London: Athlone Press.

Derrida, J. (1999). 'Hospitality, justice and responsibility: a dialogue with Jacques Derrida,' in Kearney, R. & M. Dooley (eds.), *Questioning Ethics: Contemporary Debates in Philosophy* (pp. 65-83), London: Routledge.

Dewinter, F. (2009). *Inch'Allah? De islamisering van Europa,* Brussel: Egmond.

Diallo, I. (12-03-2013). 'Tariq Ramadan sur la place de la femme dans les sociétés Musulmanes: «Tout le contraire de l'Islam»,' *Sud Quotidien, online* (Retrieved 20-03-2013 from http://www.sudonline.sn/tout-le-contraire-de-lislam_a_12829.html).

Eriksen, T. H. (2002). *Ethnicity and nationalism* (Anthropology, culture, and society), London, Sterling (Va.): Pluto Press.

Esposito, J. and I. Kalin (eds). (2009). *The 500 most influential Muslims in the world: first edition 2009,* Georgetown: Georgetown University.

Favrot, L. (2004). *Tariq Ramadan dévoilé* (Lyon Mag' hors série), Lyon: Lyon Mag'.

Ferguson, S. J. (ed.). (2013). *Race, gender, sexuality & social class: Dimensions of inequality,* Los Angeles (CA): Sage Publications.

Flobets, M.-C. (2010). 'Foreword and acknowledgments: Islam and the requirements of liberal democratic principles,' in Flobets, M.C. & J.-Y. Charlier (eds.), *Islam & Europe: crises are challenges,* Leuven: Leuven University Press, 7-22.

'Foire musulmane: Une ouverture loin des polémiques,' (28-09-2012). *Le Dernière Heure Online* (Retrieved 29-09-2012 from http://www.dhnet.be/infos/belgique/article/409529/foire-musulmane-une-ouverture-loin-des-polemiques.html).

Fourest, C. (2008). *Brother Tariq: The doublespeak of Tariq Ramadan.* New York: Encounter Books.

Fourest, C. (s.d.). 'The doublespeak of Tariq Ramadan,' *(Interview),* Retrieved 28-12-2009 from http://www.newcultureforum.org.uk/home/?q=node/236.

Fraihi, H. (2006). *Undercover in Klein-Marokko: achter de gesloten deuren van de radicale islam,* Leuven: Van Halewyck.

Geertz, C. (2001, [1966]). Religion as a cultural system, in Lambek, M. (ed.), *A reader in the anthropology of religion,* Malden (Mass): Blackwell, 61-82.

Geertz, C. (1979). Suq: the bazaar economy in Sefrou, in Geertz, C., Geertz, H. & L. Rosen, *Meaning and order in Moroccan society: three essays in cultural analysis* Cambridge: Cambridge University Press, 123-225.

Greeley, A. M. (1971). *Why can't they be like us? America's white ethnic groups*, New York (NY): E.P. Dutton.

H'madoun, M. (2011). 'Afraid of god or afraid of man: How religion shapes attitudes toward free riding and fraud' (Research paper / UA, Faculty of Applied Economics; 2011:008) (Retrieved 02-06-2012 from http://www.ua.ac.be/download.aspx?c=*TEWHI&n=95313&).

Hondelatte Dimanche (16-05-2013). 'Homosexuel et bon musulman' (Retrieved 20-06-2012 from http://www.youtube.com/watch?v=2O2J6DtKhU8, uploaded by Tariq Ramadan on 03-06-2013).

Houtart, F. (2002). 'Avant-propos. Mahmoud Mohamed Taha, témoin de l'Islam dans le monde contemporain,' in Taha, M.M. *Un islam à vocation libératrice* (Collection religion et sciences humaines. Section 1: faits religieux & société). Paris / Budapest / Torino: l'Harmattan, pp. 7-12.

Jones, R. P. (2008). *Progressive & religious: how Christian, Jewish, Muslim, and Buddhist leaders are moving beyond the culture wars and transforming American life.* Lanham (Md.): Rowman & Littlefield Publishers.

Kanmaz, M., El Battiui, M., & Nahavandi, F. (09-2004). 'Moskeeën, imams en islamleerkrachten in België: stand van zaken en uitdagingen' (Retrieved 30-04-2011 from http://www.kbs-frb.be/uploadedFiles/KBS-FRB/Files/NL/PUB_1447_Moskeeen_imams_islamleerkrachten.pdf).

LCP - Assemblée Nationale. (02-05-2012). 'Audition de Tariq Ramadan, islamologue, professeur et universitaire' (Retrieved 20-07-2012 from http://www.lcp.fr/emissions/travaux-en-commission/vod/50935-audition-de-tariq-ramadan-islamologue-professeur-et-universitaire).

Lee, M. Y. (2010). *Equality, dignity, and same-sex marriage: A rights disagreement in democratic societies*, Leiden / Boston (MA): Martinus Nijhoff Publishers.

Mahmoud, M. A. (2007). *Quest for divinity: A critical examination of the thought of Mahmoud Muhammad Taha*, New York: Syracuse University Press.

Manço, U. & M. Kanmaz (2009). Belgium. Nielsen, J.S., Akgönül, S., Alibašić, I.A. & B. Maréchal (eds.), *Yearbook of Muslims in Europe: volume 1*, Leiden: Brill, 35-48.

Moosa, E. (2007). 'Transitions in the 'progress' of civilization: theorizing history, practice, and tradition,' in Safi, O. & V. J. Cornell (eds.), *Voices of Islam: Voices of Change (Volume 5)*, Westport (CT): Praeger, 115-130.

Neirynck, J. & J. Ramadan (1999). *Peut-on vivre avec l'islam? Le choc de la religion musulmane et des sociétés laïques et chrétiennes.* Lausanne, Paris: 1999.

Ouali, N. (2012). 'Migrant women in Belgium: Identity versus feminism,' in Bonifacio, G.T. (ed.), *Feminism and migration: Cross-cultural engagements* (pp. 101-121) (International perspectives on migration, 1). New York (NY): Springer.

Ramadan, T. (2009b). (Interview by C. Mende). 'Interview with Tariq Ramadan: "We Are Europeans"'. *Qantara.de* (Retrieved 03-01-10 from http://www.qantara.de/webcom/ show_article.php/_c-478/_nr-905/i.html).

Ramadan, T. (10-05-2005). 'A response to Shaykh Dr. Ali Ali Juma'a, Mufti of Egypt' (Retrieved 05-01-2010 from http://www.tariqramadan.com/spip.php?article323).

Ramadan, T. (05-04-2005). 'An International call for Moratorium on corporal punishment, stoning and the death penalty in the Islamic World' (Retrieved 10-01-10 from http://www. tariqramadan.com/spip.php?article264&var_recherche=moratorium).

Ramadan, T. (2002). *Aux sources du renouveau musulman: d'al-Afgani à Hassan Al-Banna, un siècle de réformisme Islamique.* Paris: Éditions Tawhid.

Ramadan, T. (2002b). 'Europeanization of Islam or Islamization of Europe?', in Hunter, S.T. (ed.), *Islam, Europe's second religion: The new social, cultural, and political landscape* Westport (CT): Preager Publishers / Center for Strategic and International Studies, 207-218.

Ramadan, T. (2008a). *Face à nos peurs: Le choix de la confiance*, Lyon: Tawhid.

Ramadan, T. (2008b). *Islam, la réforme radicale: Ethique et libération*, Paris, Québec: Presses du Châtelet.

Ramadan, T. (2009). *L'autre en nous: Pour une philosophie du pluralisme*, Paris / Québec: Presses du Châtelet.

Ramadan, T. (2004b). *Le face à face des civilisations: Quel projet pour quelle modernité?* Lyon: Tawhid.

Ramadan, T. (30-04-2008). 'On education: Tariq Ramadan's first report in Rotterdam' (Retrieved 05-01-10 from http://www.tariqramadan.com/spip.php?article1441).

Ramadan, T. (28-04-2005). 'Response to the official statement of the Al-Azhar Legal Research Commission on the Call for a Moratorium published on March 30th, 2005' (Retrieved 05-01-10 from http://www.tariqramadan.com/spip.php?article308).

Ramadan, T. (29-04-2005a). 'Responses to the Muslim scholars and the leaders: The 1st response to Islamonline.net comment' (response to Dr Ahmad ar-Rawi) (Retrieved 05-01-10 from http://www.tariqramadan.com/spip.php?article311).

Ramadan, T. (29-04-2005b). 'Responses to the Muslim scholars and the leaders: The 2nd response to Islamonline.net comment' (response to Dr Taha Jabir al-'Alawani) (Retrieved 05-01-10 from http://www.tariqramadan.com/spip.php?article311).

Ramadan, T. (2004). *Western Muslims and the future of Islam*, Oxford: Oxford University Press.

'Response to Tariq Ramadan: Equal rights for GLBT Muslims "No more, no less" Declares Muslims for Progressive Values,' (s.d.). *Queer Faith News* (Retrieved 01-04-2013 from http://queerfaithnews.wordpress.com/2010/09/04/response-to-tariq-ramadan-equal-rights-for-glbt-muslims-no-more-no-less-declares-muslims-for-progressive-values/).

Safi, O. (02-05-2006). 'What is Progressive Islam?,' (Retrieved 23-04-2011 from http://www.averroes-foundation.org/articles/progressive_islam.html).

Salvatore, A. (2006). 'Public religion, ethics of participation, and cultural dialogue,' in Said, A.A., Abu-Nimer, M. & M. Sha (eds.), *Contemporary Islam: dynamic, not static* Oxon, New York (NY): Routledge, 83-100.

Seniguer, H. & B. Sambe (21-07-2013). 'Tariq Ramadan sur l'homosexualité au Sénégal: Que cache son discours?' (Retrieved 05-12-2013 from http://www.huffingtonpost.fr/haoues-seniguer/tariq-ramadan-et-lhomosexualite_b_3622915.html).

Shavit, U. (2014). *Islamism and the West: From 'cultural attack' to 'Missionary Migrant'.* Oxon / New York (NY): Routledge.

Sunier, T. (24-10-2001). 'Rol islam krijgt veel te veel nadruk' (Retrieved 05-10-2012 from http://www.trouw.nl/tr/nl/5009/Archief/archief/article/detail/2493923/2001/10/24/Rol-islam-krijgt-veel-te-veel-nadruk.dhtml).

Taylor, P. (18-03-2006). 'Canada: leading the mufti; progress in the Islamic tradition,' (Retrieved 05-05-2011 from http://www.wluml.org/node/2843).

Taylor, P. K. (23-06-2007). 'Muslims for Progressive Values Conference and Khutbah Competition Winners,' *The Washinghton Post, online edition* (Retrieved 20-04-2011 from http://newsweek.washingtonpost.com/onfaith/panelists/pamela_k_taylor/2007/06/muslims_for_progressive_values.html).

Van Amerongen, A. (2008). *Brussel: Eurabia.* Amsterdam/ Antwerpen: Uitgeverij Atlas.

van Rooy, S. & W. van Rooy (eds). (2010). *De Islam: kritische essays over een politieke religie.* Brussel: VUB-Press.

Vanlommel, S. (03-02-2012). 'De Martin Luther King van Europese jonge moslims,' *De Morgen 03-02-2012, p. 13* (Retrieved 05-10-2012 from http://www.deburen.eu/userfiles/files/2012_1/Artikel_DM_03022012_Tariq_Ramadan.pdf).

Widmann, A. (2008). 'Conference with Jürgen Habermas and Tariq Ramadan: No Europe without Muslims,' *Frankfurter Rundschau / Qantara.de* (Retrieved 19/01/10 from http://en.qantara.de/webcom/show_article.php/_c-478'/_nr-781/i.html).

Zemni, S. (2009). *Het islamdebat,* Berchem: Epo.

Zemni, S. (2006). 'The modernity of Islamism and jihad militancy,' *Studia Diplomatica, 59* (1), 199-212.

Zemni, S. (2011). The political shaping of Islam in Belgium: Between blatant Islamophobia and creeping racism, *Race & Class,* 53 (1): 28-44.

CHAPTER 4

The Contribution of Sufism to the Construction of Contemporary Europe's Islam

Eric Geoffroy

Some history

If we want to define correctly the current role of Sufism in Europe, we have to go back to the Middle Ages, as we have known for the last few decades that Islamic spirituality had something of an influence on medieval Christendom. For instance the legend of the female saint Râbia al-'Adawiyya (d. 801), who lived in Iraq, reached the court of Saint Louis, in France, and the Divine Comedy by the Italian author Dante Alighieri (d. 1321) bears the mark of the story of the heavenly Ascension of the prophet Muhammad (*Mi'râj*) (Chodkiewicz 1995: 99-100). Furthermore, the mystical doctrine of Saint Theresa of Avila and of Saint John of the Crew, in sixteenth Century Spain, may have borrowed some elements from Maghrebo-Andalusian Sufism (Chodkiewicz 1994).

Later, in the nineteenth century, European expansion in the Muslim world through exploration and colonialism enabled some European "seekers of truth" to encounter Sufism. These individuals were rejecting the positivist ideology of Europe, its mechanistic and materialistic civilization as well as the secularization of Western Christianity which, they said, had lost its esoteric content. In what they perceived as a "loss of meaning", they found a metaphysical revival in Oriental forms of spirituality like Sufism. Take the English explorer Richard Burton (d. 1890), the French Orientalist painter Etienne Dinet (d. 1929), the Swiss writer Isabelle Eberhardt (d. 1904), or the native Swede Ivan Agueli (d. 1917).

As a result of the spread of European colonialism there was a wave of Asian and African immigration in Europe, and from the 1920s Sufism appeared in Europe. One of the first Sufi orders to emerge in Europe in that period was the 'Alâwiyya order initiated by the Algerian shaykh Ahmad al-'Alâwî (d. 1934) (Geoffroy 2009b). This shaykh came to France in person in 1926, and participated in the inaugural ceremony of the Great Mosque of Paris, which was built in gratitude for the sacrifice of the Muslim soldiers during the First World War. In the atmosphere of "disenchantment" which prevailed after this appalling war, spiritualities like Hinduism and then Sufism were given the task of "colonizing people's hearts", so said shaykh 'Udda Bentounes (d. 1952), the successor to shaykh al-'Alâwî.

Not all Sufism in contemporary Europe is the result of recent migrations, however. Some Sufi orders, such as the Bektashis of Albania, Bulgaria and Macedonia, have been present in the region since the Middle Ages. Indeed, the religious culture of Muslim communities in the Balkans has largely been shaped by the legacy of Sufism.

Traditionalism: René Guénon and Frithjof Schuon

One of the greatest references in this period was René Guénon, a French author who explained to the European public that the modern West was in crisis or, worse, in a state of terminal decline, as a result of its loss of transmission of tradition during the last half of the second millennium A.D. So, for Guénon, the West had to go back to the roots of primordial truth, the primordial Tradition which underlies each of the historical religions. Having been initiated into Sufism himself in Paris in 1912 by Ivan Agueli, he aimed to set out the metaphysical thought of Perennial Philosophy in a series of books, in order to form a Western elite and to restore "traditional civilization" in the West. He settled in Cairo in 1930 and died there in 1951 but, as a universalist Sufi, he wrote much more about Hinduism for instance than about Islam or Sufism. Yet up to now he has had great influence on some Europeans who have subsequently chosen to follow the path of Sufism (Connaissance des Religions 2002; Accart 2001). His books have recently been translated into Arabic and nowadays he has larger and larger audiences in some Arabic and Turkish milieus.

In the wake of Guénon, some Traditionalists moved to Islam, since they saw in it the last expression of Revelation for this age. They all stressed the universalism of the Islamic message, in such a way that it appears to be the first real bridge between East and West, in modern times at the least. Some worked at extricating it from its oriental or Arabic context. Frithjof Schuon, a prolific spiritual author and a Sufi master of Swiss origin, highlighted the "Transcendental Unity of Religions", but in a quite distinct way from Guénon. The Sufi path he founded is devoted to the Virgin Mary and took the name of "the Maryamiyya", which explains the great influence he gained in some Western Christian circles. It may be worthwhile to note that Schuon was first affiliated to the 'Alâwiyya order, which has a "Christic" character, according to the Sufi doctrine of the "inheritance" of the prophets by Muslim saints (Chodkiewicz 1986). Schuon, who left Europe for the USA in 1981 and died there in 1998, left behind some celebrated successors in the field of Sufism and academic islamology alike, such as Martin Lings (d. 2005) in England and Seyyed Hossein Nasr, who has been teaching at George Washington University. Other representatives of Traditionalist Sufism, although less well known in America, were or are still active in Europe, adopting various positions towards exoteric Islam and sometimes having contacts with Western esoteric organizations, like Freemasonry in its spiritual tendencies (Connaissances des Religions 1999; Laude and Aymard 2002).

For some scholars like Mark Sedgwick, the Traditionalist movement is an integral part of what they call "Neo-Sufism", which may differ significantly from the standard models found in the Islamic world. It is true to say that, like Traditionalist Sufism, Neo-Sufism promotes religious and cultural pluralism and therefore the relativization of claims to religious truth. However Traditionalist Sufism takes its roots in the Qur'ân and classical Sufism, while Neo-Sufism should be considered a modern syncretism (Sedgwick 2005 and 2004; Geoffroy 2011).

The rise of Sufi orders in the West

Since the 1970s, the presence of Sufism has increased rapidly in Europe. This phenomenon was not believed to be an accident by the "oriental" Sufi masters. They saw in the West a providential land, observing that the socio-political pressure which weighs on Muslim countries may impede personal development. At the same time, and rather paradoxically, the West is truly fallow land from the spiritual point of view, where people have lost their bearings, but precisely for this reason it is also a space of freedom with broad horizons where Sufis, amongst others, can sow new spiritual seeds. For instance, by virtue of this freedom studies of the works of the great Sufi Ibn 'Arabî (d. 1240) are flourishing in the West, whereas they are denigrated and stigmatized in some Islamic countries because of the threat of fundamentalism, and even forbidden in Saudi Arabia. This explains why a few "oriental" Sufi masters settled in the West, while some Westerners who trained in the East became representatives of oriental masters or even became Sufi masters themselves.

Regardless of their origins, Sufi groups in Europe are deeply embedded in the cultures of many Muslim communities – so deeply, in fact, that it is often difficult to distinguish them from particular cultures and ethnic groups. The Tijânî and Murîdî orders, for instance, are thoroughly woven into France's West and North African communities. A small majority of the U.K.'s predominantly South Asian Muslim community are Barelwis, followers of a broad Sufi-oriented movement that encompasses a variety of orders, including the Chistis, Qadiris and Naqshbandis.

Some large Sufi orders cross multiple ethnic groups. The Naqshbandis, for example, are strongly represented across many Muslim communities in Europe. Today, it is one of the most prominent orders in the U.K. Through annual visits to Britain he was used to making from his home base in Cyprus, the Naqshbandis Haqqânî' leading *shaykh*, Nazim al-Qubrûsî, has developed a diverse following of Turks, South Asians and white or Afro-Caribbean converts in London and Sheffield, as well as a group of South Asian followers in Birmingham. In this case as in others, we can speak of "transnational" or "translocal" orders (Malik and Hinnels 2006).

Nowadays the West is the place where Sufi orders from different geographical origins can meet, as is the case for religions as a whole. Oriental religions like Hinduism, Buddhism or Islam have fruitful exchanges in the West, since here they can leave aside their different sociocultural environments which often generate conflicts.

The role of academic studies in the XXth Century

Another main factor which has contributed to a greater knowledge of Sufism in Europe and thus the spreading of its practice is the plethora of academic studies in this field. Though some Muslims criticize the European orientalists – often without discernment – there is evidence that <u>firstly</u> these orientalists knew the Islamic tradition better than these Muslims, and <u>secondly</u> that they were most likely not ill-intentioned. Famous scholars are to be found in the studies of Sufism, and those who had charismatic personalities involved themselves in spiritual quests, in Christianity or in Islam, or rather at the meeting-point between these two religions. This was the case for Annemarie Schimmel (d. 2003) in Germany and, in France, for Louis Massignon (d. 1962), Henry Corbin (d. 1978), Eva de Vitray-Meyerovitch (d. 1999), etc. Let us take the French example of Michel Chodkiewicz (born 1929). He succeeded in being at the same time the general manager of a famous publishing house, a recognized specialist of Ibn ʿArabî and Sufism, as well as being a Sufi guide himself. We could not miss William Chittick, an American scholar devoted to the studies of Ibn ʿArabî and Rûmî (d. 1273). You will not find such personal implication from scholars in the other fields of Islamic study. Many people in Europe, whether of European or Arabic origin, are still closely guided by the studies and the translations of these prominent academics and their current successors: we now have access to most major works of the universal Sufi legacy in both French and English.

Which kind of Sufism?

From a doctrinal point of view Sufism may be seen as the inner dimension of Islam, as the incarnation of Spirit in the body of the Islamic religion. It means that Sufism should be inseparable from Islam. For this reason, Guénon underlined the necessity, for a spiritual seeker, to follow one of the world religions and to aim at congruence between esoteric and exoteric practices. One cannot take a narrow, uphill path like Sufism without the protection of the wide path of a particular religion, assert Sufi masters. But, on the other hand, Sufism is not confined to the Islamic religion. So you can hear in some Islamic countries like Egypt that the mystic dimension of Christianity is called "Christian Sufism" and such is the case for Jewish mysticism.

Thus each Sufi milieu in Europe positions itself specifically in relation to Islamic orthodoxy. Most of the Sufis there remain attached to general Islamic prescriptions, and keep in contact with one Muslim country or another. Some of them have been taught in Islamic teaching institutions abroad and are well versed in Islamic sciences. But this raises the question of the adaptation of those groups to western culture, since when you have an Arabic, a Turkish or an African *shaykh* (master), you are inclined to adopt his way of life or thinking. Of course, spirituality is universal and crosses all borders, yet it is conditioned by each cultural context. Most "oriental" Sufi masters are well aware of these cultural barriers and therefore they let their Western representatives adapt their teachings to their own environment, but some of these representatives refuse to take on such freedom, contenting themselves with imitating what they have seen and experienced in the East.

In contrast, a few groups broke away from the Islamic form, believing it necessary to stress the universalism of Sufi wisdom. Opening the door to syncretism, these so-called "Neo-Sufi" groups aspire to a kind of globalization of the Spirit. Seeing in Sufism the "pure essence of all religions and philosophies", they do not speak of God but of personal development, and then present Sufism without an Islamic face. Based in England, the Indian-born Idries Shah (d. 1996) taught a philosophy inspired by his personal view of Sufism, and you may know the "Universal Order" of Pir Vilayat Khan (d. 2004), established in the USA as well as in France: if you attend one of their seminars you will not hear a word about Islam or the Prophet Muhammad. This Islam-free Sufism has had more success, no doubt, in the USA than in Europe. Amongst the reasons that explain this phenomenon, we can put forward the old historical links between the Muslim world and Europe and, concerning France, the role of Guénon in promoting a rather strict observance of a religion – whatever it might be. French Guenonism, for instance, gave birth to a highly Islamic *tarîqa*, or Sufi order, directed in Paris by the Romanian Michel Vâlsan (d. 1974), whose disciples have had a strong impact on the orientation of French Islamology. Generally speaking, European Sufism does not intend to depart from the heritage of *baraka*, the spiritual influence which comes from God and the Prophet through the initiatory lineages of the Sufi orders and which is still to be found in the Muslim world. The rituals that European Sufis need daily are also preserved in these areas. Thus, to sum up, between these two extremes, which are strict adherence to Islamic prescriptions on the one hand and Islam-less Sufism on the other, one can find a highly nuanced range of approaches (Geoffroy 2010: 200-202).

The roles that Sufism assumes or may assume in Europe

Although some Salafî Sufi groups exist, which are narrow-minded, quite fundamentalist and anti-Western, European Sufism is undoubtedly a great way of opening up to universality, firstly for the young Muslims of North African origin who are numerous in some European countries. For instance, the Sufi doctrine of the "Universal Man" (*al-insân al-kâmil*), expressed in terms adapted to our time should allow some of them to attain the inner freedom which spirituality provides. The Algerian Emir Abd El-Kader (d. 1883) should be a model for them, as he embodies the Islamic value of spiritual humanism, as shown by the fact that he was holding out the hand of friendship to the French Christian authorities while the French army was destroying his country in the 1830s and 1840s. The Emir carried out a "small" military *jihâd (al-jihâd al-asghar* in Arabic) against the invading French troops, but his true vocation was the "great" spiritual *jihâd (al-jihâd al-akbar)*, that is to say the struggle against the passions of the soul, which may lead to the enlightenment of the soul by following the Sufi path. The Emir, who was very popular in France during the five years of his detention before he left for the Near East, is an example which merits contemplation in contemporary Europe (Bouyerdene 2008: 105-134; Bentounes 2010).

More and more young Muslims in Europe reject the vision of Islam they inherited from their parents, an Islam which is often confined to a catalogue of prescriptions and prohibitions, and which appears as a kind of formalistic and insipid catechism, whereas the notion of "spiritual taste" (*dhawq* in Arabic) is central to the Sufi experience. Furthermore, this one-dimensional Islam is mixed with Arabic, Berber, African or Turkish customs, and the seminal and perennial values of Islam are absent from it. As in other social strata in Europe, these young Muslims are seeking true spirituality which makes them free from blind religious and ritualistic observance as well as from Western materialism and consumerism. In the process of a "theology of liberation" which is occurring in some European Muslim milieus, Sufism may play a decisive part (Geoffroy 2009a: 119-136). I have personally met a lot of Maghreban students in France who grew up in traditional Sufi families in their country but had subsequently given up the practice of Islam because it was a routine one and in the end they considered Sufism to be mere superstition: we can observe that they rediscovered Islam and Sufism in Europe, in a renewed context (Roy 2002: 197). Now European Sufism has itself begun to inseminate Arabic lands. In these countries Islam is often alienated by a legalist mentality as well as by ideologies like Arabic nationalism or Islamism. The everyday real-life experience of Islam there suffers from socio-political obstacles.

Now European Sufism has itself begun to inseminate Arabic lands. In these countries Islam is often alienated by a legalist mentality as well as by ideologies like Arabic nationalism or Islamism. The everyday real-life experience of Islam there suffers from socio-political obstacles.

In the present context of globalization, religion and spirituality need to get a holistic view of the world that takes into account the interdependence between man and cosmos, and this is especially possible in the West nowadays. Institutionalized religions in the world face big challenges. What is their attitude, for instance, towards modern science, economy, politics, ecology, bio-ethics and so on? We know the sentence attributed to the French author André Malraux (d. 1976): "The 21st Century will either be spiritual or will not be" (Geoffroy 2009a: 7). Most of the Third World countries have neither the economic nor the psychological means to provide answers by themselves. They need the mirror of the West. We do realize that Euro-Mediterranean relations, which have increased considerably these last few years cannot get away from taking the spiritual dimension into account. This is why politicians and company directors from both shores of the Mediterranean Sea, as well as international institutions like Unesco, are actually more and more interested in direct intervention of Sufism in the social field. In the last few decades, the West has become a big "market" of spirituality which has given rise to new forms of expression, and Sufism finds stimulation in these exchanges (Bruinessen and Howell 2007; Geoffroy 2009a: 164). Many Westerners are indeed attracted to this discipline, the most sensitive in Europe generally being women from Christian or Jewish backgrounds.

Sufi universalism: the sense of alterity

Drawing from the imaginal world (*'âlam al-khayâl*), or the world of spiritual imagination, Sufism knows how to apply its creativity to remove religious and cultural blocks. Being grounded in the vertical axis of Unicity (*tawhîd*), the Sufi should be able to contemplate multiplicity around him serenely; I mean the horizontal pluralism of cultures and religions. And it is quite obvious that Sufism serves nowadays as a link, as a necessary interface between Islam and the West, a role that it played in the past in some areas: for instance in India between Hindus and Muslims, in Central Asia between Buddhists and Muslims, in Africa between animists and Muslims, etc. Being the living heart of Islam, Sufism has always managed to adapt to new contexts and absorb ancient spiritual substrata of surprising diversity, ranging from Neo-Platonism to Shamanism.

These days, interreligious dialogue is all but a fashion: it is an obvious necessity, which concerns all believers. Those who aspire to an Islamo-Christian dialogue, for instance, assert that we are not facing a "shock of civilizations" between the Muslim world and the West, but a "shock of ignorances". Sufis have always been involved in interreligious dialogue, by virtue of the Quranic concept of *Dîn qayyim*, that is to say the Immutable Religion, the Adamic Religion considered as the trunk from which all historical religions branch (Qur'an 30:30). Islam claims the authenticity of the Old and the New Testaments, though most Muslim scholars consider them altered and distorted historically by the Jews and the Christians. Note that for some *ulema* (scholars of Islam) living in the Eastern territories of the Muslim world, the Veda, the ancient holy book of Hinduism, is recognized as a part of Revelation. Despite this founding universalism of Islam, most ordinary Muslims see in creeds other than Islam mere miscreance (*kufr*).

This is not the case for Sufis. In the Middle Ages, at a time when every civilization was focused on itself, Sufis like Ibn 'Arabî were professing that no single religion holds the whole truth, and that each one is a specific theophany, a specific manifestation of God. True religion, in their eyes, is not to be contained in any historical belief because of its narrowness and its deficiencies. It is the universal religion of Love, as Ibn 'Arabî said (Chittick, 1994). Love not as sentimentalism but as an intuitive way of knowing God. Medieval Sufis called that "transcendental unity of religions" (*wahdat al-adyân*), and Frithjof Schuon expressed it in a modern way in his famous *De l'unité transcendante des religions* (Schuon, 1948). So no surprise that nowadays Sufis like Ibn 'Arabî and Jalal al-Dîn Rûmî receive an increasingly favourable reception in the West (Chittick, 2005). Many non-Muslims are inspired by the teachings of Ibn 'Arabî, whose works are now being translated more and more into Western languages, and Rûmî is nowadays the most widely read poet in the USA.

The therapeutic function of Sufism

Another main role of Sufism is a therapeutic one. From the beginning, the Sufi master is called "the doctor of the soul", of the lower soul which is the seat of all passions and illusions. In the past, some masters practised a kind of psychoanalysis on their disciples, to free their minds from their impurities and fill them with positive thoughts and sacred knowledge (Geoffroy 2010: 149). In Europe and in the West generally speaking, the human mind is caught up in the whirl of "post-modernity", "post-Christianity" and so on, so it has largely lost its moral guidelines and the psychological protection that the old frames of reference provided. People in the West must learn how to handle their personal freedom as it sometimes makes them lose their heads!

Furthermore, many individuals sensitive to the spiritual dimension are vulnerable and ill-adapted to modernity, precisely because of this sensitivity. Some of those who converted to Islam or Sufism, for example, are former drug addicts. Young Muslims of immigrant origin are confronted with specific psychological handicaps such as: an often crude and rigid parental education in Islam, a cultural integration which is not accompanied by real acceptance by European societies and which generates a feeling of resentment against the West as a whole, etc. So, before committing to an initiatory path, which may be perilous, they have to recover their psychological health and mental stability. That is why such as the 'Alâwiyya Sufi order set up a special research group called "Therapies of the soul", which organizes seminars on Sufi therapy for various health professionals[1].

For some years, more and more political and social leaders, in the Muslim world as in Europe, have been aware that the peaceful and open Islam which the Sufis are promoting is no doubt the best antidote to the sclerotic and rigid ideas that Islamism conveys. On the other hand, some are tempted totally to separate Sufism from Islam, and this tendency certainly represents a big danger, since, as we asserted before, spirituality without religious grounding may become sterile and artificial. Sufism should not be split off from Islam, but should help it reform itself and recover its initial universalism. In the West, generally speaking, the success of Sufism makes it an easy target for mercantilism: here and there, leaflets promise to put you in a trance or in a state of being possessed, and thus the psychic and spiritual levels become totally confused. So the 'Sufi business' is in good health, and the West may change Sufism in the next few years or decades into an object of consumption, as it did for other oriental techniques like Yoga or Zen. In French we call this "ésotourisme". It may also become absorbed into the New Age spiritual tendency. Between extreme openness which dilutes the outlines of religious belonging and sectarianism which claims exclusive salvation, Western Sufism is experiencing great difficulty in finding a balance. Even then one must distinguish between American Sufism and European Sufism, the latter reputed to be more sober and undoubtedly more islamized.

Conclusion

As it did in the Muslim world, contemporary European Sufism is able to contribute to the spiritualization of everyday Islam, which is followed now by more than fifteen million people (the estimated number for just the European

Union, not the whole of Europe). Besides it may provide initiatory nourishment to a few. It may also favour the emergence of an essential Islam, freed from allegiances to the native countries (in particular the North African states) and of the search for ethnic identity. Even Islamic identity may become a factor of confinement: one must now seek universal identity. Primitive Islam witnessed such a rapid spread in the known world of that time that we can describe it as early religious and cultural globalization. But contemporary Muslims often forget that it was precisely due to the strong interest and curiosity that the first Muslims showed for all the world's cultures and religions. Most of all, Sufism may offer the Western public another view of Islam, and help European societies to consider the spiritual dimension with more interest.

Notes

1   See the site *www.therapiedelame.org/*.

References

Accart, X. (2001). *L'Ermite de Dokki. René Guénon en marge des milieux francophones égyptiens*, Milano: Archè.

Bentounes, K. (2010). 'Abd el-Kader, un modèle pour aujourd'hui', in E. Geoffroy (ed.), *Abd el-Kader – Un spirituel dans la modernité*, Paris: Albouraq, 15-20.

Bouyerdene, A. (2008). *Abd el-Kader – L'harmonie des contraires*, Paris: Le Seuil ; translated in English (2012): *Emir Abd El-Kader: Hero and Saint of Islam*; Bloomington (USA): World Wisdom.

Chittick, W. (1994). *Imaginal Worlds – Ibn al-'Arabî and the Problem of Religious Diversity*, Albany: State University of New York Press.

Chittick, W. (2005). *The Sufi Doctrine of Rumi*, Bloomington: World Wisdom.

Chodkiewicz, M. (1986). *Le Sceau des Saints*, Paris: Gallimard.

Chodkiewicz, M. (1994). 'La réception du soufisme par l'Occident: conjectures et certitudes', in C. Butterworth and B. Kessel (eds), *The Introduction of Arabic Philosophy into Europe*, Leiden: Brill, 136-149.

Chodkiewicz, M. (1995). 'La sainteté féminine dans l'hagiographie islamique', in D. Aigle (ed.), *Saints orientaux*, Paris: De Boccard, 99-100.

Connaissance des Religions, Numéro Hors Série, Frithjof Schuon, 1999.

Connaissance des Religions (2002). 'René Guénon, l'éveilleur (1886-1951)', n° 65-66 Juillet-Décembre.

Geoffroy, E. (2009a). *L'islam sera spirituel ou ne sera plus*, Le Seuil, Paris.

Geoffroy, E. (2009b). articles 'Ahmad b. 'Aliwa' and ' 'Alâwiyya', *Encyclopaedia of Islam*, 3rd edition, Leyden: Brill.

Geoffroy, E. (2010) *Introduction to Sufism: The Inner Path of Islam*, World Wisdom, Bloomington (USA).

Laude, P. and Aymard, J.B. (eds) (2002). *Le Dossier H Frithjof Schuon*, Lausanne: L'âge d'Homme.

Malik, J. and Hinnels, J. (2006). *Sufism in the West*, London-New York: Routledge.

Roy, O. (2002). *L'Islam mondialisé*, Paris: Le Seuil.

Schuon, F. (1948). *De l'unité transcendante des religions,* Paris, Gallimard.

Sedgwick, M. (2004). *Against the Modern World*, Oxford: Oxford University Press.

Sedgwick, M. (2005). 'The Traditionalist Shâdhiliyya in the West: Guénonians and Schuonians', *Une voie soufie dans le monde: la Shâdhiliyya,* under the direction of E. Geoffroy, Paris: Maisonneuve& Larose, 453-472 (new edition by Gnosis – Editions de France, Paris, 2011).

www.therapiedelame.org/.

van Bruinessen, M., and Day Howell, (2007). *Sufism and the Modern in Islam*, London - New York: Tauris.

Part II:
Secularism, Islam and Public Sphere: Turkey and Egypt

CHAPTER 5

Post-Secularism, Post-Islamism and Islam in the Public Sphere

Ihsan Yilmaz

The social-scientific debate on state-religion relations has been unresolved. Some of the former proponents of the secularization theory have declared it passé. Religion has increasingly become part (and at certain times a crucial aspect) of domestic politics in many countries and also in international relations (Fox 2001, Hurd 2007, Haynes 2007). It is doubtful whether complete secularization has ever taken place. Religions have not gone anywhere (Casanova 1994 and 2010) but have been socio-politically and also academically (Fox 2001) marginalized, vilified and suppressed. It seems that discussions and debates on state-religion relations and secularism will continue to be part of our academic and political lives in future. Islamic perspectives on this issue will, as ever, continue to be an important part of these debates and discussions.

The academic literature on secularism is full of different competing definitions: inclusive, passive, tolerant, liberal, benevolent, moderate, evolutionary, weak, ameliorative, principled distance; *laïcité plurielle, positive, de gestion* and *bien entendue* and their opposites: strong, intolerant, statist, exclusive, assertive, aggressive, or malevolent secularism are some examples (Bader 2011; Taylor 1999). In passive secularism, the secular state plays a 'passive' role, and while avoiding the establishment of any religions, it "allows for the public visibility of religion" (Kuru 2007, 571). In assertive secularism, the state tries to exclude religion from the public sphere in addition to playing an 'assertive' role as "the agent of a social engineering project that confines religion to the private domain" (Kuru 2007, 571). Until the late 1970s and early 1980s, a relatively widespread consensus had existed in the sociology of religion discipline over the privatization of religion thesis (Repstad and Furseth 2006, 97). Since then, it has been realized "that differentiation did not necessarily mean that religion would remain in its assigned place in the private sphere and not enter the public arena" (Repstad and Furseth 2006, 97). Some scholars such as Casanova (1994) have argued that during the course of the last few decades, a process of 'deprivatization' of religion has taken place in the world, and even though a historical process of religious differentiation has taken place in the West, institutional differentiation does not necessarily result in the marginalization and privatization of religion. This means that discussions on the definition and types of secularism are crucial as far as political science is concerned. When we refer to Islam when we say religion, the issue becomes much more sensitive. What is more, revival and deprivatization of Islam are more observable phenomena than in the other religions. It is thus important to see if and to what extent Islam and secularism could accommodate each other.

Islamic law recognizes the fundamental principle that people are born free (Turcan 2012, 298). In Islam, there are fundamental rights and freedoms of individuals and they do not depend on constitutions in the sense that they are or are not recognized by the law (Turcan 2012, 299). According to Islam, people should have the freedom to express themselves without being under any pressure (Gülen 2005, 451). As stressed in Shatibi's *Maqasid al Shari'a* (Major Objectives of Islamic Law), the main objectives of Islamic law are protection of religion, life, family and reproduction, intellect and property. Islamic law aims to protect these basic human rights (Gülen 2000, 134; Gülen 2001, 134-135). Some Islamic scholars have even argued that if human rights are respected by a political system, then there is no need to enter the quest for an alternative system (Gülen 2005, 451):

> If a state... gives the opportunity to its citizens to practice their religion and supports them in their thinking, learning, and practice, this system is not considered to be against the teaching of the Qur'an. *In the presence of such a state there is no need to seek an alternative state* (italics mine, I.Y.). The system should be reviewed by the lawmakers and executive institutions if human rights and freedoms are not protected enough (Gülen 2005, 451).

In Islam, people are responsible for their own fate. Thus, they have free will and freedoms. In particular, "religion, life, reproduction, the mind, and property are basic essentials that everyone must protect. In a sense, Islam approaches human rights from the angle of these basic principles" (Gülen 2000, 134, see also Gülen 2001, 134-135). These Islamic scholars have also argued that "if secularism means that state is not based on any religion, hence it does not interfere with religion or religious life and the state is neural towards all religions, then there is not a problem" (Armağan and Ünal 1999, 108 quoted in Altınoğlu 1999, 103).

This view could be said to be compatible with the Habermasian understanding of religion in post-secularist times. Habermas has revised his secularization since and has embraced the term "post-secular society" to describe the current situation with regards to religion-society issues. "Many scholars would concur that there really is something qualitatively different about the post-1970s era, enough to warrant a new term that differentiates the modern era (roughly defined as the period encompassing 1770–1970) from the postmodern" (Dillon 2012). He "has long construed the West as essentially secular since the Enlightenment" (Dillon 2012). Nevertheless, he now states that "the Enlightenment project has been partially derailed and reason subsumed by strategic market interests and political indifference, it is appropriate for him to rethink the secular... the post-secular provides him with a useful analytical device for acknowledging not so much the persistence of religion as the partial failure (derailing) of the Enlightenment, a failure that by default brings religion back and into the secular... It is not that secularization has not occurred; it is just that there are some complications that the persistence of religion has thrown on its tracks" (Dillon 2012).

It is not certain whether or not secularization has in fact taken place since there is so much differentiated evidence for and against its sociological reality (Dillon 2012). There is some ambiguity in Habermas's use of the term post-secular. While he talks about "post-secular society," it seems that he is actually talking "about a post-secular Zeitgeist, 'a change in consciousness'" (Dillon 2012). In this usage, post-secular refers to "the continued existence of religious communities in an increasingly secularized environment" (Dillon 2012). In other words, in the Habermasian understanding, "the term 'post-secular' can be applied to secularized societies in which religion maintains a public influence and relevance" (Dillon 2012). Put differently, "the 'post-secular' recognizes the public relevance of religion and of religious ideas in informing civic discourse" (Dillon 2012). In Dillon's (2012) view, the term "post-secular" is more theoretically robust if it is used "to help us understand the more general relevance of religion as a public cultural resource in all modern democratic societies regardless of their varying degrees or levels of secularism and secularization" (Dillon 2012).

I think an attempt should be made to link Habermas' understanding of 'religion in the public sphere' with his conceptualization of post-secularism. In his elaboration on John Rawls' (1997) political theory, in particular concepts of the 'public use of reason' and 'translation provisio', Jurgen Habermas (2006) has objected to this restrictive idea of the political role of religion and argued that other than the state level, public visibility of religions could be allowed at civil society and political society levels. Rawls (1997, 777) argues that "reasonable comprehensive doctrines, religious or non-religious, may be introduced in public political discussion at any time, provided that in due course proper political reasons – and not reasons given solely by comprehensive doctrines – are presented that are sufficient to support whatever the comprehensive doctrines are said to support". In response, (Habermas 2006, 7) underlines that "religious communities and movements provide arguments for public debates on crucial morally-loaded issues and handle tasks of political socialization by informing their members and encouraging them to take part in the political process". However, each time they have to "find an equivalent in a universally accessible language for every religious statement they pronounce" as part of the duty of civility (Habermas 2006, 7). This epistemic burden results in a sort of self-censorship. It is obvious that "many religious citizens would not be able to undertake such an artificial division within their own minds without jeopardizing their existence as pious persons" (Habermas 2006, 8). Habermas (2006, 8-9) concludes that "the liberal state, which expressly protects such forms of life in terms of a basic right, cannot at the same time expect of all citizens that they also justify their political statements independently of their religious convictions or world views. This strict demand can only be laid at the door of politicians, who within state institutions are subject to the obligation to remain neutral in the face of competing world views". Citizens must agree "that only secular reasons count beyond the institutional threshold that divides the informal public sphere from parliaments, courts, ministries and administrations" (Habermas 2006, 9). Religious citizens too can agree to this 'institutional translation proviso' without splitting their identity into a public and a private part when they participate in public debates and discourses. Thus, they should "be allowed to express and justify their convictions in a religious language if they cannot find secular 'translations' for them" (Habermas 2006, 10).

It seems that a post-Islamist understanding of religion-state-society relations is more compatible with this Habermasian post-secularist condition with regard to religion in the public sphere. Post-Islamism has recently been at the centre of a major debate especially in French academia regarding the historical evolution of Islamism (Lauzière, 2005: 241). Olivier Roy and some other scholars have argued that Islamism – that is, according to their definition, the holistic, populist, and often revolutionary ideology whose goal is the establishment of an Islamic state and the governance of all aspects of society according to Islamic principles – has reached a dead end and an era of post-Islamism has been dawning (Lauzière, 2005: 241). Roy (1998; 2004) claims that the reorientation of Islamists towards religiosity and away from politics is a sign of the failure of political Islam. In this usage, the term "post-Islamism" is used descriptively to refer to a shift in attitudes and strategies of Islamists after the so-called failure of Islamism (Schulze 1998, Roy 1998, 2005, Kepel 2002). In this conceptualization, post-Islamism is understood "primarily as an historical rather than an analytical category" (Bayat, 2007; 17). It prematurely suggests the end of Islamism. The critics of this conceptualization argued that political Islam is not changing, but rather that its revolutionary, top-down, version has become defunct. Thus, they argued that post-Islamism is only a variety of Islamism (Ismail 2001, Burgat 2003 cited in Bayat, 2007: 18; see also Lauzière 2005 and Sinanovic 2005). Lauzière (2005) argues that Roy's conceptualization of post-Islamism does not stand up to empirical scrutiny. Lauzière (2005: 257) shows that "[a]lthough post-Islamist theory is an attempt to systematize empirical data from the past thirty-five years into a coherent historical pattern, it relies on a narrow and selective definition of Islamism that cannot account for the particularities of the Moroccan context… It also seems better suited to cases in which the rise and failure of revolutionary Islamism has been overt and pronounced." The same could be argued in the Turkish context, for which see in detail Yilmaz (2005, 2008, 2009, 2011, 2012, 2013). Turkish Islamism has given importance, if not sufficiently, to religiosity. Besides, there have always been many observant socially active Muslim scholars such as Fethullah Gülen, individuals, groups, communities and Sufi brotherhoods that have not seen Islam in political terms. They have always been non-Islamist (Yilmaz 2009, Yilmaz 2011). There is no reason to call these people post-Islamist as Roy does, as these people were never Islamists in the first place (Yilmaz 2009). Roy also argues that the Islamists' abandonment of transnational solidarity and their new centeredness on national politics are yet other indications of failure. Again, despite the rhetoric, this has more or less always been the case in the Turkish context.

In Bayat's (2007) formulation, post-Islamism refers to both a condition and a project, which may be embodied in a master (or multidimensional) movement.

In his understanding, post-Islamism means "a condition where, following a phase of experimentation, the appeal, energy, symbols and sources of legitimacy of Islamism get exhausted, even among its once-ardent supporters" (Bayat, 1996: 45). Islamists become aware of their paradigm's anomalies and inadequacies as they try to win votes and to rule. The continuous trial and error make the system susceptible to questions and criticisms. Eventually, pragmatic attempts to maintain the system reinforce the abandoning of certain of its underlying principles. Islamism becomes compelled, both by its own internal contradictions and by societal pressure, to reinvent itself, but does so at the cost of a qualitative shift (Bayat, 2007: 18). As such, post-Islamism is not anti-Islamic, but rather reflects a tendency to resecularize religion. Predominantly, it is marked by a call to limit the political role of religion (Bayat, 1996: 45). It is clear that post-Islamist condition can only be relevant in the contexts where Islamists could participate in the electoral process.

Post-Islamism centres on the "the idea of fusion between Islam (as a personalized faith) and individual freedom and choice; and post-Islamism is associated with the values of democracy and aspects of modernity" (Bayat, 1996:45). Put differently, post-Islamism represents an endeavour to fuse religiosity with rights, faith and freedoms, Islam and civil liberties and focuses on rights instead of duties, plurality instead of singular authority, historicity rather than fixed and rigid interpretation of scriptures, and the future rather than the past. Post-Islamism is expressed in acknowledging secular exigencies, in freedom from rigidity, in breaking down the monopoly of religious truth. As nothing intrinsic to Islam – or any other religion – makes it inherently democratic or undemocratic, the question is no longer whether Islam is compatible with modernity but rather how Muslims can make these concepts compatible (Bayat, 2007: 10). The terms Islamism and post-Islamism are "primarily as conceptual categories to signify change, difference, and the root of change. In the real world, however, many Muslims may adhere eclectically and simultaneously to aspects of both discourses. On the other hand, the advent of post-Islamism as a real trend, should not be seen necessarily as the historical end of Islamism. What it should be seen as is the birth, out of Islamist experience, of a qualitatively different discourse and politics. In reality we may witness simultaneous processes of both Islamization and post-Islamization" (Bayat, 2007: 20).

In our conceptualization, post-Islamism denotes a departure, albeit in diverse degrees, from an Islamist ideological package that is characterized by universalist claims, monopoly of truth, exclusivism, intolerance, and obligation, towards acknowledging ambiguity, multiplicity, inclusion and compromise. Post-Islamists want to combine their interpretation of Islam with individual choice, freedoms, liberties and human rights. In short, whereas Islamism is defined by the fusion of religion and responsibility, post-Islamism emphasizes religiosity and human rights.

In post-Islamist understanding, there is no contradiction between Islam and democracy. Passive secularism that guarantees human rights and freedoms including freedom of religion could provide a framework to Muslims to practise their religion comfortably where other religious minorities also benefit from human rights. In this view, the faithful can comfortably live in secular environments if secularism is religion-friendly and hence does not interfere with religion or religious life. This approach to sacred-secular relations is similar to the First Amendment: "Congress shall make no law respecting an establishment of religion, or prohibiting the free exercise thereof" since, as Fethullah Gülen has highlighted, Islam does not need a state to survive and civil society or civilian realm in liberal-democratic settings is sufficient for its individual and social practice. This Muslim understanding of secularism or 'twin tolerations' (Stepan 2001) resonates with the Habermasian (2006) 'religion in the public sphere' which argues that the faithful can have demands based on religion in the public sphere and it is the legislators' job to translate these religious demands into a secular language when making laws. This is more advanced than many current liberal secular democratic political settings, and secularism will be more democratic and just if it evolves into this kind of Habermasian religion-in-the-public-sphere-friendly post-secularism. This will also be in tune with the post-Islamist approach on Islam in the public sphere.

References

Altınoğlu, E. (1999). *Fethullah Gülen's Perception of State and Society* (Unpublished Master's Thesis). Istanbul: Boğaziçi University.

Armağan, M. and Ali Ünal (ed.) (1999). *Kozadan Kelebeğe: Medya Aynasından Fethullah Gülen*. İstanbul: Gazeteciler ve Yazarlar Vakfı Yayınları.

Bader, V. (2011). 'Beyond Secularisms of All Sorts,' available online at *The Immanent Frame: Secularism, Religion and the Public Sphere*, http://blogs.ssrc.org/tif/2011/10/11/beyond -secularisms-of-all-sorts/http://blogs.ssrc.org/tif/2011/10/11/beyond-secularisms-of-all -sorts/ last visited on 26 December 2012.

Bayat, A. (1996). 'The Coming of a Post-Islamist Society,' *Critique*, 5(9): 43-52.

Bayat, A. (2007). *Islam and Democracy: What is the Real Question?*, ISIM Papers, N8. Amsterdam: Amsterdam University Press.

Burgat, F. (2003). *Face to Face with Political Islam*, London, I.B. Tauris.

Casanova, J. (1994). *Public Religions in the Modern World*. Chicago, IL: University of Chicago Press.

Casanova, J. (2010). 'Religion Challenging the Myth of Secular Democracy', in L. Christoffersen, H. R. Iversen, H. Petersen and M Warburg (eds), *Religion in the 21st Century: Challenges and Transformations*, 19-36 Surrey, UK: Ashgate.

Dillon, M. (2012). 'Rethinking secularism: Enter the Post-Secular', in Philip S. Gorski, D. Kyuman Kim, J. Torpey and J. Van Antwerpen (eds), *The Post-Secular in Question: Religion in Contemporary Society*. Social Science Research Council and New York University Press http://blogs.ssrc.org/tif/2012/08/16/enter-the-post-secular/

Fox, J. (2001). 'Religion as an Overlooked Element of International Relations', *International Studies Review* 3(3): 53-73.

Gülen, M.F. (2000). *Advocate of Dialogue: Fethullah Gülen*, compiled by Ali Ünal and Alphonse Williams. Fairfax, VA: The Fountain.

Gülen, M.F. (2001). 'A Comparative Approach to Islam and Democracy', *SAIS Review* 21(2): 133-138.

Gülen, M.F. (2005). 'An Interview with Fethullah Gülen', Translated by Zeki Saritoprak and Ali Ünal, *Muslim World* 95(3): 447-467.

Habermas, J. (2006). 'Religion in the Public Sphere', *European Journal of Philosophy* 14(1): 1–25.

Haynes, J. (2007). *An Introduction to International Relations and Religion*, London: Pearson, Longman.

Hurd, E. Shakman (2007). *The Politics of Secularism in International Relations*, Princeton, NJ: Princeton University Press.

Ismail, S. (2001). 'The Paradox of Islamist Politics', *Middle East Report*, 221:4, 34-39.

Kepel, G. (2002). *Jihad: The Trial of Political Islam*, 2nd ed., London: I.B. Tauris.

Kuru, A.T. (2007). 'Passive and Assertive Secularism: Historical Conditions, Ideological Struggles, and State Policies toward Religion', *World Politics* 59(3): 568–94.

Lauziere, H. (2005). 'Post-Islamism and the Religious Discourse of Abd Al-Salam Yasin', *International Journal of Middle East Studies*, 3: 241–261.

Rawls, J. (1997). 'The Idea of Public Reason Revisited', *Chicago Law Review* 64(3): 765-807.

Repstad, I. and Pal Furseth (2006). *An Introduction to the Sociology of Religion*, Aldershot: Ashgate.

Roy, O. (1998). 'Le post-islamisme', *Revue des Mondes Musulmans et de la Méditerranée*, 85–86: 11–30.

Roy, O. (2004). *Globalised Islam: The Search for a New Ummah*, London: Hurst and Company.

Schulze, R. (1998). 'The Ethnization of Islamic Cultures in the Late 20th century or From Political Islam to Post-Islamism,' in G. Stauth (ed.), *Islam: Motor or Challenge of Modernity*, Yearbook of the Sociology of Islam, 1, 187-198.

Sinanovic, E. (2005). 'Post-Islamism: The Failure of Islamic Activism?', *International Studies Review* 7, 433–436.

Stepan, A. (2001). 'The World's Religious Systems and Democracy: Crafting the 'Twin Tolerations,' in Alfred Stepan, *Arguing Comparative Politics,* 218-225. Oxford: Oxford University Press.

Taylor, C. (1999). 'Modes of Secularism,' in Rajeev Bhargava, ed., *Secularism and its Critics*, Delhi: Oxford University Press, 31-53.

Türcan, T. (2012). 'Anayasa Hukuku,' in Talip Türcan (ed.), *İslam Hukuku El Kitabı*, Ankara: Grafiker, 275-301.

Yilmaz, I. (2005). 'State, Law, Civil Society and Islam in Contemporary Turkey,' *The Muslim World* 95(3): 386-390.

Yilmaz, I. (2008). 'Influence of Pluralism and Electoral Participation on the Transformation of Turkish Islamism,' *Journal of Economic and Social Research*, 10(2): 43-65.

Yilmaz, I. (2009). 'Was Rumi the Chief Architect of Islamism? A Deconstruction Attempt of the Current (Mis)Use of the Term 'Islamism'', *European Journal of Economic and Political Studies* 2(2): 71-84.

Yilmaz, I. (2011). 'Beyond Post-Islamism: Transformation of Turkish Islamism Toward 'Civil Islam' and Its Potential Influence in the Muslim World,' *European Journal of Economic and Political Studies* 4(1): 245-280.

Yilmaz, I. (2012). 'Towards a Muslim Secularism? An Islamic 'Twin Tolerations' Understanding of Religion in the Public Sphere,' *Turkish Journal of Politics*, 3(2): 41-52.

Yilmaz, I. (2013). 'Türkiye'de Yeni Anayasa Tartışmaları: Din Özgürlüğü ve İslama Ters Düşmeyen Laik Devlet Üzerine Bir Yorum Denemesi,' *Yeni Türkiye*, 50: 684-693.

CHAPTER 6

The Arab Revolutions and Islamic Civil Society

Emilio Giuseppe Platti

Introduction

From February 2011 on, until Friday, August 9, 2013, when the Muslim Brothers were attacked and declared "a terrorist organization", I attended Tahrir Square in downtown Cairo and the huge demonstrations, sometimes called *milyûniyya*, a protest of one million people. I was not actually participating in the demonstrations, just observing, trying to understand and analyse the slogans, the speeches and discussions on different platforms, the Friday sermon, on most occasions given by the now famous "*Tahrir-Khatîb*", the "Tahrir-preacher" Mazhar Shaheen, imam of the nearby Omar Makram Mosque, expressing the weekly changing themes of the demonstrations.

It is obvious that the themes changed considerably, from "Raise your head! You are Egyptian!", "Egypt is one, Muslims and Copts hand in hand", "Religion is for God, Homeland is for all!"; or "the army and the people, hand in hand", to "the people wants the army to relinquish power"; or "Islamic citizenship (*muwâtana islâmiyya*), without discriminating against the Copts", and "*Sharî'a* Law is the Constitution of *al-Rahmân* (the Merciful God)", or "People want *Sharî'a* Law legislation", and "*Sharî'a* Law is the only source of Legislation"; while on October, 19, 2012, people shouted "Egypt is not the Muslim Brothers' estate (*Masr mish 'izbat al-Ikhwân*)", a slogan printed on the first page of the *al-Tahrir* newspaper...

Sharî'a Law and the Arab spring

From these very few slogans of the Revolution, out of hundreds, it becomes clear that different expressions of identity are involved, and that a fundamental ideological diversity could be found as early as in the first weeks of the Revolution, even if "freedom, citizenship and democracy" united the demonstrators in the first half of 2011, until July 29, 2011, when Muslim Brothers and Salafis suddenly overpowered the democratic youth by greatly superior numbers.

From this particular moment on, everything seemed very clear; for most observers, Egyptian society was, and still is, split into two parts, pro or contra *Sharî'a* Law, secular or Islamic; and most of the time everything is reduced to the question whether or not Islamic *Sharî'a* Law will be applied, without asking what this *Sharî'a* Law actually means in this particular society. There is a kind of presupposition that everyone knows very well what it means to apply *Sharî'a* Law.

No attention is given to the apparent contradiction in the term "Islamic citizenship" used on Tahrir Square. And the same kind of apparent contradiction is to be found in the *Constitutional Declaration* issued on March 30, 2011, by the Egyptian Supreme Council of the Armed Forces (SCAF), saying that "individual freedom is a natural right" and that "all citizens are equals in Citizenship (*Muwâtana*), with "no discrimination between them based on gender, origin, language, *religion or creed*", adding simply that Islamic *Sharî'a* Law is the main source of legislation (*al-masdar al-ra'îsî li-l-tashrî'*)!

An analysis of the different ideological bases for legitimacy expressed in the (Tunisian, Egyptian, Libyan and Syrian) "Arab Spring Revolutions" will make it clear that the "Islamic" and "Arab" nations involved do not have the same, univocal, understanding of Islamic *Sharî'a* Law, but that this *Sharî'a*, which they all still want to respect and in one way or another want to keep in their Constitutions, is mixed with elements of other bases of legitimacy. These bases are not always clearly defined, and talk about Islamic *Sharî'a* Law is mostly narrowing the perception to the simple dichotomy already mentioned.

When Mustafâ 'Abd al-Jalîl was confirmed as chairman of the National Transition Council of Libya in September 2011, the Western media quoted only one sentence from his long speech: "[t]*he new leader of Libya who says that Sharî'a Law will be used as a basis to guide the country after the fall of the Qaddhâfî regime...*". In this quotation, the term *Sharî'a Law* is not explained; it is supposed to be understood, and seems to have one well-defined meaning..., but in fact, it lacks the background of the whole of the speech, where chairman Mustafa 'Abd al-Jalîl is opening up the new horizon of Libya's future, where not only Islam and Islamic Law but also very strong tribal links are the basis for identity. Even if tribal adherence is weaker than religious identity, it is not to be forgotten, as it may in its way challenge the will to unify the citizens of the country under the only religious Law. In the post-revolutionary clashes in Libya, in Sinai and in Iraq, it became clear that tribal links are not to be underestimated. On the contrary, we will argue that *the actual challenges the Islamic Community as a whole is confronted with* are coming from the lack of a single definition of the term Islamic *Sharî'a* Law itself, which is a result of the strong presence of alternative bases of legitimacy, the Western models of society being the most fascinating and attractive challengers, with their high respect for freedom, democracy and undiscriminating citizenship.

In fact, the kind of "secular-Islamic" dichotomy put forward in analysing the situation in the Middle East can only be understood from the point of view of a kind of Islamic exclusivism, actually very much alive in extreme Wahhabi or Salafi militant thinking, and ideologically expressed by the famous Muslim Brother Sayyid Qutb (d. 1966), who wrote that an *'almânî mujtama'*, or "secular Society" (in French: *"une société laïque"*), is a kind of uncivilised, non-human, society: *"al-Mujtama' al-islâmî..., huwa wahdahu al-mujtama' al-mutahaddir"* (*"Islamic Society is the only one to be civilized"*), *"al-Islâm huwa al-hadâra"* ("Islam is the civilization") (Sayyid Qutb 1964: 116-117).

This is however not the only way to understand Islam and its Law. There are other interpretations of society given by Muslims, linked to different interpretations of *Sharî'a* Law, such as those expressed by Ahmed Osâma, a *Young Muslim Brother* (Al-Masry al-Youm 2012), representing what is called "the mainstream current", when he says that "eighty percent of the Egyptian people are religious. They fast and pray, watch television, go to theatres, walk by the Nile corniche, fall in love and get married... Some Salafis want Egypt to become like Saudi Arabia, and some liberals want Egypt to become like the United States... I don't want Egypt to become like Saudi Arabia or the American society...".

As Wahhabis and Salafis are thinking like Sayyid Qutb, we should not of course turn down as irrelevant Sayyid Qutb's interpretation. In Tahrir Square, in Cairo, I discovered through many discussions that the term *"mujtama' 'almânî"*, with an explicit reference to the French model of "laïcité", was excluded, taboo, not to be used, at least in the context of the Egyptian Revolution, as it was identified with *"lâ-dîniyya"*, a society without religion, or without God. In this sense, it was rather seen as an insult, a blasphemy...

From what we saw in Tahrir Square it was obvious that Sayyid Qutb's dichotomy "Islamic Society" (*al-mujtama' al-islâmî*") versus uncivilized society, a society in a state of ignorance ("*jâhiliyya*"), is not at all the model of society to be achieved in the future of Arab nations! On the contrary, more democratic and pluralistic models were the main inspiration of the young democrats who started the revolutions, reflecting a very deep change in the attitudes of younger generations towards the ideologies of "*Political Islam*" and its strict interpretation of *Sharî'a* Law.

This evolution is evident in the text of an interview given by the Egyptian Grand Mufti published on January 11, 2012, in the *Egypt Independent* newspaper, and summarised as follows:

> "Egypt is a liberal country governed by a democratic system approved by Muslim scholars, Grand Mufti Ali Gomaa told *Al-Masry Al-Youm* in an interview published Wednesday. Gomaa stressed that the concept of a civil state doesn't contradict Islamic law, but conforms to it. In Egypt, a civil state means a modern Nation State that is compatible with Islamic provisions, Gomaa said. He said that Egypt did not import the civil state model from the West and that the model has existed for about 150 years".

Let me simply underline that this is not a quotation from the president of one of the smaller Egyptian liberal political parties, who actually lost the elections for the new people's assembly (November 2011-January 2012), but from Dr. 'Ali Gomaa, Mufti of the Egyptian Republic, the second highest religious authority after Dr. Ahmad al-Tayyib, the Grand Imam of Al-Azhar.

Let me underline the three main ideas put forward by the Mufti, and then summarize these statements:

> First: *a democratic system in accordance with the Muslim scholars' general opinion.*
> Second: *the concept of a civil Nation-State does not contradict Islamic law.*
> Third: *the Egyptian model of a modern nation-state is embedded in Egypt's history.*

That means that there is no contradiction between a democratic system and Islamic *Sharî'a* Law. The concept of a civil nation-state – this means a *Dawla madaniyya*– does not contradict Islamic Law. This means that Dr. 'Ali Gomaa implicitly refuses the notion of *Dawla dîniyya*, *"a religious state"*. The particular history of an Islamic country like Egypt has to be taken into account: there is no general pattern of an Islamic state as the unique model for all.

At Tahrir Square, people used the complex term of *"muwâtana islâmiyya"*, "Islamic citizenship", meaning a civil nation-state (*dawla madaniyya*) with an Islamic reference or background; few want the Islamic character of Egypt to be completely erased from the new Constitution. And that is the reason why the Constituent Assembly did not want to change much of the text of the September 11, 1971, Egyptian Constitution's two first paragraphs, amended in 2007:

> Art. 1. *The Arab Republic of Egypt is a democratic state, based on citizenship...* [According to the new Constitution, approved by referendum: *The Arab Republic of Egypt is an independent sovereign state, united and indivisible, its system democratic. The Egyptian people are part of the Arab and Islamic nations (juz' min al-Ummatayn al-ʿArabiyya wa l-Islâmiyya), proud of belonging to the Nile Valley and Africa and of its Asian reach, a positive participant in human civilization*].
>
> Art. 2. *Islam is the religion of the State and Arabic its official language. Principles of Islamic Law (Sharîʿa) are the principal source of legislation (mabâdi' al-Sharîʿa al-Islâmiyya al-masdar al-raʾîsî li l-tashrîʿ).* [Identical in the New Constitution, approved by referendum, December 16-23, 2012].

It was obvious in the discussions in the Constituent Assembly that this second paragraph, which was accepted by the Muslim Brothers[1], does not express the ideas of the Wahhabi and Salafi militant islamist groups, as they proclaimed them in this way in Tahrir Square on July 29, 2011: "God the highest said: «*Sovereignty is for none but Allâh!* » (Qurʾân 12, 40). We want the Islamic Religion to be the only source (*al-masdar al-wahîd*) of legislation, not the main source (*al-masdar al-raʾîsî*) of legislation...".

The objectives of *Sharîʿa* Law

For a long time, Muslim scholars have opened the debate on a modern understanding of *Sharîʿa* Law. That is the case with the Tunisian thinker

Mohamed Talbi (1998), whose standpoint in this regard was summarized by Abdou Filaly-Ansary:

> "M. Talbi can be located in line with the Maghreb school, which places the emphasis more on the "*maqâsid*" (the objectives of the Law: *La finalité de la Loi*), and less on the "*qiyâs*", the argument by analogy whereby one sets out to imprison present day life in the patterns of the past .... In other words: one can transcend the *Sharî'a* without contradicting it, in as far as we are certain that we are still following the direction it has indicated" (Filali-Ansary 2003: 172 translated by Platti (2008: 262).

It is clear that Grand Mufti Ali Gomaa's statement mentioned before is exactly in this line, and also the two *Documents* issued by El-Azhar, referred to in paragraph 4.4, can no longer be understood according to the classical models of "*fatwa's*", the juridical advices given by Islamic legal authorities, with the "*qiyâs*" argument. These statements are very much in line with an argument based on the "*maqâsid*" the objectives of the *Sharî'a* Law (Attia 2007).

Some Muslim scholars are explicitly studying this fundamental aspect of the Islamic Law system, but none of them proposes a most detailed classification of theories on Islamic Law as Jasser Auda does in his book on the "objectives" of *Sharî'a* Law – *al-maqâsid* (Auda 2008). Extracts from his book in the following quotation make clear what we intended to say that simply referring to *Sharî'a* Law with the implicit understanding that we already know clearly what is meant is completely irrelevant and inadequate:

> "This book proposed a shift in the 'levels of authority' from the usual binary categorisation of valid/invalid evidence into a multi-level 'spectrum' of validity of evidence and sources. Current sources in theories of Islamic law are identified as Qur'anic verses, Prophetic narrations, traditional schools of Islamic law, *maṣālih* (i.e. *common interest*), rational arguments, and modern international declarations of rights. The current major 'tendencies' in various contemporary theories of Islamic law are identified as **traditionalism, modernism**, and **postmodernism** ....
>
> **Traditionalism** includes the streams of scholastic traditionalism, scholastic neo-traditionalism, neo-literalism, and ideology-oriented theories ... Neo-literalism agrees with classic literalism in being against the idea of the purposes/*maqāṣid* as legitimate source of jurisprudence. Finally,

ideology-oriented theories criticises modern 'rationality' and values for their biased 'western-centricity'.

Islamic **modernism** includes the 'streams' of apologetic reinterpretation, reformist reinterpretation, dialogue-oriented re-interpretation, interest-oriented theories, and *uṣûl* (i.e. the fundaments of Islamic Law) revision. Key contributors to Islamic modernism integrated their Islamic and Western education into new proposals for Islamic reform and 're-interpretation'. ... *Usûl* revisionism attempted to revise *usûl al-fiqh* (i.e. the fundaments of Islamic Law), through questioning the notions of 'consensus', 'authenticity' and 'abrogation', and introducing new interpretations of *maṣlaḥa* (common interest).

Islamic **postmodernism** included streams of post-structuralism, historicism, critical legal studies, post-colonialism, neo-rationalism, anti-rationalism, and secularism. The common method in all these postmodern approaches is 'deconstruction', in a Derridean style" (Auda 2008: 206-7).

Three bases of legitimacy

When the Egyptian people prepare for the elections for a new people's Assembly, and on 25th January 2013 commemorate the second anniversary of the revolution, observers have the impression that two important ideological blocs are confronting each other: the more secular, democratic, "liberal" movements, inspired by the aspirations of the new generations for "freedom, citizenship and democracy" based on the rules of a nation-state (1°), and the more radical Islamic parties, *de facto* inspired by what in the last third of the twentieth century has been called "political Islam" (2°), in the sense that Islamic *Sharî'a* Law is to be the only basis for legitimacy. We understand that the Grand Mufti expressed himself in terms of the first ideology. But the statements from the Egyptian Mufti of course remained not unchallenged, and in particular by the Salafis, the members of the *Nûr* party, the second party in the now disbanded parliament, with a quarter of the votes and 125 seats. And it is clear that their ideological background is indeed the ideology of political Islam. But let us not forget that this ideology, and the movements linked to it, became strong in the last third of the twentieth century because they were challenging the authority of the two presidents who came after Jamâl 'Abd al-Nâsir (d. 1970), Anwar al-Sadât (assassinated on October 6, 1981) and Hosnî Mubârak. They were the last representatives of a third pan-Arabic post-colonial ideology, the still influential, but very much declining nationalistic and militaristic ideology (3°). We can find reminders of the pan-Arabic nationalism, indeed, in the texts of the old and new Constitutions ("*The Egyptian people are part of the Arab and Islamic nations...: Min ummatayn, al-'Arabiyya wa l-Islâmiyya*"), and in Tahrir Square, we saw pictures of Jamâl 'Abd al-Nâsir and references to Nasserism; and the term "Arab Spring" itself has an implicit reference to pan-arabism! In Egypt, Arab nationalism was the ultimate basis of legitimacy for more than half a century, the Egyptian Revolution of July 23, 1952, with a military coup d'état staged by the Free Officers' Movement, a group of army officers led by Muhammad Naguib and Gamal Abdel Nasser. The revolution was completed by first overthrowing King Farouk and, ultimately, the monarchy with King Fuad II, born on 16 January 1952, who reigned for less than a year until 18 June 1953. King Fuad II was Egypt and Sudan's last monarch and the last of the Muhammad Ali Dynasty. But let us not forget that Arab nationalism was also the ultimate basis of legitimacy under Saddâm Husayn (Iraq), Zayn al-'Âbidîn Ben 'Alî (Tunesia), Mu'ammar al-Qaddhâfî (Libya), 'Alî 'Abdullâh Sâlih (Yemen), Bashshâr al-Asad (Syria), Yâsir 'Arafat (Palestine)...

Revolutionary Nationalism and military rule

Now that everyone has been talking about "the Arab spring", let us not forget 1998 and similar events in Indonesia, when President Suharto and his military regime were replaced by a democratic system, with an elected president. As with the Egyptian situation, there was a feeling of "Kefâya: enough is enough": Suharto was re-elected for another five-year term in March 1998, thanks to family and business associates' support. But, increasingly, people spoke out against Suharto's presidency, and university students organised nationwide demonstrations. He resigned on May 21, 1998.

It is so often said that Indonesia is the biggest "Islamic" country in the world. But what does it mean? In what sense is this country an "Islamic" country? With a population of more than 245,000,000 people and 86.1% Muslims (*World Factbook* 2011: "*Indonesia is now the world's third most populous democracy, ... and home to the world's largest Muslim population*"). The constitutional system, however, is not "Islamic": the basis of legitimacy is indeed not, in one way or another, *Sharî'a* Law, but the *Pancasila*, i.e. *the Five Principles* of the State: (1°) Belief in the one and only God, (2°) Just and Civilized Humanity, (3°) The Unity of Indonesia, (4°) Democracy and (5°) Social Justice.

Abdurrahman Wahid (who died in 2009) was the first elected president of Indonesia after the resignation of Suharto in 1998 (from 1999 to 2001), and long the president of the biggest Indonesian Islamic cultural organisation, *Nahdatul Ulama*, with perhaps 30 million members. We met him in 2005 for a long interview, in which he underlined, on the one hand, the *specific cultural relevance* of the local Islamic traditions, and on the other hand *the danger of the Wahhabi missions*, who refuse any cultural and religious diversity, propagating one single "Islamic" model for organizing society.

As was the case for Indonesia, the post-colonial period, the second half of the twentieth century, has also been characterized elsewhere by military dictatorship and nationalism. And this was the case not only in "Islamic" countries, Burma being the last example of this evolution. For "Islamic" countries, these regimes were often identified to be a typical "Islamic, non-democratic" way of organizing society. Most of the time, this had nothing to do with "Islam".

To make this case clear, allow me to analyse shortly one of the most important charters of the post-colonial period, the Constitution of the *Ba'th* Party, written for the first National Congress, held in Damascus in April 1947. As we know, the *Ba'th* ideology was the basis of the Iraqi regime (until the fall of Saddam Husayn on 30 December 2006; he had been a leading member of the revolutionary Arab Socialist Ba'th Party, and later, the Baghdad-based Ba'th Party – Ba'th meaning "*Renaissance*" – of Arab nationalism). But it is, even now, also the basis of the Syrian regime of Hâfiz al-Asad, and his son Bashshâr al-Asad.

Under the title "Constitution of the Socialist Arabic *Ba'th*-Party", we find the definition of the party:

> "*The Socialist Arabic Ba'th-Party is a national movement, popular and revolutionary, fighting for Arab's unity, freedom and socialism*". There are three fundamental principles:
> "*(1°) The Unity and freedom of the Arab Nation; (2°) The Personality of the Arab Nation; (3°) The Mission of the Arab Nation*" (Renaud 1982: 12-33).

The Arabs, spread from the Gulf of Bassora to the Atlantic Ocean, are united through their common Arabic language and culture, so that they become one motherland (*al-Umm*), which has a sacred character and an "*eternal*" mission.

The basis of legitimacy is the national, popular and revolutionary movement of the Arab citizens, united in one Arab Nation, culture and language; and nobody is allowed to divide it. Not the tribal identity (Berbers – *qabâ'il* – in Algeria, but also in Libya, Iraq, Yemen, Arabia, Sinai...), not an ethnic identity (Kurdish...), not a communitarian identity – *tawâ'if* – (Lebanon, Syria...), or a religious identity (*Sunnî, Shi'î,* Coptic, Assyrians).

In the ten pages of that *Ba'th* Constitution, no mention at all is made of Islam, Islamic Law or Muslims. It is a purely secular, National-Socialist Document.

That is the reason why Arab Christians could easily join the nationalist movements in the region (e.g. Palestine – *Fath* – and Iraq/Syria – *Ba'th*): the basis of legitimacy marginalized religious criteria of differentiation. That is also the reason why Christians in Iraq had a much better time under Saddâm Husayn than after the American intervention, when democratic elections resulted in a new power struggle between Sunni, Shi'a and Kurdish identities, Sunni and Shi'a based on religious identities, and Kurdish on a ethnic identity, unlike the pan-Arabic national identity of the *Ba'th*.

We tend to forget that this kind of post-colonial nationalist ideology represented by the Ba'th Constitution has produced most of the military regimes in power in the so-called "Islamic countries" of the second half of the XXth century, including Indonesia and Turkey, Algeria, Egypt, Palestine, Yemen, Syria and Iraq... The search for national unity is tragically represented by Jamâl 'Abd-al-Nâsir, the failed union between Egypt and Syria (1958–1961: *Al-Jumhuriya al-'Arabiyya al-Muttahida*) and the call for other unions later on.

We know how the West reacted to the different independence movements. The colonial powers France and Great-Britain did not like them. We know what happened between France and the Algerian independence movements from 1954 to 1962, and the independence war, until General de Gaulle signed the Évian accords, which led to Algeria gaining its independence from France. But we know also how the military regime crushed the Islamic movements when the FIS (Front Islamique du Salut – Islamic Salvation Front) won the first round of the parliamentary elections in December 1991, initiating a bloody civil war.

What is completely forgotten is the plot organised by Britain and the United States against Mohammed Mossadegh who was prime minister of Iran from 1951 to 1953, and was overthrown when he wanted to nationalize Iran's oil industry. We should not forget that in March 2000, Madeleine Albright, who was at that time Secretary of State, *"stated her regret that Mossadegh was ousted"*, as *"it was a setback for Iran's political development"*, and it is now *"easy to understand why many Iranians continue to resent this intervention by America"*.

A completely different ideological movement was appearing: Islamic radicalism. From Khomeini's time on, these Western powers started to reconsider their position. The West, and France in particular, supported the military regimes of the Middle East, considered to be more "secular", more *"laïc"*, and useful allies in their fight against "Islamic terrorism". France's sympathy towards the military regime in Algeria was unshaken during the second civil war between 1990 and 1993, while it became clear that the radicalization of the Islamists and the violent uprisings that dominated political life in 1992 and 1993 resulted from the revived political authoritarianism led by the army...

But it became clear very soon that from the seventies on, the nationalist ideologies lost much of their credibility.

The Islamist ideology of Political Islam

Under President Anwar as-Sadât, and much more under Hosni Mubârak, the legitimacy of the regime, based on the nationalist ideology, vanished altogether, in the same way as happened in Algeria, in Iraq, in Indonesia and even in Palestine, where the national liberation movement of *Fath* has been challenged since the appearance of *Hamâs*. Based on the principles of *"Political Islam"* gaining momentum throughout the Arab world in the 1980s, *Hamâs*, (*Harakat al-muqawwama al-islâmiyya*, the Movement of the Islamic Resistance), was founded in 1987, during the first *Intifâda*.

But Hamâs was not the only movement of its kind; it was the political expression of another ideology, more profoundly rooted in the culture of Muslim peoples, unlike the nationalist ideologies influenced by Western thinking.

The ideology of "Political Islam" is indeed a completely different source of legitimacy, and fundamentally challenges all nationalist ideologies. In the eighties and nineties it became stronger to the extent that the military regimes lost all credibility. It was and is still very much a pan-Islamic ideology, and can be traced back to the early thirties of the twentieth century, when Hasan al-Bannâ in Egypt, followed by the Muslim Brother ideologist Sayyid Qutb (executed in 1966), and Abû l-Aʿlâ Maudûdî (d. 1979) in India, were propagating a new, coherent and modern way to understand the social and political implications of traditional Islamic thinking; radically purifying the Islamic *Way of Life* from non-essential, devotional or Western-inspired practices. Their systematic way of thinking, based on a neo-literalistic reading of the Qurʾân[2], is still very much the primary source of inspiration of all radical Islamic movements who want the application of *Sharîʿa* Law (*tadbîq al-Sharîʿa*), all over the world, to conform to their literalistic understanding of God's Law (Sabanegh 1980; Bellani, and Borrmans 1986).

An incredible rush towards the Arabic-Islamic literary heritage – *al-turâth al-ʿarabî al-islamî* – was one of the consequences of their vision of the *Revival* of the pan-Islamic community, with new-born Islamic States, based on the unique legitimacy of Islamic Law and Constitution, basically rediscovered in the fundamental texts of the Arabic-Islamic literary heritage. But, as the eminent scholar Mohamed Arkoun (d. September 2010) wrote in his last book, "The way this Arabic-Islamic literary heritage is used in modern times is *"anachronistic"* (Arkoun 2010: 53). We agree completely with this statement, and will make it clear in analysing Maudûdî's way of considering *Sharî 'a* Law, analysed later on.

As was the case with the nationalistic ideology, the West was again unable to grasp the profound impact of this until 1975 mostly hidden, ideology, until the dramatic events of the Iranian revolution in 1979 and 1980, and the assassination of president Anwar as-Sadat on October 6th, 1981.

Observers in the West did not realize the impact of this ideology on the whole of the Islamic world: I saw people reading Maudûdî's booklet *Towards Understanding Islam* in Brussels[3], in Manila, in the metro in Paris, in London, and of course in Cairo... For many Muslims, at least, after centuries of decadence, of Western arrogance, revival was possible, based on the very principles of their revealed Book, explained in a simple and apparently modern way.

The military regimes understood the threat of Political Islam's legitimacy much better. The repression was ferocious: emergency law in Egypt and continuous persecution of Muslim Brothers and more radical Muslims until the fall of Mubarak; civil war in Algeria; the massacre of Hama in February 1982 under Hâfiz al-Asad; what has been described as one of *"the single deadliest acts by any Arab government against its own people in the modern Middle East"*, Hâfiz's son Bashshâr doing even worse... On the other hand, the most radical groups of this "Islamic" political movement became more and more violent and evolved towards action identified as "terrorism" by the West...

In the most ambiguous political situation of Pakistan and its political instability since independence from British rule and *Qâ'id A'zam* leader Muhammad Ali Jinnah (d. September 11, 1948), with continuous interaction between democratic legitimacy, military rule, and Islamic political traditions, it was Abû l-A'lâ Maudûdî who presented a coherent alternative, called revolution (Maudidi 1947; 1991), based on the principle that *"no man made Law, only God's Law"* has legitimacy (Platti 2008; Maudidi 1978 and 1964)[4].

We know now how deeply these ideas were absorbed by radical Muslims all over the world, even if Maudûdî did not intend to incite to violence. Maudûdî was very explicit in defending his global vision on the fact that Islam and Western civilization *"are in conflict with each other"* (Maudidi 1991). He remained fundamentally peaceful, arguing that only education can bring about a global change, and not a sudden, violent revolution. Nevertheless, we saw how some of his main ideas, expressed in his articles in "*West versus Islam*", became a terrible reality on September 11, 2001: radical Muslims made Huntington's book *The Clash of Civilizations* (1996) look like a prophecy in the sense of "*Islam versus West*".

According to Maudûdî, the Muslim community has its own "*complete code of life*" (Maudûdî 1985: 30), which is diametrically opposed to that of the West, the latter being based on foundations different from those of Islam. The West, for example, has detached economic and social existence from the ethical principles of religion on account of its "struggle for liberation" from the church and from clericalism. Maudûdî claims that, as a consequence of this historical evolution, therefore, Western society is established on three principles: **nationalism**, whereby the nation is the ultimate ground of all legitimacy and not universal human dignity rooted in the oneness of God; **democracy**, whereby the law is dependent on alternating majorities made up of different interest groups and not on the difference between justice and injustice; **the absence of religion from matters of state**, whereby alternative interests are *de facto* at work and not the question of ethical responsibility; this is the real agenda of the West (Maudûdî 1987).

The impact of Maudûdî's Islamic Political System based on the principle of God's Sovereignty – *Rubûbiyya* – cannot be underestimated (Maudûdî 1992: 72). Even in Tahrir Square, on July 29, 2011, this principle was clearly proclaimed by militant Salafis: "*Islam admits no Sovereignty except that of God and, consequently, does not recognise any Law-giver other than Him*"; so the slogan in Tahrir Square said: "*Inna al-Hukm illâ li-llâh. Ad-Dîn al-islâmî huwa al-masdar al-wahîd li-t-tashrî*": "*Sovereignty belongs to God. The Islamic Religion is the only source of legislation*", not even the primary source of legislation, as proposed by the *Supreme Council of the Armed Forces*, the SCAF, in their constitutional document of March 31, 2011.

Since the turn of the new century, it has, however, become clear that Maudûdî's Islamic political system has a fundamental weakness. His vision of Islamic Law is not compatible with any modern apprehension of natural causes and natural law[5]. The negation of the historical dimension of the Islamic tradition and of the particular roots of Islamic civilisation not only leads to the refutation and rejection of global multiculturality and the idea of an evolving Islamic way of life; it also reveals an overwhelmingly crushing image of God[6]. History and culture, human engagement and freedom to engage lose their consistency. The point of reference par excellence is a univocally understood statement from the Qur'an: *al-ḥukm li-llah* – legitimacy belongs to God alone.

And it is exactly this verse from the Coran that was exhibited by Salafis on Tahrir Square: "« *Sovereignty is for none but Allâh!* » (Qur'ân 12, 40); We want Islamic Religion to be the only source of legislation, not the main source of legislation: let us stop combining his legislation with other legislations *(an nushrika maʿa tashrîʿihi tashrîʿâtin ukhrâ!...)*".

For these radical Islamists, there are no such things as subsidiarity, no delegation, no consistent human (co-)creative engagement, no legitimacy of any kind in human interference with God's Law: all of that is considered *shirk*, polytheism (the use of "*nushrika*" in the Salafi slogan is already suggestive!). It seems to me that all of this, however, represents a flagrant contradiction of the Qur'anic concept of *khalīfa* – the human person as the *locus tenens* of God! – and the ebullient creative and inventive activities of older Islamic civilisations. Human contingency is driven to its extremes by the Islamists, monotheism is stretched to its limits, and nothing ultimately exists apart from God.

Maudûdî was given the first prestigious King Faisal Prize in 1979, some months before he died. This event symbolizes the recognition by the two-centuries-old Wahhabi movement of the similarity of Maududi's action to the Wahhabi *jihâdî* revival. It goes back to Muhammad Ibn ʿAbd al-Wahhâb (d. 1792) and his disciples' action against "polytheism" – *shirk* -[7].

A short analysis of Muhammad Ibn ʿAbd al-Wahhâb's most important book, *Kitâb al-Tawhîd (Book on Monotheism)*, shows:

(1)   Its extreme exclusivist attitude: characterized as "*Shirk*" are the Shiʿa (with the "saints" of the Family of the Prophet), the Sufis (with their "mystic saints"), and Christians (with their icons, tombs, saints...). *Shirk* has to be extirpated by way of *Jihâd*.

(2)   The importance of obedience to God's Law: and God's attribute of Justice. "islam" is almost reduced to his casuistic interpretation, and the rulings of fatwas.

(3)   The strict (and literal) interpretation of *Sharîʿa* Law as a unique model for the Islamic Way of Life.

At a certain moment of the Egyptian revolution, in April-May 2011, Salafi and Wahhabi movements attacked Sufi shrines in Cairo and Alexandria: « *In Alexandria, ... at least 16 historic mosques belonging to Sufi orders are targeted by members of the Salafi movement, who attempted to demolish tombs of important*

Islamic scholars because they oppose the veneration of saints as heretical. One of the mosques allegedly attacked by Salafis is the historic mosque of al-Mursī Abū l-ʿAbbās, which dates back to the 13th century and is a popular site for visits by Egyptians from across the country. …) There are about half a million registered Sufis in Alexandria, which has a population of 4.1 million people. The city contains 36 of Egypt's 76 registered Sufi orders » (Al-Masry Al-Youm 2011).

This reminds us of the terrible attack on July, 1, 2010, in Lahore, on the shrine of the great mystic Abû l-Hasan ʿAlî al-Ghaznawî al-Hujwayrî (d. 1074), the author of the famous book on Islamic mysticism, *Kashf al-Mahjūb* (Nicholson 1990). This attack, with more than forty pilgrims killed, against one of the most prestigious Muslim-Sufi shrines, reminds us of other attacks against Sufi and Shiʿa shrines in Libya, Mali and Iraq.

In the minds of these radical Muslims there can be no other model of living Islam than the way of life of the "*Salaf*", the early companions and ancestors, who lived, according to them, the pure life of Muslims according to the Qurʾân and the Sunna, the way of life of the Prophet. They reject all other practices seen as "innovations", different from the simple rituals from Muhammad's time, like visiting the tombs of saints, or the Sufi "prayer" of *dhikr*. Sometimes, they refer to the medieval scholar Ibn Taymiyya (Taqî al-Dîn Ahmad Ibn Taymiyya, 1263 – 1328), who refuted radically any mediation by saints or holy people between God and humans. Ibn Taymiyya indeed also condemned the Sufi's *dhikr*, mentioning God's name (Bannerth 1974; Michot 2012; Ibn Taymiyya 1996).

It is obvious that the ideology of "Political Islam" is influencing extremist and exclusivist groups, using violence against Sufis, Shiʿites and Christians, or Western societies in general. But it is too easy to reduce Islamic activism or even fundamentalism to this kind of "radical extremism". In the same way Islamic *Shariʿa* Law can be understood in different ways, to characterize a society as "Islamic" does not mean that the ideology of "Political Islam" is the only basis for legitimacy in that society. Society can have intertwined ideological bases. This is indeed the case in the first paragraph of the new Egyptian Constitution, bringing together pan-Arabism and Islam: *the Egyptian people are part of the* **Arab** *and Islamic Nations (juzʾ min al-Ummatayn* **al-ʿArabiyya** *wa l-Islâmiyya)*!

Democracy and the liberal Nation-State

The ideology of "Political Islam" was already conceived decades before Western public opinion became aware of it between 1975 and 1981, with the Iranian

Revolution and the murder of president Anwar al-Sadât, and much later on with terrorism and al-Qâ'ida. In the same way the ideas of democracy, freedom and citizenship were already expressed long before democratic youth movements started the "Arab Spring" revolutions, taking Western public opinion by surprise. The legitimacy of the old regimes was shaken long before 2011. But in Tahrir Square the authority of the old regime is openly de-legitimized: corruption, arbitrary action, violence, repression and falsified elections are to be replaced by "a Nation-State with citizenship, justice and democracy" (*min ajl Dawlat al-muwâtana wa l-'adl wa l-dîmuqrâtiyya*). At the same time, a religious state (*dawla dîniyya*) based on a purely Islamic model of society is banned: "May the Crescent live together with the Cross!" (*'âsha al-Hilâl ma'a al-Salîb*). The old Wafd party was happy to remind the Egyptians of their slogan from the time of Egyptian independence from British rule (1922) and their hero Sa'd Zaghlûl (d. 1927): "Religion is for God and Homeland is for all" (*al-Dîn li-llâh wa l-Watan li l-jamî'*).

In the time when militants of "political Islam" were still persecuted and imprisoned, intellectuals were already discussing secularism… In the eighties of the twentieth century Fouad Zakariyya criticized "political Islam" and its revival (Zakkariyya 1989)[8]. Judge Muhammad Sa'îd al-Ashmâwî argued for enlightenment instead of "political Islam", the title of his most renowned book (al-'Ashmâwî 1987; Anawati 1989). And Faraj Fûda, who was murdered in 1992, dared to write *On Secularism/Laïcité* in his book *Hawla l-'almâniyya* (1987). Some Tunisian intellectuals were very explicit in defending modernity. We have already mentioned Mohamed Talbi; Saâd Ghrab, Hmîda Ennaïfer and Abdelmajid Charfi analysed secularization trends already active in Arab countries (Charfi 1996; Ghrab 1996; Ennaifer 1996).

In India, Syed Alam Khundmiri (d. 1983) criticized the theological principles of modern Islamic fundamentalism, referring to al-Ash'arî (d. 938) and Ghazâlî (d. 1111), whose theology implied, according to him, that "human agents have no role to play, no creativity or initiative. Human beings are determined objects and not active, creative subjects". For this Indian philosopher, this means that modern Islamic fundamentalism is in fact traditionalism and stagnation, and is "not a victory for the Prophetic Tradition" (Ansari 2011: 34, 48).

The most interesting evidence of a personal evolution from militancy for "political Islam" towards an open and tolerant Islam is given by the Indian scholar Maulana Wahiduddin Khan in his book *Islam rediscovered* (2001: 152).

Khan joined the Indian branch of Maudûdî's movement in 1949, but left it in 1962, convinced that the view of Islam represented by Maudûdî was "a grave misinterpretation": "What made matters worse ... was the emergence of certain Muslim leaders in the first half of the twentieth century, who expounded their own political interpretation of Islam, according to which Islam was a complete system of State and Muslims had been appointed by God to fulfill the mission of establishing this Islamic State throughout the world. Some well-known names associated with this interpretation are the following: Syed Qutb in Egypt, Ayatollah Khomeini in Iran, and Syed Abul Ala Maududi in Pakistan. This political view of Islam, in spite of being a grave misinterpretation, spread rapidly among Muslims".

In this context, it is interesting to see how Professor Vali Nasr, who was the author of the most comprehensive analysis of Maudûdî's life and work (Reza Nasr 1996; 1994), has been feeling the radical change going on in the Middle East, referring to the Turkish model as a "promising way forward for the wider region" in his book published in 2009 with this subtitle: "Why the new Muslim Middle Class is the key to defeating Extremism" (Nasr 2009). Other sociological analyses are needed to link this statement to the democratic youth connected by the Internet and Facebook who were the driving force of the Arab revolutions. It is however clear for me that economic and social problems in Tunisia and Egypt were also very much at the back of the insurrections. We cannot forget the pre-revolutionary movement of 6 April (*Harakat 6 April*) involved in the 2008 strike at the textile factories of Mahalla al-Kubrâ in the Egyptian Delta.

We started by referring to the second highest religious authority in Egypt, the Mufti Shaykh Ali Gom'a, and his interview on "democracy". In this context, the most spectacular document coming from the highest Islamic authority in Egypt is certainly the Document for *Basic Freedoms in Society* (January 11, 2012) issued by the Shaykh al Azhar, Dr. Ahmad al Tayyib. Nobody can ever say after this Document that democracy, citizenship and freedom are alien to Islam. It is clear that Al-Azhar is very much aware of the radical changes in Islamic societies and wants the Islamic community to integrate the globalized world, upholding an open, tolerant and Islamic identity, in dialogue with international institutions. In this sense, this Document on freedoms is a step further than the first Document, a *Statement about the Future of Egypt* (June 19, 2011).

The most important articles (out of the eleven) of this first Document describe modern post-revolutionary Egypt as follows (excerpts):

First. A modern and democratic State, according to a Constitution..., ... This Constitution should establish rules, guarantee the rights and the duties of all the citizens equally (*musâwât*) .... It differs from other states which rule according to the model of a "religious and clerical state" (*dawla dîniyya kahnûtiyya*). ... Islamic *Sharî'a* Law is the fundamental source of legislation (*al-Sharî'a al-islâmiyya hiya al-masdar al-asâs li-l-tashrî'*).
Second. Al-Azhar embraces a democracy based on free and direct voting which represents the modern formula for achieving the Islamic precepts of "*Shura*" (consultation).
Third, commitment to fundamental freedoms of thoughts and opinions (*al-hurriyyât al-asâsiyya fî l-fikr wa l-ra'y*), with full respect of human, women's and children's rights (*huqûq al-insân wa l-mar'a wa l-tifl*).
Fourth. Al-Azhar supports dialogue and mutual respect between citizens ....
Fifth. Commitment to all international conventions ....

The basic rights of citizens are formulated in the four articles of the second Document (excerpts):

First: *Freedom of Belief*
Freedom of belief and the associated right of full citizenship for all – which is based on complete equality in rights and duties – is regarded as the cornerstone in the modern social structure. This freedom is guaranteed by the authentic conclusive religious texts and the clear constitutional and legal principles. Almighty Allah says, {*There shall be no compulsion in the religion. The right course has become clear from the wrong...*} (Qur'ân, *Al-Baqarah* 2: 256). And He also says, {*So whoever wills – let him believe; and whoever wills – let him disbelieve...*} (Qur'ân, *Al-Kahf* 18: 29). Accordingly, any aspect of compulsion, persecution, or discrimination on the basis of religion is prohibited ....

Second: *Freedom of Opinion and Expression*
Freedom of opinion is the mother of all freedoms, and it is most manifest in the free expression of opinion by all different means, including writing, oratory, artistic production, digital communication.

Third: *Freedom of Scientific Research*
            Serious scientific research in humanities, physics, mathematics, etc., is
            the driver of human progress and the means to discovering the laws of
            the universe so as to use them for the goodness of humankind .... Great
            Muslim scholars, such as Ar-Râzî, Ibn Al-Haytham, Ibn An-Nafîs,
            were the leaders and pioneers of knowledge in the East and the West
            for many centuries. It is time now for the Arab and Muslim world to
            make a comeback to the race of power and the age of knowledge.
Fourth: *Freedom of Literary and Artistic Creativity*
            There are two types of creativity. One type is scientific creativity, which
            was tackled earlier. The other is literary and artistic creativity, which
            comprises different genres of literature, such as lyric and dramatic
            poetry, stories and novels, theatre, biographies, and visual plastic arts,
            and cinematic, television, and musical arts, in addition to other forms
            newly introduced to all these genres.

It has to be underlined how much these two documents contradict the current
negative image of "Islam" essentially influenced by the Salafi, Wahhabi or
Maududian ideologies and their inherent censorship, completely in contrast
with the last paragraph of al-Azhar's second document: "*[t]he more the reasonable
freedom is entrenched in society, the clearer the proof of its civilization. Literature
and arts are the mirror of the consciences of societies and the true expression of their
variables and invariables. They paint a bright picture of their aspirations for a
better future. We implore Almighty Allah to guide us to that which is good and
right*".

Conclusion

Dozens of times I went to Tahrir Square, observing the Egyptian revolution
evolving from the formidable *milyûniyya*s in January-February 2011 towards
the vibrant acclamation of Dr. Muhammad Morsi as the new elected President
of Egypt on Friday, June 29, 2012, at 6 p.m., and the Friday, October 19, 2012
manifestation against the Muslim Brothers and the draft of the New Constitution.
From everything I saw and heard, I tried to understand the background,
sometimes confronted with apparent contradictions in one and the same Friday
sermon, let alone the differences between the women's emancipation platform

and the Salafi candidate Hâzim Abû Ismâ'îl's discourse in the same square. And so I came to the conclusion that it was, and still is, impossible to reduce everything to some simple univocal concepts, but, on the contrary, that different projects for building a new society were intertwined, conforming to the complexity of the Egyptian society and the Middle East realities.

From everything I have read since I visited Pakistan in 1992, I was able to distinguish the three fundamental ideologies of Nationalism, Political Islam and Democracy[9]. All three are clearly influential in the so-called "Arab Spring", now more and more evolving towards political activism and unresolved conflicts. But as freedom of speech became a reality, none of these ideologies had the absolute upper hand, as was the case under Nasser and is still the case in Saudi Arabia; but for how long? It has been evident in Egypt since the new century that, intellectually speaking, the third ideology of freedom and democracy is slowly becoming stronger and the pan-Arabic option weaker. And younger generations are no longer fascinated by their parents' struggle for political Islam as they were in the eighties and nineties.

In Tahrir Square, democratic activists were killed by anonymous adherents to the old regime. This was the case for the most eminent Sheikh, 'Emâd ad-Dîn 'Effat, Director for Fatwa's at Dâr al-Iftâ', who was gunned down in the square on December 16, 2011,and proclaimed a Martyr of the Revolution with many others. Salafis and Muslim Brothers and Sisters were liberated from prison and showed new strength. But ultimately, they were not able to impose their views completely. It is a kind of "Islamic citizenship" (*muwâtana islâmiyya*) which is ultimately prevailing. Nobody was able to silence the newly discovered consequence of the Revolution: freedom of expression and pluralism (*ta'addud*), legitimized by Egypt's supreme religious authority in his second Document.

A clear sign of this evolution, but above all of the complexity of the new realities, is this sentence in that second Document, mixing freedoms and *Sharî'a* Law: "The basic freedoms ... are the freedom of belief, the freedom of expression, the freedom of scientific research, the freedom of literary and artistic creativity. All these freedoms should have their roots in serving the objectives of the *Sharî'a* (*maqâsid al-Sharî'a!*) and grasping the spirit of modern constitutional legislation and the requirements of human knowledge advance".

The diversity of interpretations of the fundamental concept of *Sharî'a Law*, clearly analysed by Auda, is in itself a sign that a great number of Muslim scholars are really joining the actual globalisation of intellectual life in our world, leaving behind dictatorial regimes, but also the narrow-minded identity of *"Political Islam"*.

Post-scriptum (August 31, 2013)

On October 19, 2012, people on Tahrir-square shouted "Egypt is not the Muslim Brothers' estate". It was the beginning of increasing criticism towards the way president Morsi and the Muslim Brothers were governing the country. There was, on November 22, 2012, the Constitutional Declaration issued by president Morsi bringing him beyond the bounds of judicial supervision. A new Constitution is pushed through and endorsed by referendum (December 25, 2012); there is however nationwide protest against article 219 specifying how article 2 ("principles of *Sharî'a*-law") has to be understood in a very restrictive way: according to the principles and rules of the Islamic Law-system (*qawâ'id usûliyya wa-fiqhiyya*) and the four Sunni-schools of the Islamic community (*madhâhib Ahl al-Sunna wa l-Jamâ'a*); excluding other possible interpretations. On the second anniversary of the revolution, January 25, 2013, anti-Morsi protesters fill Tahrir-square. In February-March, opposition increases, given the total inefficiency of the government in basic social and economic matters. Anti-Brotherhood sentiment is on the rise: the "narrow-minded identity of Political Islam" becomes obvious, and, more important, his fundamental inability to address social problems. On Tahrir-square, speakers reject the Muslim Brothers: they are seen as "traders in religion – *tujjâr al-Dîn*", "they follow al-Bannâ's *Sharî'a* and not Muhammad's *Sharî'a* (sic)"! It appears clearly that the Brothers' slogan "Islam is the solution – *al-Islâm huwa al-hall*" is not at all realized. And the Sinai Peninsula becomes increasingly a war-zone against jihadist infiltrators. From May on, an anti-Morsi campaign called *Tamarrud* – Rebellion, aims to force Morsi out of office by collecting 15 million petitions. On the evening of Sunday June 30, millions gather on squares and streets in all the big cities of Egypt to support *Tamarrud*. The opposition to Morsi's regime is such that general Sisi, the Defense minister, appears on television on the evening of July 3, with high ranking commanders of the army, the great-Imam Ahmad at-Tayyib, the Coptic Patriarch Tawâdros and representatives of the opposition and the Salafi Nûr-party – all of them together symbolising the unity of the Egyptian people. They present a Declaration removing Muhammad Morsi from office, describing a road-map towards new elections and democratic institutions, and the appointment of Adly Mansour as

Egypt's interim President. The Muslim Brotherhood's reaction is furious: they try to convince the world that this is simply a military coup (*inqilâb ʿaskarî*), and not a popular uprising representing the Nation's legitimacy (*al-sharʿiyya*). On July 26, a similar *milliûniyya* in favour of Sisi and the removal of Morsi will be seen as a confirmation of the Egyptian people's will for radical change. On August 14, there is the violent intervention of the security forces and the army against the Muslim Brothers on Râbiʿa al-ʿAdawiyya and Nahda-squares, with the following repression of the Muslim Brotherhood.

From the three intertwined ideologies, fundaments of legitimacy, explicitly present on Tahrir-square, one is out (for the time being): Islamist movements imposing « Political Islam », a « religious State » (*dawla dîniyya*) (1°). Representatives of the democratic tendencies have been dominating the (new) constitution-drafting process, and they abolished article 219, seen as imposing too strict an interpretation of *Sharîʿa*-law on Egyptians. These democrats want a *«liberal» Nation-State* with freedom and citizenship, without discrimination between Christian Copts and Sunni Muslims (*dawla madaniyya*) (2°). In July, some pictures of ʿAbd al-Nâsir appeared more frequently on Tahrir-square: but it doesn't mean that Nasser's post-colonial nationalism can be revived; it is certain however, that Egyptian nationalism was overwhelmingly present on Tahrir-square in July. Demonstrators wanted national unity: a strong Egyptian Nation (*dawla wataniyya*) (3°). Evolving towards a new military rule? Nobody knows what the military has in mind for the future... Hopefully, they will hold firm to the new, more liberal, post-Morsi, Constitution, in a context of polarization and violence; a tragic situation not at all conform to the ideals of the January 2011 "Arab Spring Revolution".

Notes

1   As we know, the Democratic Alliance, guided by the *Party for Freedom and Justice*, won a 47% majority out of 498 seats in the November-January 2011-2012 elections. This party is directly linked to the movement of the *Muslim Brothers* founded in 1928 in Egypt by the Islamic scholar and schoolteacher Hasan al-Bannâ (who was shot and died on February 12, 1949, in Cairo). At these elections, they won 234 seats for the People's Assembly which was later dissolved by the court.

2   For a modern Western mind it is amazing that society is to be organized according to commentaries of revealed texts: (Maudidi 1988; Qutb 1999).

3 Syed Abul A'la Maududi (all editions have different transcriptions of his name Sayyid Abu l-A'lâ Maudûdî), *Towards Understanding Islam* (Delhi: Markazi Maktaba Islami, 1989, 14th Ed.), (Leicester: The Islamic Foundation, 1980 reprint); translation in French and Dutch: *Comprendre l'Islam* (Leicester: The Islamic Foundation, 1983); *De Boodschap van de Islam* (Den Haag: Moslim Informatie Centrum, 1992, tweede druk).

4 In our book (Platti 2008: 199-225), we analysed Maudûdî's "Political Islam", and in particular his book *Islamic Law and Constitution* (Lahore: Islamic Publications, 1955: cf. the second part: *"Political and Constitutional Thought of Islam"*, on *Political Theory of Islam, Political Concepts of the Qur'ân, First Principles of the Islamic State, Fundamentals of Islamic Constitution*.

5 See the discussion on the contradictions in Maudûdî's thought: Frank Griffel (2007). Griffel is referring to my article "La théologie de Abû l-A'lâ Mawdûdî", in *Philosophy and Arts in the Islamic World: Proceedings of the Eighteenth Congress of the Union Européenne des Arabisants et Islamisants* (ed. U. Vermeulen and D. De Smet), (Leuven: Peeters, 1998), 242-51; see p. 60: "Emilio Platti's observation that Mawdudi held a contradictory position regarding the relationship between Shari'a and natural law" (...). "Since the believer is unable to establish natural law from any source other than Shari'a, he must obey Shari'a and not what he may think natural law is"; "Sayyid Qutb and Mawdûdî respond to the scientific and modernist claim that nature is the realm of reason with the alternative concept that equates Shari'a with the moral laws established in 'nature'".

6 See also: Wael B. Hallaq 2004, "Theory, however, is one thing, reality another. A most central and vexing problem remains, and the solution to it seems thus far untenable. The question that today's Muslims must answer is to what extent they are willing to subscribe to modernity and to adopt its products. To reject it completely is obviously out of the question..." pp. 47-48.

7 Muhammad bin Abdul-Wahhab, *Kitab at-Tauhid, The Book of Monotheism* (Riyad: Darussalam, 1996/Hidjra 1416). Interesting is the report of a French diplomat written in 1806, on the Wahhabis attacks, e.g. on the Shi'a shrine of Husayn in Kerbelâ' (Iraq), and their extreme rigorism: *La « purification rigoriste» des wahhabites qu'évoque un rapport français de 1806: Mémoire sur les origines des Wahabys, sur la naissance de leur puissance et sur l'influence dont ils jouissent comme nation.* (Rapport de Jean Raymond daté de 1806), (Le Caire: IFAO, 1925): « *L'Alcoran dans toute sa pureté. Restauration morale (...). Abdul-Aziz fils de Saoud: le Coran dans une main, le glaive dans l'autre. Victoires éclatantes, glorieux butin, la terreur alentour...* ».

8 Some of his articles were translated with this typical French title: Fouad Zakariya, *Laïcité ou islamisme. Les Arabes à l'heure du choix* (Paris-Le Caire: La Découverte-Al-Fikr, 1991).

9 I have been very much inspired in this research by professor Van de Putte's analyses: (van de Putte 2000; van Leeuwen and Tinnevelt 2005).

References

al-'Ashmâwî, Muhammad Sa'îd (1987). *Al-Islâm al-siyâsî*, Cairo: Sînâ li l-nashr.

Al-Masry Al-Youm, February 28, 2012.

Al-Masry Al-Youm, Friday, 8 April 2011, English edition.

Anawati, G.C. (1989). *Un plaidoyer pour un islam éclairé (mustanîr): Le livre du juge Mohammad Sa'îd al-'Ashmâwî*, in Mideo 19, pp. 91-128.

Ansari, M.T. (ed.) (2001). *Secularism, Islam and Modernity. Selected Essays of Alam Khundmiri*, New Delhi: Sage.

Arkoun, M. (2010). *La question éthique et juridique dans la pensée islamique*, Paris; Vrin.

Attia, G.E. (2007). *Towards Realization of the Higher Intents of Islamic Law: Maqāṣid al-sharî'ah a Functional Approach* (Transl. from Arabic by Nancy Roberts), London-Washington: The International Institute of Islamic Thought.

Auda, J. (2008). *Maqâṣid al-Sharî'ah as Philosophy of Islamic Law. A Systems Approach*, London-Washington: The International Institute of Islamic Thought.

Bannerth, E. (1974). 'Dhikr and Khalwa d'après Ibn 'Atâ' Allâh,' in *Mideo* 12, 65-90.

Bellani, R. and Borrmans, M. (1986). 'Débats autour de l'application de la Sharî'a,' in *Études Arabes*, Roma: Pisai.

Bin Abdul-Wahhab, M., (1996). *Kitab at-Tauhid, The Book of Monotheism*, Riyad: Darussalam.

Courants actuels du Monde Arabe (1982) Le Ba'th. Première partie, Roma: Pisai, 12-33.

Filaly-Ansari, A. (2003). *Réformer l'islam? Une introduction aux débats contemporains*, Paris.

Frank Griffel, F. (2007) 'The Harmony of Natural Law and Shari'a in Islamist Theology,' in Abbas Amanat and Frank Griffel (eds), *Islamic Law in the Contemporary Context. Shari'a*, Stanford: Stanford University Press, 38-61.

Fûda, F. (1987). *Hawla l-'almâniyya*, Cairo: al-Mahrûsa. Translated: *L'islamisme contre l'Islam* (Paris-Le Caire: La Découverte, 1989).

GRIC, (1996). *Pluralisme et laïcité*, Paris: Bayard-Centurion.

Hallaq, Wael B. (2004). 'Can the Shari'a be restored?,' in Y. Yazbeck Haddad and B. Freyer Stowasser (eds), *Islamic Law and the Challenges of Modernity*, Walnut Creek: Altamiran, 21-53.

Ibn Taymiyya (1996), *Les intermédiaires entre Dieu et l'homme*, Paris: Éd. AEIF.

Maududi, S. Abul A'la (1947). *The Process of Islamic Revolution*, Lahore: Islamic Publications.

Maududi, S. Abul A'la (1967). *The Meaning of the Qurân I-XVI*, Lahore: Islamic Publications.

Maududi, S. Abul A'la (1985). *Islamic Way of Life*, Lahore, Islamic Publications, 1973), reprint Kuwait: Sahaba.

Maududi, S. Abul A'la (1987). *Al-Islām wa l-madaniyya al-hadītha*, Jeddah: Al-Dâr al-Sa'ûdiyya.

Maududi, S. Abul A'la (1988). *The Meaning of the Qurân I-XVI*, Lahore: Islamic Publications.

Maududi, S. Abul A'la (1989). *Towards Understanding Islam*, Delhi: Markazi Maktaba Islami, Leicester: The Islamic Foundation, 1980 reprint).

Maududi, S. Abul A'la (1991). *The Islamic Movement. Dynamics of Values. Power and Change*, Delhi: Markazi Maktaba Islami.

Maududi, S. Abul A'la (1991). *West vs Islam*, Delhi: International Islamic Publishers.

Maududi, S. Abul A'la (1992). *Islamic Law and Constitution*, Islamic Publications.

Maududi, Abul A'la (1978). *Man made Law. Divine Law*, Delhi: Crescent.

Maududi, Abul A'la (1964). *Political Theory of Islam*, Delhi: Markazi Maktaba Islami.

Michot, Y. (2012). *Ibn Taymiyya. Against Extremisms*, Beirut: Al-Bouraq.

Nasr, Seyyed Vali Reza, (1994). *The Vanguard of the Islamic Revolution. The Jama'at-i-Islami of Pakistan*, London-New York: Tauris.

Nasr, Seyyed Vali Reza, (1996). *Mawdudi & the Making of Islamic Revivalism*, New York-Oxford: Oxford Univ. Press.

Nasr, V. (2009). *The Rise of Islamic Capitalism*, New York-London: Free Press.

Nicholson, R. A. (ed.) (1990). *The Kashf al-Mahjub. The oldest Persian treatise on Sufism by 'Alî b. 'Uthmân al-Jullâbî al-Hujwîrî*, Karachi: Darul-Ishaat.

Platti, E. (2008). *Islam, Friend or Foe?*, Leuven: Peeters.

Qutb, S. (1964). *Ma'âlim fî al-tarîq (Milestones)*, Cairo: Dâr al-Shurûq.

Qutb, S. (1999). *In the Shade of the Qur'ân (Fî Zilâl al-Qur'ân) 1-18*, Leicester: The Islamic Foundation.

Qutb, S. (1999). *In the Shade of the Qur'ân (Fî Zilâl al-Qur'ân) 1-18*, Leicester: The Islamic Foundation.

Renaud, E. (1982). '*La Constitution du Parti Ba'th*', in *Études Arabes. Dossiers* 63-2.

Sabanegh, E.S. (1980), 'Débats autour de l'application de la Loi islamique (Sharî'a) en Égypte', in *MIDEO* 14, 329-384.

Talbi, M. (1998), *Plaidoyer pour un Islam modern*, Paris. Ccrcs.

van de Putte, A. (2005), 'Burgerschap in een multiculturele wereld', in B. van Leeuwen and R. Tinnevelt (eds), *De multiculturele samenleving in conflict. Interculturele spanningen, multiculturalisme en burgerschap*, Leuven-Voorburg: Acco, pp. 79-91.

van de Putte, A. (2000) 'De Natiestaat en de multiculturele samenleving. Een politiek-filosofische beschouwing', in B. Raymaekers and A. van de Putte (eds), *Krachten voor de toekomst. Lessen voor de eenentwintigste eeuw*, Leuven: Universitaire Pers Leuven-Davidsfonds, 367-378.

CHAPTER 7

The Muslim Brotherhood and the Democratic Experience in Egypt

Roel Meijer

Introduction

The Egyptian Spring seems to be in limbo. It has taken a zigzag course over the past two years. The Muslim Brotherhood has played a special role; joining belatedly on 28 January, but saving the revolution from defeat, but then working mostly alone. Having won the general elections in January 2011 it believe to have the first step to gaining power, but then on 14 June the Supreme Constitutional Court declared that the earlier parliamentary elections were illegal and that parliament should be dissolved. Three days later the Egyptians chose the leader of the party of the Muslim Brotherhood Muhammad Mursi as their new president, while the Brotherhood had promised before not to take part in the presidential elections. But even before the results were announced the military had limited his powers.

Aside from the continuous struggle with the Egyptian military and the tactics of the Brotherhood, the question is what the Muslim Brotherhood will do the coming years? Is there a line in the policy of the Brotherhood or is it simple political opportunism? For example, what does it mean if the Brotherhood claims to have won the general elections in December-January on the basis of "the will of the people" (*iradat al-sha'b*)? In short what does 'politics' mean for the Brotherhood?

These questions are also relevant for the Muslim Brotherhood in Europe because the Brotherhood is viewed with particular skepticism there. Since the 1990s the Brotherhood has been portrayed as power-hungry, opportunistic and willing to speak with a forked tongue, a radical one for its followers, and a moderate one for the European audience. All of this just to gain power. In French this called "*le double langage*". Is this also the case in Egypt?

My argument is that one of the problems with the Brotherhood is not that it mingles religion with politics but that in the past it has not embraced the political sufficiently (Meijer 2012). It is still to a large extent a religious movement, that has included politics as one option. After the fall of Mubarak it has been unable to reform itself quick enough and fell back on its old proven exclusivist strategy of "going alone" or *Alleingang*.[1] It did establish a political party, the Freedom and Justice Party (FJP) during the first year of the revolution, but it was unable to make a long-term coalition with other political groups and form a broad social movement to sustain the so-called Revolution of 25 January as these might jeopardize its vested interests. Only when it suited its own interests of putting pressure on the military did the Brotherhood enter Tahrir and form coalitions with other groups. In the end it depended on its own organization, the *Tanzim*, and alienated potential allies.

The lessons for Europe are difficult to make. As several researchers have pointed out, it is extremely difficult for the Brotherhood to implement the same hierarchical organization in Europe as in the Middle East, (Roald 2012) and the Muslim Brotherhood is a loose web of European and national organizations (Vidino 2010).

Liberalizing the Muslim Brotherhood

The biggest problem with the Muslim Brotherhood is that when the revolt started at the end of January 2011 it was in the process of reform. This process had been going on for decades. Since its founding in 1928 its slogans had been Islam is "a total system" (*al-nizam al-kamil*), "Islam is all-encompassing" (*shumuliyya*), and "Islam is state and religion" (*al-islam al-din wa-l-dawla*), since the end of the 1970s this was changing. The totalitarian pretentions were gradually crumbling and realism started to gain the upper hand over utopia.[2] As the claims to the Truth diminished, more room was created for internal debates, and working together and forming coalition with other groups became possible. Party politics, previously discarded as a threat to the "unity of the *umma*" and leading to a "degenerate political system", was becoming increasingly accepted as a means---besides *da'wa*---to transform society. In 1984 the Brotherhood for the first time took part in general elections, after it had accepted the notion of "partyism" (*hizbiyya*).[3] Until the fall of Mubarak it would participate in eight elections, winning 88 seats in 2005.

It was especially the next generation of the rising new generation of leaders in the Brotherhood who supported parliamentary democracy and believed in greater openness. Well-educated and much more worldly than the older generation who had known the founder Hasan al-Banna personally, they wanted to transform the Brotherhood into a broad centrist political party, and separate the movement from the political party. The remarks that the French sociologist Olivier Roy made at the time that political Islam revolves around virtue and piety and "the rest of sin, plot and illusion" no longer applied when he wrote these words in 1992 (Roy 1992: 27).

One of the major Islamist presidential candidates, Abd al-Mun'aym Abu al-Futuh, who lost in the first round but received 18% of the votes is a good example of this generation, which has experienced a metamorphosis in this period, transforming from radical pietism to political realism.[4] In many respects they are comparable to the left-wing intellectuals of the 1960s in Europe that evaluated from Marxism to social-democracy.

These changes did not however take place without struggle. The General Guide at the time Mustapha Mashhour still was able in the 1990s to declare that the Christian minority the Copts would be treated as *dhimmis* in the new Islamic order if it were established (El-Ghorbashi 2005). But the outcry that these words provoked within the movement indicated that things were changing.

At the beginning of this century this reform process accelerated. The political program the Brotherhood published in 2006 is usually regarded as the most liberal document until that moment. The document underwrites for the first time numerous liberal rights, such as the freedom of speech, organization, independence of the judiciary, separation of powers, and defense of human rights. As Asef Bayat has argued before, this is part of post-Islamist trend of claiming rights instead of. But I would argue that it is more. It is part of a larger process to accept politics. For the first time the Brotherhood is accepting politics as a process.

This is apparent in the way the faction in parliament was building a reputation as a constructive opposition becoming adept at parliamentary work. Not so much the implementation of the *sharia* or the veiling of women were the major themes. Rather, concrete politics, such as revealing corruption and combating poverty, were some of the topics with which the Brotherhood tried to discredit the Mubarak regime.

In this manner the Muslim Brotherhood represented what is the most prominent aspect of the uprising against Mubarak: the unprecedented politicization of the public and the primacy of politics. After decades of the 'politics of identity' and symbolism, politics really had something to say. It dealt with rights, concrete demands, programs. In short, it touched upon the fundamental relations between citizen and state. Egyptians had become aware of the relations between corruption, the huge expansion of the police state, and the unprecedented enrichment of the clique around the sons of Mubarak and the deterioration of public services and impoverishment of the people. The Brotherhood had contributed to this rise of political consciousness, to the extent that even members of the Brotherhood had become embarrassed by the populist rhetoric of its electoral slogan "Islam is the solution".

Tanzim

The question is to what extent the embracement of the political has been made by the movement as a whole. Despite the new tendencies within the movement it had retained its authoritarian and secretive structure---called the *Tanzim* (the "Organization").[5] The *Tanzim* duplicated the state in all respects. The General Guide acted as president, the Maktab al-Irshad (politburo) as cabinet of ministers and the Majlis al-Shura as a parliament. It retained the same divisions as the state, and penetrated the state except for the military and the police.

In itself the existence of the *Tanzim* is not remarkable. When the Brotherhood was established and experienced its rapid growth in the 1930s and 1940s, this was the worst period of totalitarian political ideologies and hierarchical disciplinary forms of organization. The cell structure, or "family" (*usra*) system, that the Brotherhood had adopted from the Communists still constitutes the backbone of the movement.[6] According to this system an aspiring member has to spend six years in training before a normal member. Ideologically this discipline is legitimized on the Quranic principle of "hearing and obeying" (*al-sam' wa-l-ta'a*). All new members, and when a new General Guide is appointed, all members have to pledge their allegiance (*bay'a*) to the new leader.[7]

Ultimately, the *Tanzim* allowed the Brotherhood to survive sixty years of dictatorship and semi-authoritarian rule (1952-2011). The major problem was that when the Mubarak regime fell, the *Tanzim* as a closed organization posed a threat to democracy and was outdated. Like in the Communist parties, it were not the creative intellectuals but the apparatchiks who ruled the movement. The present leader Muhammad Badi', Khayrat al-Shater as well as Muhammad Mursi are the embodiment of the *Tanzim*.[8]

Ambivalence

In the new more opener democratic political context after the fall of Mubarak the *Tanzim* became as much an asset as a liability. Not everyone was happy with the closed structure that worked like a state within the state and was a semi-clandestine organization that was still illegal but was tolerated. Since the new parliament convened for the first time on 23 January 2012, legislators have protested against the illegal status of the Brotherhood and the secrecy of the *Tanzim*. MPs have demanded that it be registered as a NGO and that it should come under the strutiny of the Ministry of Social Affairs.[9] They feared the power of the movement. But its power was ambiguous.

Due to its strict discipline the *Tanzim* was like no other organization able to mobilize large numbers of people during the 18 days of Tahrir demonstrations and sit-ins in January-February 2011. The *Tanzim* also enabled the Brotherhood to play a crucial role in the struggle with the military during the rest of the year.

On the one hand, the Brotherhood wanted to weaken the Supreme Council of Armed Forces (SCAF). For that purpose it called out its troops in May and in July and August and again in November. When in October the military opened fire on peacefully demonstrating Copts outside Maspero, the Brotherhood has exactly where it wanted SCAF: they were losing rapidly their popularity because they had reneged on their promise not to fire on the population when they had evicted Mubarak.

On the other hand, the Brotherhood needed SCAF to achieve its main purpose. When immediately after fall of Mubarak it became clear that free elections would be held it formulated its primary goal: winning the general elections that would be held (eventually) in December/January 2011-2012. Already on 14 February, three days after the fall of Mubarak, it announced its intention to found a political party (al-Hayat 2011:5). On 2 May it presented the new leadership of the FJP. Convinced that the party would win the elections, because the other groups were in disarray and did not have the organizational capacity the Brotherhood had in the form of the *Tanzim*, the Brotherhood formulated a majority strategy to grab as many seats in parliament as possible.

This did not mean that the Brotherhood no longer supported the protests on Tahrir Square; it only supported them when it served its own purpose to weaken SCAF and secure a majority in parliament. In order to limit the chances that its troops would become embroiled in violent encounters with the police and the military, it ordered its members to refrain from taking part in "open (permanent) sit-ins" and return home. Cooperation with other groups remained restricted.

It is true the Brotherhood did make concessions to its critics to change its provocative slogans "Islam is the solution" into "in the interests of Egypt". And by officially striving for the establishment of a "civil state" (*al-dawla al-madaniyya*) instead of a "religious state" (*al-dawla al-diniyya*), but the restriction that it would be within the parameters of "religious sources" (*al-marja'iyya al-diniyya*) seemed to limit these concessions.[10] Highly religious remarks by its leaders which seemed to contradict the more liberal interpretation did nothing to assuage the fears of the liberals, Copts and democrats who feared the power of the Brotherhood and were highly suspicious of its majority strategy.

The result was that the Brotherhood acquired a bad reputation among the Tahrir youth groups as well as established parties and liberals who at first were willing to give the movement a chance after years of repression by the Mubarak regime. It seemed as if the Brotherhood was constantly taking away with one hand what it had given with the other. Its reputation of being opportunistic and power hungry was fed by its reneging on earlier promises to take only limited part in general elections and not to take part in presidential elections. Among secularists, it lost its last vestiges of reputation when it announced in March 2012 that it would taken part in the presidential elections.

However, despite the growing unease with Brotherhood, its majority strategy seemed at first to have been brilliantly successful. Due to the superb organization of the *Tanzim* the FJP gained 235 seats in parliament (47% of the votes). Together with the much more doctrinaire Salafi Nour Party the Islamists won 75% of the parliamentary seats and the liberals and secularists were decimated. These results seemed to underline the Brotherhood's claims that it represented the "will of the people" (*iradat al-sha'b*).[11]

Representing the *volonté générale* – and not the will of God (although some leaders were not able to discern the difference) – seemed to dovetail nicely with its strategy to inherit the Revolution of 25 January by means of winning the general elections.

In hindsight the majority strategy should however be regarded as a major mistake. Had the Brotherhood understood what the Revolution of 25 January had been about? Had not the fundamental distrust of power, authority, hierarchy, and the return of the political driven the youth at Tahrir to protest against Mubarak? And had not the old-fashioned hegemonic thinking been replaced ideological pluralism and horizontal activism? Moreover: did the Brotherhood not highly exaggerate its own power by claiming to represent the *volonté générale*? Must people regarded the normal support base of the Brotherhood at 25% of the population and certainly not the majority.

Critique

Critique of the majority strategy of the Brotherhood – or what the famous American commentator Fareed Zakaria calls "illiberal democracy" (Zakaria 2003) – was enhanced by the fact that the Brotherhood also internally sinned against the new trend that had manifested itself at Tahrir. At an early stage the more critical and liberal figures in the Brotherhood, like Abd al-Mun'aym Abu al-Futuh, had been thrown out of the politburo, or had even been evicted from the movement.

It is interesting to glance at the alternative route he had envisioned for the Brotherhood. Abd al-Mun'aym Abu al-Futuh's goal had been to establish multi-religious, conservative but democratic religious political party, comparable to the Christian Democratic parties. When when the politburo of the Muslim Brotherhood decided to appoint the leadership of the FJP from its own ranks this option was clearly buried.[12]

When members of the Brotherhood were not only forbidden to vote for other parties than the FJP but also were not allowed to establish their own parties, it was clear that the democratic–centralism of the Brotherhood had prevailed and that any democratic alternative had been dismissed. All political reform was submitted to gaining political power.[13]

As a result, a second exodus occurred, this time an important section of the Brotherhood youth no longer accepted the slavish principle of "hearing and obeying" and rejected and left the movement in June 2011.

All these groups that have left the Brotherhood have evolved where the Brotherhood had left off in its ideological evolution. With them the implementation of the *sharia* hardly plays a role anymore.[14] Politics has emancipated itself from religion and become a field of activity in itself. Although not overt secularists, this forms an important step towards secularization of politics. According to the youth, politics should be based on civil rights, equality (*masawa*), and recognition of "pluralism" (*ta'addudiyya*), "recognition of difference" and freedom of the individual to make choices. They make a clear distinction between politics that is meant combat the authoritarian state and religion which is a non-political field and should not be mixed.

Abd al-Munaym Abu al-Futuh's programme is, for instance, based on terms such as "tolerance", "openness", "dialogue" with other political groups and religions.[15] According to him a Copt and a women can become president. The same applies to former Brotherhood youth groups who have organized themselves in the Egyptian Current (al-Tayyar al-Masri) and refuse to call themselves an Islamic party.[16] They regard religion more as an ethical code rather than religion of minute rules that has relevance for politics.

Especially in tactical and organizational respect these groups differed from the Muslim Brotherhood. Whereas the Brotherhood held its lines closed, they were prepared to work together with other groups and to take part in "open sit ins" and refused to be bullied by the *Tanzim*, regarding their "allegiance to the nation more important than the allegiance to the *Tanzim*".[17] They criticized the Brotherhood for being undemocratic and not separating politics from *da'wa*.[18] Insofar they took part in the elections they joined the Socialist People's Alliance.

None of this means that the liberals had completely disappeared with in the Brotherhood. Leaders like Muhammad al-Biltagi succeeded in challenging party discipline. He appeared on Tahrir even against the wish of the General Guide and dared to say that sharia was totally irrelevant for day-to-day politics and the solution of the major problems Egypt faced. On the other hand, their weight declined as their words were almost immediately undermined by the actions of the political leadership.

Constituent Assembly

Eventually the majority strategy of the Brotherhood was the most damaging to themselves. Nowhere was this more apparent than during the issue of the Constituent Assembly. Nowhere did the ambiguity and shortsightedness of the Brotherhood become recognizable for liberals and alienate them.

The drawing up of a new constitution was justifiably seen as the major challenge of the new regime after the fall of Mubarak. Liberals like Mohamed al-Baradai, the former director of the International Nuclear Agency (?) in Vienna, argued in favor of speedy installation of the Constituent Assembly in order mark the new ear and establish the basic rules of a new democratic system. He and all those in support of a revolutionary change believed that the new constitution should be in place before general elections and presidential were held.

This was for the liberals the chance to provide Egypt with a liberal constitution that would lay down civil rights, equality before law, freedom of expression and organization, freedom of religion, independence of the judiciary, the division of power between the legislative, the executive and the judiciary.

Only the Muslim Brotherhood opposed this move and blocked this opportunity. It made a deal with the military to support a revision of the existing constitution of 1971 of eight article that were necessary to allow for a free parliamentary and presidential elections. About such crucial issues as the powers of the president and the relations between parliament and the executive the revision did not say anything. The Brotherhood supported the campaign to vote in favor of the amendments during the referendum held on 17 March 2011, which passed with 77% of the votes. At the end of March SCAF issued the Constitutional Declaration that contained far more revisions than the referendum.

The Brotherhood also supported the Constitutional Declaration of 30 March 2011 although the military had added their own amendments. The reason was probably that it contained the by now notorious art. 60 that stipulated that "parliament will choose the Constituent Assembly".

During the period preceding the elections liberals would make several attempts to revise art. 60 and have the Constituent Assembly appointed by an independent body in order to make it representative of the country as a whole. Their attempts became all the more insistent as it became apparent that the Brotherhood would win the general elections. In the summer of 2011 a campaign "the Constitution First" was launched, but it was opposed by the Brotherhood and Salafis with the argument that a man-made constitution can never prevail over the *shari'a*.

The Brotherhood was able to undermine these attempts when it became clear that liberals were increasingly willing to make concessions to SCAF and allow the military certain privileges in return for a liberal constitution guaranteeing individual rights. This became clear in the autumn of 211, just prior and during the first phase of the elections, with the Ali Silmi plan. Ali Silmi was the Wafdist vice-Prime Minister who had drawn up a document, the "Principles of the Constitution" that reflected this liberal-military deal, allowing the military their privileges and control over their budget in exchange for liberal rights. The Brotherhood however torpedoed this project with the argument that it allowed SCAF to remain in place. In order to block it the Brotherhood mobilized its troops to protest at Tahrir. It withdrew, however, when the clash with the military escalated into violence at Muhammad Mahmud Street and Qasr al-Ayni in November 2011. It let the Tahrir youth groups do the fighting against SCAF, being the primary beneficiary of the violence and the weakening of SCAF.

The last episode in this constitutional battle occurred when the Brotherhood had won the general elections in January 2012. As predicted the Brotherhood, reneging again on its promise not to go for a majority, Insisted with the Salafis on appointing the majority of the members of the Constituent Assembly. In response the liberals went to court and on 10 April the administrative court declared the Constituent Assembly illegal because "it did not represent the different sections of the Egyptian people.

From these examples, it is clear that though its majority policy the Brotherhood in the end lost everything. By alienating since the electoral victory in January almost everybody, ranging from liberals, leftists, liberal Islamists, and even Salafis, the Brotherhood allowed the military to revive the forces in support of the Mubarak regime, play on the fears of the liberals act and disband parliament.

Conclusion

Events since the early summer have been as surprising as the previous one and a half years. Less than a month after having been elected in June 2012 Mursi fired head of SCAf Muhmmad al-Tantawi. These developments confirm the previous trend: politics determines the future of the Muslim Brotherhood. This also means that the Brotherhood has learned from its mistakes of pursuing a majority strategy. After Mursi only attained 24,9% during the first round of the presidential elections the Brotherhood knew it was in trouble and had to draw in wider support and make wider coalitions in order to prevent Ahmad Shafiq form winning the elections. Although it was largely unsuccessful, it did win enough support to prevent the old regime from winning the elections. This was a wake-up call. When Mursi became president he announced that he would be president for all Egyptians. Much of this is rhetoric, but the Brotherhood has realized its popularity can plummet it if it does not comply with the laws of politics instead of ideology. This process had started thirty years earlier.

What does this mean for Europe? Of course we do not know the immediate effects, but in the long run it can have important implications. One, the more realistic (political) the Brotherhood becomes the more it will be accepted by Europe and the less ideologically it will respond to its leadership. Second, the more it tries to be a political party and the less it is a religious movement, the greater the chances of becoming a broad political party that can attract different adherents across religious divides. Third, the more it adheres to the rules of the political game and does not try to impose its views, the less it will provoke opposition. In the end, if the transition to a normalization of the political system is achieved, it could have a positive effect on Islam in Europe. The Brotherhood, like the Ennahda Party in Tunisia, has experienced, long years of oppression. Its inclusion into the political process will hopefully also enhance its gradual transition to a political movement or party, which in the end will also lead to a process of internal democratization. In that case the need for the *Tanzim* is no longer felt.

Notes

1   This is a major precondition for the success of any social movement and explains why the coalition of Tahrir fell apart so quickly after the fall of Mubarak.

2   The trend is to regard that Islamism has reached a post political stage. I argue that in fact it has become increasingly political. For more on Roel Meijer (2009: 25-28, 34-37).

3   For more on the transition in the 1980s and 1990s see Roel Meijer (2012: 293-319).

4   Abd al-Mun'aym Abu al-Futuh has written his memoires in which he describes his early years as a member of the Gama'at al-Islamiyya. Journalists often confuse this very broad movement with the later movement that came into conflict with the state. (Meijer 2009)

5   For more on the *Tanzim*, see Hussam Tamam (2006).

6   For the earlier period, see the description in Mitchell.

7   Membership of the Brother differs. According the former member Sameh al-Barqy estimates its membership at one million. As each member is expected to pay 8% of his salary to the movement, and estimated yearly income of the members is around 12.000 Egyptian pounds, the Brotherhood would have a yearly income of 1 billion Egyptian pounds. Others estimate the numbers between 40.000 and 50.000 members with between 400.000 and 500.000 sympathizers. For more on this theme, see "Muslim Brotherhood Operating Outside the Law? *Egypt Independent*, 16 February 2012, http://www.egyptindependent.com/news/ muslim-brotherhood-operating-outside-law, and Khalil Inani, "The Embattled Brothers," *Egypt Independent*, 19 April, 2012, http://www.egyptindependent.com/node/783431. Hussam Tamam, believed the *Tanzim* consisted of between 100.000 and half a million members, Hussam Tamam, *Tahawwulat al-Ikhwan al-Muslimun*, p. 9.

8   Ibid.

9   "Muslim Brotherhood Operating Outside the Law? *Egypt Independent*, 16 February 2012, http://www.egyptindependent.com/news/muslim-brotherhood-operating-outside-law

10 The ambiguity has also been pointed by others. For more see the excellent paper by Nathan J. Brown, Amr Hamzawy and Marina Ottaway (2006).

11 Its General Guide, Muhammad Badi'

12 *al-Masri al-Yawm*, maart 11, http://www.almasry-alyoum.com/article2.aspx?ArticleID= 290166&IssueID=2071

13 *al-Masry al-Yaum*, 29 March 2011, http://www.almasry-alyoum.com/article2.aspx?Article ID=291935&IssueID=2089. See also *al-Quds al-Arabi*, 30 maart, (hc). P. 10.

14 This applies to Abd al-Mun'aym Abu al-Futuh, see the long interview with him where he said the sharia was already being applied, *al-Masry al-Yaum*, 22 januari 2012, http:// www.25yanayer.net/?p=27188

15 *al-Quds al-Arabi*, 30 maart, (hc). P. 10.

16 Lang Interview met al-Qassas, 13 november, http://www.onislam.net/arabic/newsanalysis/ special-folders-pages/new-egypt/egypt-after-the-january-25/135090-2011-11-13-11-47-12. html

17 Al-Masry al-Yaum, 1 april, http://www.almasryalyoum.com/node/381912

18 *al-Yaum al-Sabi'*, 21 juni 2011, http://www.youm7.com/News.asp?NewsID=439866. Zie ook de meningen van Muhammad Qassas over deze issues: Muhammad Qasas, *al-Dustur*, 11 april 2011, http://www.dostor.org/opinion/11/april/26/40815

References

Brown, N.J., Hamzawy, A. and Ottaway, M. (2006). 'Islamist Movements and the Democratic Process in the Arab World: Exploring Grey Zones', *Carnegie Papers*, no. 67, March.

El-Ghorbashi, M. (2005). 'The Metamorphosis of the Egyptian Muslim Brothers', *International Journal of Middle East Studies*, vol. 37, 373-395.

al-Hayat, 16 februari 2011.

Lorenzo, V. (2010). *The Muslim Brotherhood in the West*, New York: Columbia University Press.

Meijer, R. (2012). 'The problem of the political in Islamist movements', in A. Boubekeur and O. Roy (eds). *Whatever Happened to the Islamists? Salafis, Heavy Metal Muslims, and the Lure of Consumerist Islam*, London/New York, Hurst/Columbia University Press, 2012, 27-60.

Meijer, R. (2009). *Towards a Political Islam*, Clingendael Diplomacy Papers.

Meijer, R. (2012). 'The Muslim Brotherhood and the Political: An Excercise in Ambiguity', in R. Meijer & E. Bakker, *The Muslim Brotherhood in Europe*, 293-319.

Roald, Anne S. (2012). 'Democratisation and Secularisation in the Muslim Brotherhood: The International Dimension,' in R. Meijer and E. Bakker (eds), *The Muslim Brotherhood in Europe*, London: Hurst, 87-109.

Roy, O. (1992). *The Failure of Political Islam*, London: I.B.Tauris.

Tamam, H. (2006), *Tahawwulat al-Ikhwan al-Muslimun: Tafakkuk al-Idjulijiya wa-l-nahiya al-Tanzim* (The Transformation of the Muslim Brotherhood: Ideological Splits and the End of the Tanzim), Cairo: Maktaba Madbuli.

Zakaria, F. (2003). *The Future of Freedom: Illiberal Democracy at Home and Abroad*, New York: W.W. Norton & Company.

Part III:
Contemporary Islamic Social Activism

Social Work, Poverty, Inequality and Social Safety Nets: Voluntary Welfare Organizations

Jonathan Benthall

The Islamic tradition

Voluntary welfare provision by Muslims has much in common with other charitable traditions, though with some differences relating especially to Qur'anic doctrine. All Islamic authorities agree on the vital importance of charity.[1] *Zakat*, the Islamic tithe, is a major support in the standard Islamic case against the evils of both capitalism and communism. It draws the sting of Marxism, depriving it of a legitimate argument against private property, and property of any objectionable features; it turns the main contradiction in capitalism into a virtuous spiral of redistribution, and it lucidly answers the communist refusal of the right to possess. It solves the problem of poverty with the consent of the rich, and punishes those who hoard and monopolize and try to corner markets. Under the ideal scheme that wide observance of *zakat* would make possible, the rich do not become poor, but the poor are poor no longer. *Zakat* is a reminder that all wealth belongs to God (as in Judaism and Christianity); but there are several verses in the Qur'an that tolerate economic inequalities even though the dignity and fundamental equality of all human beings as children of Adam are also recognized. Islam accepts – so the argument runs – that there are inevitably differences among human beings that will in every society result in economic inequalities. Wealth ought to be cherished in moderation, but not to be (as we might say today) fetishized. The Qur'an condemns the competitive multiplication of wealth, and deprecates ostentation. Provided that believers obey the rules enjoined, there is no need for them to feel guilty about their inability to measure up to an ideal morality: there is no need for the well-to-do either to give away all their wealth or to feel guilty about not being poor. Nor would Islamic teaching commend, as does the Christian Gospel, the widow who gives away her last farthings.

The Christian concept of charitable action bears connotations of spiritual love that are absent in the Qur'anic terms *zakat* and *sadaqa*.[2] *Zakat* bears lexical connotations of both purity and growth. The meaning is taken to be that, by giving up part of one's wealth, one purifies that which remains, and also oneself – through a restraint on one's selfishness and indifference to others' privations. The recipient, too, is purified – from being jealous of those who are well off. *Sadaqa* – optional almsgiving over and above what is mandatory – bears connotations of justice, but is so closely associated with *zakat* that the key verse in the Qur'an that defines the purposes of *sadaqa* (Q 9:60) is treated as referring also to *zakat*. *Zakat* is closely linked in Islamic teaching with prayer, held to be ineffective if the *zakat* obligation is not met, and with sacrificial offerings.

Though *sadaqa* is also an important principle today, especially because it is less rule-bound, *zakat* is the third of the five pillars (*arkān*) of Islam. Muslims are enjoined to donate about one-fortieth of their assets, after deducting the value of their homes and working necessities, to a list of eight categories of people. These are (to borrow the most usual descriptions): the poor; the destitute; those employed to administer the *zakat*; those who might be converted to Islam, or assist in the cause; slaves; debtors; those committed to the 'way of God'; and travellers in need. Theologians have debated the interpretation of this list. For instance, 'slaves' may include prisoners of war, or the subjects of oppressive regimes. The 'way of God' is taken to mean the same as *jihad*. *Jihad* is an elusive concept whose nearest equivalent for Christians is the idea of the Church Militant warring against the powers of evil. Jihad can have warlike connotations in some contexts,[3] but can also mean a spiritual commitment to master one's weaknesses and lead a better life. Effective compassion for the disadvantaged is one important expression of this commitment.

The Qur'anic injunctions on *zakat* have much in common with Hebraic tithing – the obligation to give a tenth of annual agricultural produce – which, though replaced in early Christianity by the idea of freewill offerings, was later revived in various forms by some Churches. Some denominations, such as the Mormons, still practise strict tithing in the same way as devout Muslims. The Qur'an not only urges generosity, but also tells Muslims that they should encourage others to be generous. *Zakat* with its purifying power is specially enjoined, and bestows special merit, during the holy month of Ramadan, which has become the major fund-raising season, similar to Christmas. Alms given discreetly rather than publicly are best. Those whose personal wealth is below a fixed threshold are exempt from almsgiving.

At various points in Islamic history, *zakat* became a mere vehicle for extracting taxes. In no present-day state is *zakat* organized exactly as Islamic teaching prescribes. However, great efforts have been made to explain how the original injunctions should be interpreted in response to economic and political realities. It is used as a fund-raising device by charities both in Muslim countries and among Muslims resident in Western countries. Such charities often supply their supporters with printed tables to enable them to calculate their *zakat* liability. *Zakat* is one of the two major Islamic institutions adapted for modern fund-raising. The other is the *waqf*.

The institution of *waqf*, the Islamic equivalent of the charitable trust or foundation, known alternatively as *hubs* (Arabic plural *ahbas*, French *habous*) in North Africa, dates back virtually to the founding of Islam. With its legal status consolidated in the eighth century, it spread over almost the whole of the Islamic world, so that, for example, between a half and two thirds of the lands of the huge Ottoman Empire were *waqf* at the start of the nineteenth century. The great exception was sub-Saharan Africa, in whose history *waqf* is mentioned only in a limited area around certain cities such as Timbuktu: west African largesse tended to be personalized in prestigious individuals, and wealth was concentrated in moveable property such as cattle. During the nineteenth century, centralizing states were already chipping away at the independence of local *waqfs*. In Egypt and some other countries, all *waqfs* have been nationalized as state assets and the term is often popularly understood as referring only to mosque properties. Since the 1960s the institution has been given new life in some jurisdictions, partly as an Islamic response to the worldwide upsurge of voluntary organizations, but sometimes with a strong admixture of political motivation.

Another term that needs explanation is *da'wa*. *Da'wa* in Arabic means the call to Islam, missionary activity, and sometimes by extension the provision of religious education and practical social services with a view to reviving the faith of a community. It is part of Islamist ideology that politics, religion, economics, morality and charitable works form a seamless whole – *shumuliyyat al-islam*. There is scope for debate as to how much this is a pious ideal; how much a strategy for domination in some circumstances and survival in others; and how much it should make us reflect sociologically on the interconnectedness of these spheres in every society, though it is normal in the West to try to segregate them. While this ideal of seamlessness has contributed to the success of Islamist organizations, it has also exposed them to substantial trouble in some political contexts. Whereas *da'wa* is a spiritual and moral principle, not an institution, Israeli and American counter-terrorist experts used the term to signify a range of Islamic charitable organizations in the Palestinian Territories as allegedly fronts or façades for Hamas (during the period 1994–2007), on the grounds that the social services they provided were the base which supported all of Hamas's military and political operations. I and others have argued that this is an unconvincing interpretation of the reality in Palestine, since the principle of *da'wa* is much wider and has been accepted by many Palestinians who do not endorse Hamas's political and military aims but attach great importance to the principles of *da'wa* and *zakat* as means to sustain the steadfastness and solidarity of the Palestinian population at times of acute stress.

Donors and recipients

One feature common to all religious traditions of charity is that donors gain spiritual merit by their beneficent acts – laying up treasures in Heaven, as the New Testament Gospel puts it. Through some theological lenses, the poor can be seen as essential to the salvation of the well-off. This was true of the medieval Church, as described in Bronislaw Geremek's history of poverty: God could have made all men rich, but He wanted there to be poor people in this world, so that the rich might be able to redeem their sins (Geremek 1994). Thus there is only a limited incentive for the well-off to abolish poverty. That this theological assumption is by no means obsolete today is shown in an article by two Dutch anthropologists, comparing the impact of Pentecostal Christian and Sufi Islamic charitable networks in two African countries, Ghana and Senegal (de Bruijn and van Dijk 2009). In both their case-studies, it seems that charity and beneficence neither aimed at nor resulted in reducing the vulnerability of the populations, since individual salvation of the donor was the main goal. Many contemporary Faith Based Organizations, however, work hard to rebut by their policies and actions the objection that charity, including charity inspired by religion, has the effect of consolidating inequality. Moreover, political campaigns to abolish poverty through the introduction of communist or socialist systems are today more or less defunct, so that – though it can be always be argued that charity tends to address the symptoms rather than the causes of poverty and distress – voluntary personal donations are now widely seen again as essential to the promotion of social cohesion, which is in keeping with the Islamic texts. I have argued that government aid from North to South should be seen as an institutional form of charity (*pace* many development experts), insofar as it is voluntary rather than an entitlement that the beneficiaries can enforce (Benthall 2012).

Much attention has been given by scholars, especially historians but increasingly social scientists too, to the study of charity as an ideology and as a practice. Research on charity tends to stress the perspectives of donors. It is also possible, however, to give a counterbalancing weight to the recipients' point of view, in terms of an expanded concept of social security, defined by Franz and Keebet von Benda-Beckmann as 'the dimension of social organization dealing with the provision of security not considered to be an exclusive matter of individual responsibility' (Thelen et al. 2009: 2). The von Benda-Beckmanns have identified five 'layers' of analysis and I will look at these briefly in turn with special reference to the Muslim world.

First: ideological, that is to say cultural and religious, notions with regard to risk and caring. In addition to the overarching Islamic concepts of *zakat*, *sadaqa*, *waqf*, and *da 'wa*, we may single out the emphasis on orphans in the Muslim world – defined as children without a father or breadwinner, as opposed to the West where the term is generally reserved for 'double orphans'; but the category may also include children born out of wedlock. Orphan programmes are a popular, almost universal feature of Islamic charities. The Prophet Muhammad was an orphan. For a Muslim, the gesture of crossing two fingers alludes to a saying of the Prophet that whoever looks after an orphan will be 'like this' with him in Paradise. Islamic charities provide a wide range of services, from residential homes and day-care centres to individual sponsorship, and paying for school uniforms, textbooks or special clothes for festival days. Islamic charities are also specially focused on widows and on refugees. As well as these religious predispositions, cultural norms in traditional societies impose webs of obligations on relatives and patrons that are more binding than for most northern Europeans.

Second: institutional (often legal) provision, based on clearly defined rights. Where these are extensive and enforceable, as in our Welfare State, private charity becomes of relatively minor importance; though it follows that when the Welfare State comes under threat, as in most of the industrialized world today, private charity has to fill the void. In most Muslim-majority countries other than the petrodollar states, government provision is quite inadequate, and inevitably the private charities that substitute for it can become vehicles for political contestation, so that the government tries to control them.

The third level is actual social relationships between providers and recipients, as opposed to what these relations should be in an ideal world. The American anthropologist Erica Bornstein's studies of Christian and Hindu charity are a benchmark for ethnographic research which has not yet, as far as I know, been carried out in such depth with regard to Muslims (Bornstein 2012).[4]

Fourth, concrete social security actions. There are various ways in which these can be described and evaluated, with the constant risk of rhetorical distortion and unconscious observer bias. In politically charged regions, it is common for painstaking reports to be compiled and then shelved because the conclusions are inconvenient to those in power. For instance, in the early 2000s the United Nations Development Programme prepared a comprehensive study of social welfare provision, the Poverty Participation Project, for every governorate of the Palestinian Territories, for the benefit of the Palestinian Authority and funded by the British Government to the extent of about £600,000. The distinctive aim of the project was to document the views of poor people rather than administrators. It revealed a wide dissatisfaction with the integrity and effectiveness of the welfare services provided by the Palestinian Authority; the much smaller Islamic charity sector came out on the whole rather better (UNDP n.d.). Corroborating evidence from other sources suggests that the extent of corruption during this period was very high, including abuse of the voluntary sector by means of fabricated NGOs set up to siphon funds from international donors. Unsurprisingly, the report has been more or less ignored despite the deepening welfare crisis since 2005, when the study was completed, whereas such an exercise ought to have been seen as a baseline for future research on welfare provision.

The fifth level of analysis is the social and economic consequences of social security practices for both providers and recipients. As regards the providers, we may include here, for example, the political advantage gained by charity entrepreneurs who in some cases use their local reputation to stand for elective office and/or build up commercial networks for their own benefit. As regards the recipients, we may note the creation of 'aid economies' such as Jordan or, to take a more extreme case, the Gaza Strip, which result in excessive chronic dependency.

I believe that the style of analysis proposed by the von Benda-Beckmanns and their Dutch- and German-speaking anthropological colleagues has the potential to introduce a new rigour into reflection about these problems, because the concept of 'social security' as refined by them is as near value-free as we are likely to get, whereas concepts such as 'charity', '*zakat*', 'aid', 'development' and 'humanitarianism' are all highly contentious.

European Islamic charities

One of the focuses of this book is on Europe. It is clear that networks of voluntary assistance among European Muslims do exist, but mainly at a local or informal level – and they have so far attracted little attention from researchers. Nearly all the research effort to date has focused on international charities operating *from* Europe,[5] rather than for the benefit of populations *in* Europe. This is justified because Muslim populations in Europe generally prioritize charitable giving to the South, on the grounds that 'real' poverty hardly exists in Europe because of welfare safety nets. One example is a charity called Al-Muntada Al-Islami, 'the Islamic Foundation', originally founded by Saudi students in Britain, which runs in west London an unusually enterprising mosque complex, with a primary school attached and a range of varied social, sports and educational facilities. It has been active and successful in mediating between disaffected young Muslims in London and the police. But all its publicity is focused on its overseas relief and development work in Africa. The recently founded Muslim Charities Forum, an umbrella group, is restricted to British Islamic charities that work overseas. Such charities may be seen as organized in parallel with diaspora remittances (financially much larger but generally restricted to particular nationalities or ethnic groups).

Very recently, however, the economic crisis since 2008 has impelled Muslim Aid, previously concentrating on overseas aid, to launch its Warm Hearts Winter Campaign which distributes 'keep warm kits' to homeless and other vulnerable people in Britain itself; and this is a trend likely to intensify as the gap between rich and poor in Britain increases. There are also many charities founded in Britain by groups of Muslim women to confront problems such as domestic violence.

A rare exercise in scholarly analysis of 'domestic' Muslim charity in Britain has been undertaken by Sufyan Abid in his research on Muslim businessmen and entrepreneurs in Birmingham. Common to their local and very public charitable giving is the conviction that by doing so they purify their profits and ensure their future commercial success; but the choice of charitable organizations is determined by their particular religious affiliations – Barelvi, Deobandi or Salafi, with subdivisions within each group (Abid 2013). As well as remitting funds overseas, these Birmingham Muslims are committed to such local services as Muslim funerals, day care centres, radio transmissions, vocational courses and anti-narcotics programmes, as well as assisting poor communities with their access to state benefits.

By contrast with the Islamic charities that were built up from the Arabian heartlands since the late 1970s, forming a parallel system of foreign aid hardly mentioned until recently in the analysis of international aid flows,[6] European Islamic charities, especially from Britain, have been much influenced by the 'aid culture' of present-day Europe – with its emphasis on professionalism, transparency, accountability and non-discrimination. They have joined the international aid system, while skilfully making use of Qur'anic injunctions (such as the need to care for orphans), the religious calendar and visual symbols, to appeal to their Muslim donors. Efforts are also made to address the causes rather than the symptoms of poverty, in common with other agencies that are committed to longer-term development as well as immediate relief for victims of disasters and conflicts. Older interpretations of *zakat*, which insisted that only Muslims could be beneficiaries, have been dropped in favour of a commitment to bringing aid to the poorest whoever they are. There is an emphasis on working in Muslim-majority countries, but in defence of this practice they argue that the extent of need and deprivation among Muslims is undeniable.

The success in Britain of NGOs such as Islamic Relief Worldwide and Muslim Aid not only has benefited their recipients overseas but also (it will be argued here) is a major factor for integration of Muslims in Britain itself. As in the Christian world, it may be that a measure of authority is moving away from traditional religious office-holders to new humanitarian bureaucracies. The rise of Islamic Relief Worldwide is especially impressive. Founded by some Egyptian medical students in Birmingham in 1984, it is now the largest Islamic NGO in the world – unless you count the Aga Khan Foundation, which is a special case – and it has steered its way with assurance through political minefields. It has a fundraising branch in Belgium. In the UK, for some years it has been a member of the Disasters Emergency Committee, the elite grouping of 13 leading British overseas NGOs which combine their efforts to raise funds through the media and the banks on the occasion of major disasters. I felt that Islamic Relief had really gained acceptance just after the Kashmir earthquake of 2005, when the general manager of Islamic Relief fronted an appeal on television on behalf of all the British aid agencies – evidently because Islamic Relief was better placed to coordinate practical assistance in Pakistan than any of the secular or Christian aid agencies.

Whereas in some respects the European Islamic NGOs are strongly secularized – for instance in providing medical or disaster relief services directly – they also work through local Islamic organizations and individuals in developing countries. Here lies perhaps their greatest potential contribution, in that such partnerships are able to cut through government welfare structures which are often corrupt and ineffective. In several countries, domestic Islamic charities have helped preserve the cohesion of local populations during periods of great stress.[7]

The Egyptian case

Understandably, Islamist movements of this kind are accused of making political capital by their charitable activities. When the state fails to provide, however, it is normal that the dominant religion will muster its resources to fill in the gap, just as in 2012 and 2013 the Orthodox Church in Greece was feeding many thousands of citizens suddenly impoverished as a result of the economic crisis. Let us consider the case of Egypt. After a serious earthquake in Cairo in 1992, killing some five hundred people, the Muslim Brotherhood took a leading role. Again, when Egypt was hit by serious floods in November 1994, the government's response was slow and ineffective. It was the Muslim Brotherhood and similar organizations which gave refuge in the mosques to families who had lost their roofs. In the late 1990s, at least half of all welfare associations in Egypt were Islamic in character, often based on mosques built and controlled by the people rather than the state, providing services to millions. It is widely agreed that such Islamic community activities often outdo their secular counterparts, as well as stimulating other voluntary organizations and the state sector to do better. Yet after a national disaster in February 2002 – a serious railway accident at Al-Ayatt, 70 kilometres south of Cairo – the Muslim Brothers were reportedly forbidden by the Egyptian government to raise funds or organize help for the victims.

The Muslim Brotherhood was founded in Egypt in 1928 by Hassan al-Banna, a schoolteacher opposed to European colonialism and the Westernization of Islam. It has always pursued a dual goal of socio-economic development and political campaigning. In 1945, at the height of its success, it was required by the Egyptian government to split into two: a section concerned with politics and a section concerned with welfare. It was for many years denied registration either as a political party or as an NGO, but it continued to enjoy popularity under the Mubarak regime, and in 2012, after the popular uprising, succeeded in winning – together with the more conservative Salafis – a majority in the Egyptian Parliament. In an astonishing turn of events, the disastrous twelve-month presidency of Mohamed Morsi resulted in his removal from power in July 2013 and later to the banning of the Brotherhood as an allegedly terrorist organization. Among its traditional roles were public health and responding to crises such as epidemics. Although the movement has been compared to Latin American liberation theology, it was not based on any belief in liberating the poor, but aimed rather to 'reislamize' the whole of society. It was generally paternalistic, supported by politically marginalized professionals as much as by the poor.

In 1966, the Muslim Brothers had acquired a martyr in the intransigent, charismatic Sayyid Qutb, an Egyptian intellectual who travelled to the US in 1949 and returned with a contempt for what he saw as Western racism and sexual permissiveness. Imprisoned as a subversive by the Egyptian government and finally hanged, Qutb left behind him militant tracts urging violence against infidel governments and commending *zakat* as the basis of an ideal Islamic state. He condemned Muslims who refused this challenge, as well as the whole of the West, as belonging to the *jahiliyya*, the 'time of ignorance' before the Islamic revelation. Qutb's influence pervades Islamist extremism to this day but is widely rejected by more moderate Islamists. More than in Egypt, the Muslim Brothers in Jordan have earned a reputation for moderation, constituting a kind of 'loyal opposition' to the Hashemite monarchy while adhering to the principles established by the Egyptian founders, which include deep-seated hostility to Zionism and building up effective welfare services as an adjunct to their political commitment. In Syria, the organization was violently suppressed in the early 1980s and mere membership became a capital offence. The Muslim Brotherhood is a loosely knit international organization, Egypt remaining (at least until 2013) its centre of gravity, which has meetings in different cities and regular elections; but the weighting given to political, religious and welfarist goals differs in different countries. One of the founding principles of the Muslim Brothers was 'avoidance of the domination of notables and important men; since rising movements attract them and mean riches and benefits for them'. The organization remains opaque at the international level.

The voluntary sector in Egypt is huge and complex. The American researcher Mona Atia has shown how during the Nasser period an extensive Welfare

State was built up, including education, housing, employment and health care, but this began to contract after the 1980s as a result of Structural Adjustment programmes. Diminished state funding was unable to keep up with the needs of an increased population. Atia comments that she has found Islamic charitable associations to play a far deeper role than providing services: writing before the so-called Arab Awakening in 2011, she wrote that 'they provide developmental, personal and communal growth. They are also important because they are a few of the only spaces left where people can safely articulate a desire for social change, particularly one that incorporates the institutionalization of Islamic values' (Atia 2008: 246). In common with the rest of the voluntary sector, the Islamic associations had moved away from traditional ideas of welfare to development through programmes of training, income generation, microcredit and the like. Until 2013, the Muslim Brotherhood of Egypt was split between those who continued to be committed to the 'social question' and a wing that was more aligned with the interests of the middle class. It was already argued by Janine Clark in 2004 that the Muslim Brothers of Jordan had swung very much in the direction of providing services for the middle class rather than the poor (Clark 2004).

Let us consider two examples of voluntary institutions in Egypt at opposite ends of what one could call the media spectrum. At one end: the Mustafa Mahmoud Mosque Complex in Cairo, whose founder, a medical doctor, became what one might call (borrowing the Christian term) a 'born-again' Muslim and a highly successful interpreter of Islam for a scientific age. Though lacking theological qualifications, Mustafa Mahmoud, who died in 2009 in his late 80s, gained such a personal following by means of television and cassettes that he became one of the most important moral authorities in Egypt. The mosque complex is highly professionalized and is focused partly on health services but also on human development, with an emphasis on helping the poor to lift themselves out of poverty. The preacher and his work have been extensively documented by Western social scientists (e.g. Salvatore 2000).

At the other extreme is a huge organization, the biggest in Egypt, about which practically nothing is known outside the country: the Gamiya Shariya or Islamic law association. Founded by Sheikh al-Subki in 1913, it has about 450 branches and is responsible for some 6,000 mosques, with between 2.5 and 5 million adherents. It shuns publicity to the extent that practically nothing is known about it by researchers: one paper by an otherwise well-informed Egyptian scholar consists of little more than a reflection on the difficulties of researching it (ben Néfissa

2007). It has received large donations from wealthy Egyptians that enabled it to found clinics and other welfare institutions which make no charge to those using them. During the Mubarak era, it seemed that both the Government and the Muslim Brothers tried to get control over it, but that it managed to play the various parties off against one another and to remain relatively independent.

The voluntary sector in Egypt has been highly politicized for many years, much penetrated by the intelligence services, and in 2013 was embroiled in the trial of strength between the Army, the Islamists and the mainly secular revolutionaries, while measures taken against foreign NGOs generated major tensions with the country's principal benefactor, the United States.[8] As this book goes to press, the future of Islamism and the voluntary sector in Egypt is impossible to predict.

The Palestinian Territories

In the Palestinian Territories, where I have concentrated my own research, it is easier to read the political fields of force. Since 2007, after the Hamas takeover of Gaza, it has been agreed by all observers that the *zakat* committees and other Islamic charities have been politicized by both administrations: the Fatah-dominated Palestinian Authority in the West Bank and the Hamas de facto government in the Gaza Strip. What is more relevant to the future of the voluntary sector, in the event that Palestine will finally gain the full status of a nation, is to try to reconstruct analytically in retrospect the true nature of the *zakat* committees during what has been called the 'Oslo period' between 1994 and 2007.

I have already mentioned that the Israeli and US governments hold that during this period the Palestinian *zakat* committees were fronts or façades for Hamas. It is conceded even by the sternest critics of these committees that they had a high reputation for financial probity and cost-effectiveness. Emanuel Schaeublin's work and mine have been associated with the Islamic Charities Project, sponsored by the Swiss Federal Department of Foreign Affairs between 2005 and 2013,[9] and we have arrived at the hypothesis that, on the contrary, the principle of *zakat* was, on the whole, one that persuaded the various factions to form 'social coalitions' to administer welfare and health services based on *zakat*, consisting of some individuals who were politically active but also independent Islamists not affiliated to any political party, as well as the pious middle class, and practical businessmen such as you would find running charities in medium-sized towns all over the world. Until 2007, these were beginning to tap into the international aid system for funds, while also remaining close to their communities and earning considerable popular trust – unlike the officials of Fatah; also responding to local priorities rather than the agendas of international aid agencies. Compared to the extensive services provided by the Palestinian Authority and the United Nations Relief and Works Agency (UNRWA), those for which the *zakat* committees were responsible were relatively small in scale, but they had an iconic value for the beleaguered and stressed population, standing for the Islamic values of solidarity and compassion (Schaeublin 2009, 2011). Fatah and Hamas declared in 2011 that regularizing the position of charities would be one of their goals in seeking political reconciliation. This seemed still elusive in early 2014, but it is possible that all those concerned in the Palestinian Territories will eventually see value in negotiating a 'political hands-off' so that Islamic charitable principles can be put into practice with as little interference as possible.

When Islamic charities from Europe or North America seek to engage with local intermediaries of this kind, they often attract political controversy because of the shadow that has fallen on Islamic charities since the attacks on the USA on 11th September 2001, as a result of allegations that some Islamic charities were implicated in terrorist financing. This has applied particularly to local Palestinian charities (and European and American charities remitting funds to them) which have become embroiled in the conflict with Israel, especially because of Hamas's policies (now apparently abandoned) of suicide bombing attacks against Israelis.

Islamic charities today

All Islamic charities based in the Gulf, which have tended to form a kind of parallel structure of aid very little connected to the rest of the international aid system, have fallen under suspicion. By way of background, we must recall the history of the Afghan war of the 1980s, when Western and Gulf-based organizations were united in supporting the *mujahideen* in order to bring down the Soviet empire. US regulation of its overseas aid charities did not set a rigorous example (Benthall 2011). Since 2001, the Gulf-based charities seem to be slowly moving away from their traditions of secrecy to submit to the kind of public monitoring and regulation that are taken for granted in the West, so as to reduce the risk of abuse of the privileges of charities for nefarious purposes (Juul Petersen 2014, Lacey and Benthall 2014).

Where government policies are relatively uncontentious, it is possible for transnational Islamic aid to make progress at the grassroots without much difficulty. This was the case in Mali when I undertook fieldwork there in 2006 (Benthall 2006), but six years later the whole country was destabilized as a result of a revival of civil unrest in the north and a military coup in the South.

To conclude by bringing the discussion back to Europe: at the risk of seeming to be chauvinistic, it is Britain that has led the way in encouraging international Islamic charities, thanks to a constructive and sympathetic approach on the part of the Charity Commission, which is the national regulatory body appointed by the Government but acting independently. It has done much to stimulate not only Islamic but all diaspora-based charities, for instance Hindu and Sikh, to grow in compliance with the principles of accountability and non-discrimination. Early in 2011 the major Islamic charities met in a committee room of the House of Commons for a public discussion of relief aid following the massive flooding in Pakistan, for which the UK Islamic charities had raised some 20 million pounds. In the United States, where there was an equally buoyant Islamic charity sector before 9/11, a much more repressive policy with regard to charities has set in because of the threat of terrorism (ACLU 2009). Many people working in the humanitarian field, however, hold that there should be no incompatibility between security and humanitarian concerns. If a 'humanitarian vacuum' is allowed to form because of repressive policies, there is a danger of that vacuum being penetrated by extremists, as it has been already to some extent in some countries such as Pakistan stricken by disaster, poverty and civil strife; also most notoriously during the terrible civil war in Syria.

A buoyant and carefully regulated Islamic charity sector is in everyone's interests – all the more so because of the pressures on traditional (non-Muslim) aid budgets since 2008, which are impelling the international aid bureaucracy to reach out for funding shortfalls to be met by so-called 'new humanitarian donors'. It is often forgotten that Islamic humanitarianism has a long history – a tradition that should be treated with guarded respect rather than with opportunism.

Notes

1   For further commentary on Islam and charity, see Benthall and Bellion-Jourdan 2003, Benthall 2012.

   The present article is concerned only with Sunni Islam. Shi`a Muslims are obliged to pay a religious tithe known as *khums* to an imam, amounting to one fifth of their annual income after deduction of expenses. The imam is responsible for distributing the funds for religious teaching, education, welfare and relief aid. Through this mechanism, networks of Shi`a charity have developed internationally.

2 Another key concept in Christian moral theology is service – in Greek, *diakonia*. The social teaching of the Gülen Movement, which has been realized in such organizations as the Istanbul-based international aid organization Kimse Yok Mu ('Is there anybody there?'), is consistent with modern interpretations of the Qur'anic *zakat* prescriptions, but gives much more emphasis to the concept of *hizmet* – a common Turkish word meaning 'service', used in both secular and religious contexts – which is indeed an alternative name for the Movement (Harrington 2011: 11-13). Arabic Bibles translate διακονία as *khidma*, which does not appear in the Qur'an (unlike the term *'abd*, 'slave', which is used to signify devotion to God). As far as I know, the question of a possible influence of Christian moral theology on the Gülen Movement has not yet been studied.

3 Some scholars have argued that there is an important difference between traditional Christian charity and *zakat*, since a proportion of the funds raised by *zakat* could legitimately be spent not only on 'good works' but on various other authorized purposes including the military defence of religion (Kuran 2004). But current English charity law, like the historic Islamic *zakat* rules, accommodates military objectives to some extent in that one of the charitable purposes permitted under the Charities Act 2001 is 'the efficiency of the armed services of the Crown'.

4 There are, however, published papers by Victoria Palmer, on Islamic Relief's work in Bangladesh with Muslim refugees from Burma (Palmer 2011), and by Bruno De Cordier of the University of Ghent on the work of Islamic aid agencies in Pakistan and central Asia (De Cordier 2009).

5 For instance, the part of Marie Juul Petersen's monograph that deals with British Islamic charities (Juul Petersen 2014).

6 For discussion of this sector, see Lacey and Benthall 2014.

7 I have analysed the role of Islamic charities in Algeria, from the pre-independence period to the present day, in Benthall and Bellion-Jourdan 2003, pp. 93-98.

8 Since 2013, Saudi Arabia has provided massive funding for the post-Morsi government, reducing Egypt's dependence on US aid.

9 Formerly known as the Montreux Initiative.

References

Abid, S. (2013). 'Contesting Islamic reformisms and multiple interpretations of being a 'true Muslim': Everyday life experiences and religious practices of Birmingham Muslims.'

Unpublished paper, South Asian Anthropologists' Group, University of Sussex conference, 11 September.

ACLU (2009). *Blocking Faith, Freezing Charity: Chilling Muslim charitable giving in the 'war on terrorism financing'*. New York: American Civil Liberties Union.

Atia, M. (2008). 'Building a house in heaven: charity in neoliberal Egypt'. University of Washington doctoral thesis.

Ben Néfissa, S. (2007). 'Citoyenneté morale en Egypte, une association entre Etat et Frères Musulmans' [the Jam`iyya Shar`iyya], in S. Ben Néfissa et al. (eds), *ONG et gouvernance dans le monde arabe*. Cairo: CEDEJ and Paris: Karthala.

Benthall, J. (2006). 'Islamic aid in a north Malian enclave', *Anthropology Today*, August, 22.4.

Benthall, J. (2011). 'Islamic humanitarianism in adversarial context', in E. Bornstein and P. Redfield (eds), *Forces of Compassion, Humanitarianism Between Ethics and Politics*, Santa Fe: SAR Press.

Benthall, J. (2012). 'Charity' in Didier Fassin (ed.), *Companion to Moral Anthropology*, Oxford and New York: Wiley-Blackwell.

Benthall, J. and J. Bellion-Jourdan (2003). *The Charitable Crescent: Politics of Aid in the Muslim*, London: I.B. Tauris. Reprinted in paperback with new Preface, 2009.

Bornstein, E. (2012). *Disquieting Gifts: Humanitarianism in New Delhi*. Stanford: Stanford University Press.

de Bruijn, M. and R. van Dijk (2009). 'Questioning social security in the study of religion in Africa: the ambiguous meaning of the gift in African Pentecostalism and Islam', in C. Leutloff-Grandits et al. (eds), *Social Security in Religious Networks: Anthropological perspectives on new risks and ambivalences*, New York and London: Berghahn, 105-127.

Clark, J.A. (2004). *Islam, Charity, and Activism: Middle-class networks and social welfare in Egypt, Jordan, and Yemen*, Bloomington: Indiana University Press.

De Cordier, B. (2009). 'The "Humanitarian Frontline", Development and Relief, and Religion: what context, which threats and which opportunities?', *Third World Quarterly*, 30 (4), 663-684.

Geremek, B. (1994). *Poverty: A History*. Oxford: Blackwell.

Harrington, J.C. (2011). *Wrestling with Free Speech, Religious Freedom, and Democracy in Turkey: The political trials and times of Fethullah Gülen*, Lanham, MD: University Press of America.

Juul Petersen, M. (2014). *For Humanity or for the Ummah?*, London: Hurst & Co.

Kuran, T. (2004). *Islam and Mammon: The Economic Predicaments of Islamism*. Princeton, NJ: Princeton University Press.

Lacey, R. and J. Benthall (Eds)(2014). *Gulf Charities and Islamic Philanthropy in the 'Age of Terror' and Beyond*, Berlin: Gerlach Press.

Palmer, V. (2011). 'Analysing "cultural proximity": Islamic Relief Worldwide and Rohingya refugees in Bangladesh', *Development in Practice* 21:1, February, 96–108.

Salvatore, A. (2000). 'Social differentiation, moral authority and public Islam in Egypt: the path of Mustafa Mahmud', *Anthropology Today* 16: 2, 12-15.

Schaeublin, E. (2009). 'The West Bank Zakat Committees (1977 – 2009) in the Local Context', CCDP Working Paper 5, Geneva: Graduate Institute of International and Development Studies.

Schaeublin, E. (2011). 'Gaza Zakat Organizations (1973 – 2011) in the Local Context', CCDP Working Paper 9, Geneva: Graduate Institute of International and Development Studies. Both available for download at http://www.graduateinstitute.ch/ccdp/home/ccdp-research/projects/completed-projects/religion_politics/religion-politics-islamic-charities.html

Thelen, T., Leutloff-Grandits, C. and A. Peleikis (2009). 'Social security in religious networks: an introduction', in C. Leutloff-Grandits et al. (eds), *Social Security in Religious Networks: Anthropological perspectives on new risks and ambivalences*, New York and London: Berghahn, 1-22.

UNDP (n.d.). 'National Report on Participatory Poverty Assessment (Voice of the Palestinian Poor)', Jerusalem: United Nations Development Programme.

CHAPTER 9

Tradition and Modernity in Social Islam: The Case of Muslim NGOs in Jordan

Egbert Harmsen

This chapter deals with a particular form of Muslim social activism, namely the activity of Muslim voluntary welfare organizations delivering services of a varied nature (financial and in kind support, advice, employment, education etcetera) to socially vulnerable target groups such as the poor, orphans, single parent families, children at risk and the disabled. It analyses this activity from the perspective of the respective roles of tradition and modernity, especially in relation to civil society theory.

In the first section, the issue of defining tradition and modernity is dealt with, especially in relation to the concept of civil society and the role of reflexivity and a critical relationship toward tradition. Special attention will be paid to the way in which reflexivity and a critical relationship with tradition took shape in the Muslim Arab world.

Subsequently, a historical sketch of modern Islamic welfare activism in Jordan will be given. After that, a closer look will be taken at Muslim NGOs in Jordan on which I carried out fieldwork myself. The Muslim Brotherhood-affiliated Islamic Center Charity Society will be dealt with, as well as more liberal Muslim NGOs. Special attention will also be paid to the issue of gender in discourse and practice by Muslim NGOs. These associations will be dealt with from the point of view of reflexivity and a critical relationship toward tradition as markers of their modernity. The difference between more collectivist and system-oriented approaches toward modernity and more individualized and pluralized versions of modernity will be dealt with as well.

In the conclusion, an attempt will be made to answer the question of the extent and the way in which tradition and modernity play a role in the work of current Muslim NGOs in Jordan.

Tradition and modernity

This chapter wishes to reflect on the role of tradition as well as modernity in Muslim social welfare activism in Jordan, and especially in their accompanying (Islamic) discourse. In this regard, it is important to reflect on the meanings of both concepts. Tradition and modernity are often regarded as opposites. In orientalist thought and discourse, "the West" and "Islam" have been contrasted to one another in a way in which the former represents modernity and progress superseding traditions, while the latter represents the inability to supersede traditions and therefore constitutes a hindrance and obstacle to modernization. This assumption, not only about Islam but also about the relationship between tradition and modernity as such, has been criticized in more recent scholarship. In the work *Islam and Modernity, Key Issues and Debates*, Armando Salvatore states, for instance, that tradition is a dynamic cultural dimension of a civilization and that it serves, therefore, as an important source of modernization. Radical western religious movements, for instance, have laid an important basis for political modernity in Europe, as well as for religious and political fundamentalism. In this case, modernization was even unthinkable without (religious) tradition as a cultural resource to draw upon.[1]

Concepts of tradition and modernity also play a central role in theories on civil society. Civil society can be conceived as the realm in which citizens associate themselves on a voluntary basis in order promote their interests, ideas, beliefs, values and/or ideals in society. The voluntary nature of civil society associations distinguishes them from groupings with a membership of an ascribed nature (i.e. acquired by birth and/or blood-ties), such as families, tribes, geographic regions, nations or religious communities. The term "ascribed" has often been equated to traditional identity, and "voluntary choice" to a modern one. Following Habermas, Civil Society theoreticians Cohen and Arato describe, for instance, traditional (pre-modern) European society as one in which people were first of all ascribed members of extended families and communities. In this society, there was no modern differentiation between various institutional realms. There was no differentiation, for instance, between childrearing in families and education in schools. Socialization of children was undertaken by these extended families and communities in an undifferentiated fashion. These families and communities were decisive for the identity of their members in every sense. Something like a public identity based on voluntary membership of associations, collectives and groups independent of ascribed identity hardly existed. Likewise, there was originally no clear differentiation between the religious, the artistic and the scientific. There was even no distinction between private and public in a modern sense.

Modernization of society, Cohen and Arato maintain, entailed a process of differentiation between all these spheres; specialized institutions started to assume special tasks: the (increasingly nuclear) family became responsible for childrearing and the school for formal education; science was taken out of the monasteries and became largely a university affair, and businesses and associations came into being whose members and/or employees did not join them on the basis of their familial ties. This also entailed the progressive liberation of personal identities and interpersonal relations from the unquestionable acceptance of traditional values and institutions. In turn, this resulted in a more reflexive and critical relationship towards tradition. Reflexive forms of association, publicity, solidarity and identity came into being. Norms, established patterns and definitions of situations were increasingly questioned and reinterpreted by the members of society. This resulted also in a new type of voluntary association, with equal rights of membership, freed from kinship, patriarchal and other ascriptive restrictions on belonging and holding office. This type of association renews its forms of solidarity primarily in the free interaction of its current members.[2]

According to Cohen and Arato, a *critical* and *reflexive* relationship towards tradition is essential to modern civil society, but not the abolition of tradition. This approach may also include forms of traditional identity, such as tribal and religious life, within the realm of civil society. Within such forms of life, people may also engage in common voluntary activities to serve their aims, interests and convictions. Such voluntary engagement presupposes a kind of reflexive consciousness regarding values, ideals and preferences on the part of individual participants. However, no individual develops his or her values, ideals or preferences entirely detached from relations with other individuals and from the general social, cultural and economic environment in which he or she lives. And from (religious) tradition, for that matter.[3]

On the basis of Cohen's and Arato's theory on civil society, one could suggest that reflexive consciousness and a critical relationship towards tradition are typical for modernity and constitute the features on the basis of which a modern society is to be distinguished from a traditional one. However, should we assume that "traditional", or pre-modern, societies were really unreflective and uncritical towards tradition? Some Muslim thinkers, who are proponents of the *Mujtamma' ahli* thesis[4] and often sympathetic to moderate versions of Islamism, maintain that pre-modern Muslim society already knew something like a civil society. This civil society or *Mujtamma' ahli* consisted of institutions like guilds that organized craftsmen, *awqaf* (endowments) that served the public good, cultural associations and religious groupings. They used to integrate individuals, families and social groups into their social networks. They protected the members of the community and constituted a sphere that was relatively autonomous vis-à-vis state power. Through this *mujtamma 'ahli*, Islam preserved its emancipatory essence, according to the proponents of this thesis.[5] The thesis has been criticized, however, by secular Arab as well as western scholars ranging from Aziz al-Azmeh and Sami Zubaida to Ernest Gellner. Zubaida, for instance, maintains that these pre-modern Muslim societal institutions were often "uniformly patriarchal and authoritarian, often coercive". Positions of authority within, as well as general membership of these formations were usually based upon family-ties and inheritance from father to son. All of them stressed values of authority, loyalty and obedience. [6] In other words, these institutions were a far cry from a modern civil society.

We do face a methodological problem here. This problem is that we cannot be absolutely certain about the extent and nature of reflexivity in pre-modern times, certainly not about the reflexivity, or lack thereof, among the vast illiterate majority of the (Muslim) population. Were they really so uncritical and unreflective in their attitude as a binary conception of tradition versus modernity suggests? What we can observe is that (contemporary) modernity in Muslim Arab societies has been shaped during the last two centuries by colonial rule, the development of relatively modern bureaucratic state structures, urbanization, the pervasiveness of globalization and the world market and, last but not least, the spread of mass education and mass media. Especially the last development gave rise to the emergence of a new and modernly educated middle class, consisting of members originating from the more traditional Muslim lower- and middle classes where traditional religious values continued to prevail. [7] Due to this modern education as well as mass media, these new middle class members were capable of reflecting on the Islamic message in a new, more modern, way. A way in which every Muslim can read/hear and interpret Islamic messages more or less autonomously and reflect on their meanings and relevance to the contemporary problems and dilemmas of the Muslim individual, family and society at large. And in which they can rationally debate these reflections and interpretations amongst each other. This state of affairs can be contrasted with the situation until at least the end of the 19th century, when the usual educational methods in the *madrasah* (mosque college) were largely focused on repetitive methods, such as memorization, recitation, grammar as well as ritual purity. And when explanation and interpretation of the Islamic textual sources was still the monopoly of a small class of specialized religious scholars.[8]

The newly emergent modernly educated Muslim Arab middle class of the latter part of the 20th and the beginning of the 21st century faced many frustrations with the policies and modernization programmes of the secular and/or western-oriented elite of the state and the society they lived in. These policies and programmes failed to bring the bulk of the population meaningful prospects and prosperity. Their actual implementation was characterized by corruption, nepotism and the repression of dissidence. The newly educated (young) Arab Muslims were largely excluded by the dominant system from opportunities of social mobility and advancement and ended up in situations of un- or underemployment. Many of them became attracted to cultural and political trends that drew upon traditional Islamic values, albeit in a form that had been profoundly adapted to modern society.[9] These trends, the Muslim Brotherhood most prominent among them, presented an alternative to the current unjust and frustrating state of affairs in a secular-dominated society. They presented a sociocultural as well as political ideal based upon Islamic social values such as piety, care, compassion, honesty, trust and mutual solidarity. They provided many (young) members of the modernly educated but excluded middle class with a sense of self-worth as well as social, moral and political orientation by involving them in various activities. Examples of these activities are religious preaching, ethically correcting one's own as well as another's behavior, political activity and, last but not least, organized social work carried out through religiously inspired voluntary welfare associations.

The history of Islamic voluntary welfare activism in Jordan

Very central to the history of organized Islamically inspired voluntary welfare activism in Jordan was the establishment of the Muslim Brotherhood there in 1945. At that time, it was actually licensed under the Ottoman law of Associations as a charitable association. [10] The native merchant Abu Qura, a native from the town of Salt which is located between Amman and the Jordan valley, became its General Guide. [11] Already years before, he had been known for his great religious zeal. This zeal was accompanied by his charitable works as well as by his interest in the Palestinian cause. [12] In fact, he stood in a (Muslim as well as Christian) tradition of religiously inspired social involvement and charity that goes many centuries back in time. This tradition obtained an modernly organized form in the area for the first time in 1912, when members of the Greek Orthodox community in the town of Madaba, to the southwest of Amman, established the Dur al-Ihsan (homes of charity) Association. This association was dedicated to serving the Greek Orthodox community, especially its needy children.[13] From the 1920s onwards, its example was followed by the establishment of other voluntary associations established by Jordan's religious and ethnic minorities and aiming to provide charitable services to their own religious or ethnic community, such as the Greek Orthodox, the Circassian or the Hijazi.[14] In the 1940s, women's societies were established in Jordan that were patronized by Princess Misbah, mother of Jordanian Crown Prince Talal. They focused on improving the social condition of Jordanian women by raising their educational level, assisting them in the care and upbringing of their children and raising their awareness of health and welfare issues, apart from the more traditional activity of assisting the poor and needy. [15] The Muslim Brotherhood, for its part, emphasized Islamic education in order to bring about a "new Arab culture" based on Islamic principles. As part of this endeavour, it organized Boy Scout Clubs where social (including charitable) and athletic activities as well as religious study took place.[16]

When Jordan had to absorb so many Palestinian refugees in 1948, the Muslim Brotherhood was one of the major players providing those refugees with the necessary aid, including food, shelter and healthcare. In subsequent years and decades, the Islamic movement further developed and professionalized its voluntary welfare activism. In 1963, the Jordanian Brotherhood's leadership established the Islamic Center Charity Society. This NGO soon evolved into the largest voluntary welfare association in the country, apart from the associations led by members of Jordan's royal family. It runs schools, some institutions of higher education, medical centres, some hospitals and centers offering financial and in-kind aid, vocational training and income-generating projects as well as (religiously inspired) educational and cultural activities to orphans and poor all over the country. Its greatest source of pride is the modernly equipped and commercially run Islamic hospital in Amman.

Many more religiously inspired Muslim voluntary welfare associations have been founded in Jordan since the 1960s, often, but not always, by politically engaged Islamists, members of the Muslim Brotherhood as well as others. Like the Islamic Center Charity Society, their activity is to be found in the realms of health, education and poverty alleviation, in addition to religious awareness raising.

After a period of 32 years of martial law and severe state repression against anything perceived as opposition against Jordan's monarchical regime, a process of limited liberalization started in the country in 1989. This provided space for Muslim Brothers and other Islamists to establish associations focusing on cultural issues. In 1991, for example, the Society for the Preservation of the Holy Qur'an was established by prominent Muslim Brothers. It opened centres for religious education all over the country. In 1993, another important addition to the community of Islamist NGOs was made when prominent Muslim Brotherhood member Abdul Latif Arabiyyat established with others the Al-Afaf Welfare Society. This NGO specializes in marriage and family issues and has organized well publicized annual mass weddings, intended as a model of a „better Islamic society" of chastity, social solidarity and harmony. [17]

Discourse and activity by Islamic voluntary associations in Jordan

Before we deal with the Jordanian Muslim NGOs themselves, something about the modernization of Islamic thought and practice concerning welfare in general must be clarified. Much of traditional Islamic discourse surrounding social aid and solidarity has centered around the notion of *Zakah*, one of the five pillars of mainstream Islam. The general idea behind this wealth tax originating from the earliest days of Islam and destined for, amongst others, the poor and needy, is that by giving up a portion of one's own wealth, one purifies the rest of it as well as one's own spirit – since the *Zakah* functions as a restraint on one's selfishness, greed and indifference to other's sufferings. The needy recipient, in turn, is purified from jealousy and hatred of the wealthy. [18] In societal terms, this purification implies social stabilization and harmony between the economic classes. While being enforced as a law in the early Muslim community, historical studies have shown that in subsequent centuries, *Zakah* was merely considered as a matter of conscience and moral obligation left to the (prosperous) Muslim individual to act upon. In the Ottoman empire, for instance, voluntary Zakah transfers used to flow to the most visible poor, such as servants of the donors or the beggars who lived in the latter's own neighborhood, rather than toward the neediest. Little thought was given to the challenges of overcoming the sources of need.[19]

Modernization of Islamic thought and discourse on *zakah* and on social aid in general has in the course of the twentieth century led to innovative approaches toward this concept. Donating *zakah* became increasingly motivated by notions of socio-economic and cultural development of the Muslim community as a whole. Nowadays, Islamic banks invest the *zakah* donations they receive in a great variety of social projects for needy Muslim communities, ranging from relief aid after natural disasters to the establishment of religious and cultural centres. Ideas of promoting the economic self-reliance and empowerment of the needy have also been translated into ways of spending *zakah* donations by Islamic banks as well as by Muslim NGOs. Both of them are participating in the trend of shifting from traditional charitable aid to supporting the launching of small and medium-sized businesses by needy families themselves. The traditional Islamic (and Qur'anic) idea of the "right" of the poor to assistance from the rich is expanded through the notion that the latter face the moral duty to help the former rid themselves of their own state of dependency, become self-supporting (by setting up their own businesses or by other means, such as vocational training) and, therefore, fully integrated into an economically secure Muslim society. [20]

We see here that traditional Islamic notions on the duty of the rich to give *zakah* and the right of the poor to receive are capable of being modernized and innovated. Such modernization and innovation are justified by referring to Qur'anic verses and hadiths which seem to point toward self-reliance and empowerment. Examples are the *qur'anic* verse stating that God only helps those who help themselves, and the *hadith* stating that it is better to give a needy person an axe to earn his own bread than simply a piece of bread. How do Muslim welfare NGOs of various backgrounds in Jordan deal with this Islamic tradition and this modernization?

The Islamic Center Charity Society

Traditional Islamic notions on the spiritual as well as social function of giving aid are clearly discernable in the activities of centres for orphans and poor belonging to the nationwide Muslim Brotherhood-affiliated NGO called Islamic Center Charity Society (ICCS) in Jordan. Such centres give their financial and in-kind assistance first of all to so-called orphan families, meaning fatherless and mostly single-parent families that lack a regular income-provider. They offer educational, social and cultural activities to these target-groups as well.

At one ICCS-centre for orphans and poor in a Palestinian refugee camp in Amman I regularly visited in 2003, the dependency relationship between its workers and its needy target group could be clearly observed, especially during distributions of financial and in-kind aid. The mothers of the orphan families had to wait patiently and quietly in rows in a hall until they were called upon to receive their modest benefits. This was obviously not an example of self-organization by the underprivileged fighting for their own rights. Rather, this was a welfare initiative established and implemented by Muslims from the middle class delivering services to the needy. The centre received the resources for financial and in-kind assistance mostly from local individual donors and sometimes donors in the Arab Gulf States.

Many of the ethical messages in folders, brochures, and pamphlets are addressed to potential donors and supporters. In the spirit of traditional Islamic social ethics outlined above, they are called upon to give selflessly to the poor and orphans *fi sabillillah*, for the sake of God. Fulfilling this duty is supposed to counter one's greed and egoism, to have a morally purifying effect, and to improve the chances of divine reward in the afterlife. The poor recipients, in turn, are told to find inner peace in God by being thankful for that which He provides them, and by cultivating a patient attitude in life. Wholly in line with traditional Islamic ethics, this entails countering their greed and jealousy vis-à-vis the better of. The perfectly just Islamic society is supposed to be realized through a pious mentality or attitude of all the believers, regardless of rank, status or wealth. Such an attitude has to be translated into honest, selfless and helpful behaviour.

This orientation on duty is also reflected in the way the centre uses its financial and in-kind assistance as a means of pressuring the orphans and their mothers to participate in its educative and cultural programme. Religious ideology, in my experience, plays a central part in these educational efforts.

During a language class for orphan boys that I attended, for instance, only religious material was used. Among this material was a poem about the life of the prophet Muhammad. The teacher stressed the importance of understanding the poems' meaning. He drew a parallel between levels of aggression against the Prophet and his followers in Mecca and the present situation, during which Muslims were once again humiliated and threatened by others, especially the United States and "the Jews". The message was that Muslims had to regain power by restoring their mutual solidarity as a community of believers with its common faith in God and in His revelation. Similar political messages were expressed in a satirical play that the orphan girls in the center were staging. In this play, they mocked Arab rulers who betray their own people by collaborating with the Americans and the Israelis. At that occasion, the orphan girls and the centre's women workers also sang a song about Eid al-Fitr, the feast which concludes Ramadan. A message of social solidarity as well as protest was clearly discernable in the song. It dealt with the fate of an orphan family that was economically unable to celebrate while wealthier people celebrated the feast in luxury, a state of affairs which betrayed the holy month's true spirit and meaning of equality and solidarity among the believers.

In such messages, one can discern how the Islamic tradition is used in a modern fashion, and for modern purposes. The stress on understanding the meaning of religious sources and not merely ritually memorizing them is, as has been pointed out above, typical for the more recent Muslim Arab generations who have enjoyed a relatively modern (secular) education and been exposed to modern forms of mass media. Moreover, the centre's workers endeavor to disseminate this understanding and knowledge among the orphans who are from the lower classes, and do not keep it to themselves as past generations of *ulama* often did with their own understandings of scripture. Their vision of the *umma* or community of believers could be seen as modern as well. They propagate in their religious messages a united *umma* which is strong and independent and in which mutual solidarity and equality among the believers reigns. Islam is meant to overcome problems and to achieve progress (in this regard, the prophet's own background as an orphan is stressed as well) and not to resign itself to injustice and suffering. Therefore, orphans should take good knowledge of the content and meaning of Islamic scripture, in order to translate it into reflection, behavior and action.

Interviews with workers as well as orphans reveal that reading and reciting the Quran and the Hadith, and following the behavioural injunctions contained within both sources, play a central role in the activities and group discussions at the centre. Duties and responsibilities in the field of rituals, civilized and pious eating habits, ways of communication and modest dress, especially in the case of women, and the duty of older children to take care of smaller ones and of children in general to respect and obey the elderly or their older siblings are stressed.

Hence, when it comes to values pertaining to individual behaviour and to family relations, we see a rather traditional Islamic approach. However, tradition is also harnessed here to empower the orphans to function effectively in modern society as well as to change it for the better, which has a modernizing impact. Conversations with the orphan girls revealed that they understood the Islamic injunctions in terms of notions of dignity, taking one's responsibility, and developing and utilizing one's capabilities for the sake of beneficial purposes. There is a strong emphasis, for instance, on the importance of knowledge and education and high school achievements. The centre also tries to tutor orphan children in their homework for school. It emphasizes the value of work as a means of self-sustenance, and tries to obtain jobs for the older orphan boys by using its social networks. Furthermore, it offers the older orphan girls and their mothers training and some income in a sewing workshop and a bakery. Traditional Islamic notions of duty towards God are equated in this vision to a modern sense of duty and responsibility of every believer to contribute to the development of a better, stronger and harmonious Islamic society.

Research carried out by Danish researcher Marie Juul Petersen at another ICCS-centre for Orphans and Poor in Amman has shown that reinterpretation of Islamic scripture and tradition along modernist lines can go even further. She mentions projects organized by this centre that expressly aim to empower women and liberate them from oppressive traditional customs that are regarded as unislamic. One of these projects was called The Woman Can. It taught women that they can express themselves and can do what men can do. One of the centre's women teachers told her: "a woman should choose a career, she should not be dependant, she can earn money for the family". Petersen states that while traditional conceptions of gender roles among many Muslim voluntary welfare associations still limit endeavours of empowerment of women seriously, even the most conservative among them encourage girls to pursue their education and criticize views denying women their educational rights. [21]

Within the ICCS, there are differences in opinion about the nature of a correct Islamic welfare approach within modern society. Everybody in the organization seems to adhere to a vision of Islam with its laws and injunctions as constitutive of all aspects of life, of the ideal society and of their own work. Some of them, however, equate this Islamic approach to modern notions of empowerment and human (including women's) rights while others criticize such a developmentalist discourse as an essentially un-Islamic attempt to please the West. Petersen observes that the latter view draws on models of a collectively binding Islamic order while the former one relates to more pluralist and individualistic interpretations of Islamic traditions. [22] The difference between these two approaches is not so much a contrast between tradition and modernity. Both of them legitimize themselves on the basis of Islamic tradition and each of them represents another version of (Islamic) modernity: one focusing on sharia-based collective discipline as a model for society, and the other on individual reflection and choice as a believer.

It must be stressed that collectivist notions of an Islamic order are dominant within the ICCS. This is reflected, for instance, in the expectation of all of their staff members to pray and (especially in the case of women) to wear proper Islamic dress; frequent references to *Qur'an* and *Hadith* as the authorizing rationale for their own work; an emphasis on "family atmosphere" and "a sense of solidarity"; and the inclination to contrast their own Islamic welfare approach, supposedly based on love and charity, with secular welfare approaches, supposedly based on money and self-interest. However, Petersen notes that several ICCS workers also emphasize their experience of personal growth and individual creativity as an important aspect of their motivation for, and gratification in, their work. Women workers mention, for instance, how they acquired new skills in the field of teaching, lecturing and speechmaking through their work. In the self-imagination of ICCS-workers, a more classical modern sense of collective (Islamic) identity and a post-modern sense of individualized (also Islamic) modernity often seem to exist side by side. [23]

A rights-based and secular Islamic approach towards orphans and their families

Other Muslim NGOs are not engaged in an endeavour to bring about a collectively organized Islamic order in society. They rather formulate their goals in terms of working for the rights of their target groups, albeit out of an Islamic inspiration. Al-Faruq Welfare Society for Orphans, which is mainly active in the Palestinian refugee camp of the northern city of Irbid and where I conducted field research as well, has no affinity with political Islam. It provides nonetheless the same type of services to orphan families (in the sense of fatherless one parent families) as the Muslim Brotherhood-affiliated centers for the poor and orphans are doing. Its educational and cultural programs, however, are much less one-sidedly based on a religious doctrine. It pays as much attention to globally formulated human, children's and women's rights. Its methodology towards orphan children and their upbringing is to an important extent adopted from UNICEF. This approach is focused on letting children discover their own individual qualities and taking their own individual feelings and thoughts seriously, rather than on conformity with strictly conceived religious injunctions. However, the Society organizes Quran courses as well, and uses Islamic concepts in its discourse. A female social worker of the Society, for instance, saw in the Quranic principle of *himaya*, or protection of the woman, a basis for the struggle against women's abuse and domestic violence. The social workers use religious concepts like *rahma* (compassion), *tasamuh* (forgiveness and tolerance), and *sabr* (patience) to redirect communication within client families in the direction of mutual empathy, understanding, and respect and to counter practices of verbal and physical violence. Al-Faruq Society's approach is decisively tilted toward a more individualized and pluralist conception of (post-)modernity, and is more secular as well. Secular not in the sense of absence of religion, but in the sense of limiting religion's function to that of a moral and ethical inspiration in general terms for progressive change, rather than considering it in a reified sense as an absolute basis for an all encompassing Islamic societal order and system.

Gender discourse as a reflection of Islam vis-à-vis tradition and modernity

A field in which mutual tension between as well as intertwinement of tradition and modernity comes strongly to the fore in the case of Muslim NGOs in Jordan is that of gender. Al-Afaf Society, another Muslim Brotherhood-affiliated association, specializes in issues of marriage and family. The founders of this society were motivated by a sense of alarm about the lack of access to marriage for many young Jordanians. This is due to the traditionally high financial and material demands attached to marrying and to the wedding party in Jordanian society, along with the costs and demands involved in starting a family. Al-Afaf Society starts from a strong anti-materialist and anti-consumerist ideology. According to Mufid Sarhan, the Society's general manager, Jordanians set their priorities incorrectly if they wait until they have obtained a well-paid job, a spacious home and a beautiful car before they decide to marry. "According to Islam", Sarhan argues, "martial life and love is fundamental for the well being of the human being. One shouldn't cherish too high material expectations in this regard ... material expectations should be lowered, and a higher priority should be put to the importance, the warmth and the love of marriage".[24]

According to the Society's members, this lack of access to marriage leads to the spread of sexual immorality, mental disorders and frustrations and to the disintegration of the social fabric of Muslim society. They see this development also as part of a deliberate campaign directed against this society. Arabiyyat laments, for instance, the "absence of authentic values which govern individual and collective social conduct and customs ... in a framework of projects for Westernisation which are backed by wealth, experience and deadly means". Therefore, the Society states in one of its publications: "Let us sow the seeds of goodness in a good society ... let us set up the pillar of the Muslim home without overspending and extravagance, in order to shut the society's doors in the face of the winds of the foreign ... corruption and let our slogan be "Afaf".[25]

Al-Afaf Society tries to put its vision of an Islamic society and family characterized by modesty, cooperation and compassion into practice by annually organizing a mass wedding for young Jordanian couples. Wealthy donors and companies contribute financially and in-kind to these weddings, in which the participating couples receive bridal gifts and interest-free loans. [26]

What we see in this case is a critique of a certain traditional habit, the tendency toward extravagant spending and luxury in weddings and marriage, that is at the same time related to modern, western-inspired patterns of consumerism and materialism. The answer to this (from Al-Afaf Society's point of view) imbalanced, vicious and even dangerous state of affairs is to be found in the original true model of Islam. Islam provides the model for a correct way of life and a society where piety, justice and solidarity reigns, and in which the insights from the tradition of Islamic faith are in full harmony with those from modern science and are optimally utilized.

Al-'Afaf Society also organizes lectures and workshops on marriage and family issues and publishes booklets on these topics. Behavioral values of harmony, patience, mutual respect and understanding are stressed in these events and publications. In the Society's vision, the traditional role division between the husband as solid head and provider of the family and of the wife as patient mother and housewife are of fundamental importance to a unified, harmonious and warm family life. At the same time, the circumstances of modern society are reflected in the Society's vision. Its members and workers criticize certain indigenous traditional habits they consider to be un-Islamic as well as detrimental to familial well being in a modern context. An example of such habits is the interference of relatives, in particular the husband's mother, in the affairs of the married couple. This is a practice which all too often leads to increased pressures on the wife, psychologically as well as in the sphere of household duties. In the name of respecting the privacy of the nuclear family and simultaneously of maintaining harmonious relationships with the extended family, Al-Afaf Society disapproves of this habit.

Another example is traditional patriarchal authority. While the Society upholds, in the name of Islam, the principle of obedience of the wife toward her husband as head of the family, it firmly rejects what it considers physical or verbal abuse of the wife. [27] A husband who had married at one of the Society's mass weddings told me that an important lesson he received at one of its workshops was the prohibition of abusing one's wife and the need to respect her dignity. Traditional habits, he pointed out, sanction this abuse, and he mentioned as an example his own mother who had suffered serious abuse from his father. One of the prominent women volunteers of Al Afaf Society explained to me that the Muslim wife's obedience toward her husband should not be understood in a military sense of following orders. It means, she said, that the wife should coordinate her activities outdoors and her desires in this regard with her husband, and respect his judgments in his role as head and provider of the family. She criticized the traditional lifestyle of her own parents, in which her mother unquestionably followed her father in everything and in which she did not have much of a life of her own outdoors. She cited reports on the behaviour of the prophet Muhammad in support of women's rights as well as on the duty of the husband to assist his wife in their household duties. We are obviously witnessing here the discourse of a modernly educated Muslim middle class which sees in the Islamic message the true (modern) answer to modern dilemmas in the sphere of gender, marriage and family.

Other Muslim NGOs, and especially women's associations among them, are more outspoken on this line and explicitly advocate the rights of women in the wider society, including the public domain. Their argument centres on women's need to use their skills and education to contribute to Jordanian and Muslim society at large, and not just her own home and family.

One example is the Al Aqsa Association led by Nawal al-Fauri. She is an Islamist activist for women's and children's rights who left the Muslim Brotherhood during the 1990s out of frustration with the conservative and patriarchal attitudes among the organizations' leadership. With the support of several Western embassies, her association had implemented micro-credit projects enabling needy women to set up agricultural and stockbreeding farms. Moreover, it carries out awareness raising activities for underprivileged women on social, cultural and political issues, including gender. In the name of Islam, Al-Fauri stresses that women have a right to participate in economic, social and political life that is equal to that of men, and that a husband has to assist his wife in household tasks and the upbringing of children. Women, she states, should follow the will of God as it is revealed in the Islamic sources, and not the arbitrary and self-interested traditional habits invented by men. This constitutes a somewhat more radical critique of local patriarchal traditions in favour of modernization of gender relations in the name of Islam as compared to the discourse of Al-Afaf Society. [28]

Another example of this is an Islamic women's association in a poor suburb in the industrial city of Zarqa, working for the empowerment of school dropout girls and their mothers from broken and socially weak families. Some of these mothers are even working as prostitutes in order to survive. Methods used by this association are literacy courses, a creative handicraft project, confidential discussions of personal and social affairs and recreational outings. It is led by a woman who is also working as a religious teacher and social worker in a mosque. She wears orthodox Islamic dress, including a *niqab* or full face veil. She was, at the same time, trained by a British development organization supporting projects for children at risk. In the name of the Islamic concept of *karama* or dignity, this association endeavours to raise the self-esteem of the girls and their mothers, and to counter traditional habits that discriminate against females regarding their social and educational opportunities.[29] Marie-Juul Petersen has visited this association as well. Its head told her that people often asked her why she did not just focus her efforts on getting the girls married, but no, she said, I want these women to be able to take care of themselves. One of the beneficiaries told Petersen that the association made her aware of her rights and capabilities and helped her to stand up for herself. [30]

Conclusion

The examples of the voluntary associations dealt with in this chapter demonstrate that tradition and modernity can relate to each other in many different ways and are not necessarily at odds with each other. All of these associations were established by members of modernly educated Muslim generations which were already exposed to mass media for several decades and became more recently well versed in information technology as well. These people were able to study the

Islamic sources by themselves and reflect on their relevance to their own lives and their own society, in conjunction with their own experiences with modern life and society and their dilemmas. They adhere to the Islamic message and tradition and find them relevant for modern society, but the way in which they define this relevance differs from one association to the other.

In the case of the Muslim Brotherhood-affiliated NGOs Islamic Center Charity Society and Al-'Afaf Society, we find a strong emphasis on Islam as an all-encompassing model and system for life and society. Their views are in line with the more classical version of modernity which emphasizes humanity's need for the most desirable and just societal *system* in order to become happy and prosperous. In this version, the human agent needs to exert the necessary collective efforts in order to realize this ideal system or order. Therefore, it strongly emphasizes the duty of each individual to contribute to this collective effort. The Muslim Brotherhood-oriented NGOs emphasize that such a desirable and just order pertains to all aspects of life and behaviour and can be derived from the injunctions of the *Qur'an* and the words and example of the Prophet Muhammad and his companions. However, even within these NGOs we find a (new) tendency to put this 'Islamic solution' into the perspective of the realities and dilemmas of modern life and society, to reinterpret the message accordingly, to put a greater stress on individual empowerment and rights and to acknowledge pluralism. The sense of an Islamic *umma* being under threat from its enemies (e.g. the West and Zionism) seems to be conducive to a classical modern collectivist conception of the good Islamic life and society, while criticism of oppressive indigenous patterns and customs, especially regarding the treatment of women and children, seems to go hand in hand with a more individualized and rights-oriented 'post-modern' approach.

The rights-oriented approach is most central in Al-Faruq Society, the Khawla bint al-Azwar Association and the Al Aqsa Association. We do see differences, though, with regard with to place of Islam within these approaches. In regard with the conviction and discourse of the, in terms of ideological and professional backgrounds of its members most secular Al-Faruq Society, Islam is an important element of Arab society's cultural and ethical heritage and at the same time an evolving part of its development and modernization, rather than an absolute and all-encompassing basis for society. In the Khawla Bint al-Azwar Association, the Islamic revelation and its injunctions are more dominant. It interprets the goals of this revelation, however, as the promotion of human dignity and social justice through the empowerment of the deprived. The same goes for the Al-Aqsa

Association, which also emphasizes the importance for Muslims meaningfully to learn from and cooperate with the non-Muslim world.

Being the product of a modernly educated Muslim middle class, all of these associations provide examples of being part of modernity on the basis of an inspiration from Islamic tradition. This orientation may entail criticism of Western political, economic and cultural domination, as well as indigenous customs that are being regarded as un-modern as well as unislamic. Even though the validity of Islamic tradition is itself not questioned, it is used as a basis for criticizing existing patterns of society, including aspects of traditional culture. Therefore, these associations belie any dichotomy between (religious) tradition and modernity.

Notes

1   Armando Salvatore, "Chapter 1, Tradition and Modernity within Islamic Civilisation and the West" in Armando Salvatore, Muhammad Masud and Martin van Bruinessen eds., *Islam and Modernity, Key Issues and Debates*, Edinburgh, Edinburgh University Press, 2009, pp. 11-14 and pp. 30-31.

2   Jean L. Cohen and Andrew Arato, *Civil Society and Political Theory*, Cambridge and Massachusetts, MIT Press, 1992, pp. 434-436.

3   As for how (religious) tradition shapes modern forms of reflexivity, debate and civil society, one could consult the works of Talal Asad, *Genealogies of Religion, Discipline and Reasons of Power in Christianity and Islam* (1993, Baltimore and London: The John Hopkins University Press), Charles Hirschkind, "Civic Virtue and Religious Reason: an Islamic Counterpublic", *Cultural Anthropology* Volume 16 No. 1, pp. 3-34 and Saba Mahmood, *Politics of Piety, the Islamic Revival and the Feminist Subject* (2005, Princeton, US and Oxford, UK: Princeton Univesity Press).

4   *"Mujtamma' Ahli"* can be translated as "popular-" or "peoples society".

5   Amr Hamzawi, "Normative Dimensions of Contemporary Arab Debates on Civil Society. Between the Search for a New Formulation of Democracy and the Controversy over the Political Role of Religion" in Amr Hamzawi ed., *Civil Society in the Middle East*, Nahost-Studien 4, Berlin, Verlag Hans Schiler, 2003, pp. 28-29.

6   Sami Zubaida, *Civil Society, Community and Democracy in the Middle East* (unpublished version), pp. 3-5 en 13-14.

7   Francois Burgat, *Face to Face with Political Islam*, London and New York, I.B. Tauris, 2003, pp. 43-48.

8   Gregory Starett, "The Hexis of Interpretation: Islam and the Body in the Egyptian Popular School", *American Ethnologist*, 22 (4): 1995: p. 960.

9   Burgat, pp. 43-48, Gilles Kepel, *Jihad, the Trail of Political Islam*, London and New York, I.B. Tauris, 2003, pp. 62-68 and Oliver Roy, *De globalisering van de islam* (original title: *L'islam mondialisé*, translated into Dutch by Walter van der Star, Amsterdam, Van Gennep, 2003), p. 16.

10   Marion Boulby, *The Muslim Brotherhood and the Kings of Jordan 1945-1993*, Atlanta, Scholars Press, 1999, p. 46.

11   Shmuel Bar, *The Muslim Brotherhood in Jordan*, Tel Aviv, Moshe Dayan Center for Middle Eastern and African Studies, 1998, p. 10.

12   Ali Abdul Kazim, "The Muslim Brotherhood, the Historic Background and the Ideological Origin" in: Jillian Schwedler ed., *Islamic Movements in Jordan*, Amman, Al-Urdun Al-Jadid Research Centre, 1997, p. 15.

13   Waleed Hammad, *Jordanian Women's Organisations and Sustainable Development*, Amman, Al-Urdun Al-Jadid Research Centre, 1999, p. 25 and Katja Hermann, *Aufbruch von Unten, Möglichkeiten und Grenzen von NGOs in Jordanien*, Münster, Hamburg and London, Lit Verlag, 2000, p. 62.

14   Musa Shteiwi, *Voluntarism and Volunteers in the Arab World, Case Studies,* no location, The Arab Network for NGOs, 2001, pp. 39-40, and Hammad, p. 25.

15   Laurie A. Brand, *Women, the State and Political Liberalization, Middle Eastern and North African Experiences*, New York, Columbia University Press, 1998, pp. 120-121.

16   M. Boulby, p. 42-46.

17   Egbert Harmsen, *Islam, Civil Society and Social Work, Muslim Voluntary Welfare Associations in Jordan between Patronage and Empowerment*, Amsterdam, Amsterdam University Press, 2008, pp. 151-155, 159 and 163-164.

18   Jonathan Benthall, Financial Worship in Benthall and Bellion Jourdan eds., *The Charitable Crescent, Politics of Aid in the Muslim World*, London and New York, I.B. Tauris Publishers, 2003, p. 9.

19   Timur Kuran, "Islamic Redistribution Through Zakah" in Michael Bonner, Mine Ener and Amy Singer eds., *Poverty and Charity in Middle Eastern Contexts*, Albany, State University of New York Press, 2003, pp.. 283-284, Miriam Hoexter, "the Poor and Distribution of Alms in Ottoman Algiers", pp. 151-158 and Eyal Ginio, "Living on the Margins of Charity, Coping with Poverty in an Ottoman Provincial City", pp. 165-184 in the same volume.

20   Benthall and Bellion-Jourdan in Benthall and Bellion-Jourdan eds., pp. 42-44.

21   Marie Juul Petersen and Sara Lei Sparre, *Islam and Civil Society, Case Studies from Jordan and Egypt*, Danish Institute for International Studies Report no. 13, Copenhagen, Danish Institute for International Studies, 2007, pp. 39-41.

22 She made these observations in a document unpublished at the time of writing, entitled "We think that this job pleases Allah": Islamic Charity, Social Order and the Construction of Modern Muslim Selfhoods in Jordan".

23 Ibid.

24 Egbert Harmsen, "Islamic Voluntary Welfare Activism in Jordan" in *ISIM Newsletter* no. 13 (December 2003), p. 30.

25 Quoted by Quintan Wiktorowicz and Suha Taji Farouki in: "Islamic NGOS and Muslim Politics: a case from Jordan in *Third World Quarterly* Volume 21 No. 4 (2000), p.691-692.

26 Egbert Harmsen, *ISIM Newsletter* No. 13, 30. I have attended one of these mass weddings, in July 2003.

27 Even though they do adhere to the qur'anic ruling that in cases of persistent disobedience by the wife, she may be disciplined by means of "light" or "moderate" beatings.

28 Egbert Harmsen, "Between Empowerment & Paternalism" in *ISIM Review* no. 20 (Autumn 2007), p. 11.

29 Ibid.

30 Petersen, *Islam and Civil Society*, pp. 39-41.

References

Abdul Kazim, A. (1997). 'The Muslim Brotherhood, the Historic Background and the Ideological Origin,' in J. Schwedler (ed.), *Islamic Movements in Jordan*, Amman: Al-Urdun Al-Jadid Research Centre and Friedrich Ebert Stiftung, 11-43.

Asad, T. (1993). *Genealogies of Religion, Discipline and Reasons of Power in Christianity and Islam*, Baltimore and London: The John Hopkins University Press.

Bar, S. (1998). *The Muslim Brotherhood in Jordan*, Tel Aviv: Moshe Dayan Center for Middle Eastern and African Studies.

Benthall, J. (2003). 'Financial Worship,' in J. Benthall and J. Bellion-Jourdan (eds), *The Charitable Crescent, Politics of Aid in the Muslim World*, London and New York, I.B. Tauris Publishers, 7-28.

Boulby, M. (1999). *The Muslim Brotherhood and the Kings of Jordan 1945-1993*, Atlanta: Scholars Press.

Brand, L.A. (1998). *Women, the State and Political Liberalization, Middle Eastern and North African Experiences*, New York: Columbia University Press.

Burgat, F. (2003). *Face to Face with Political Islam*, London and New York: I.B. Tauris.

Cohen, J.L., and Arato, A. (1992). *Civil Society and Political Theory*, Cambridge and Massachusetts: MIT Press.

Ginio, E. (2003). 'Living on the Margins of Charity, Coping with Poverty in an Ottoman Provincial City,' in M. Bonner, M. Ener and A. Singer (eds), *Poverty and Charity in Middle Eastern Contexts*, Albany: State University of New York Press, 165-184.

Hammad, W. (1999). *Jordanian Women's Organisations and Sustainable Development*, Amman: Al-Urdun Al-Jadid Research Centre.

Hamzawi, A. (2003). *Civil Society in the Middle East,* Nahost Studien no. 4, Berlin: Verlag Hans Schiler.

Harmsen, E. (2007). 'Between Empowerment & Paternalism' in *ISIM Review* no. 20 (Autumn), 10-11.

Harmsen, E. (2008). *Islam, Civil Society and Social Work, Muslim Voluntary Welfare Associations in Jordan between Patronage and Empowerment*, Amsterdam: Amsterdam University Press.

Harmsen, E. (2003). 'Islamic Voluntary Welfare Activism in Jordan,' in *ISIM Newsletter* no. 13 (December). 30-31.

Hermann, K. (2000). *Aufbruch von Unten, Möglichkeiten und Grenzen von NGOs in Jordanien*, Münster, Hamburg and London, Lit Verlag.

Hirschkind, C. (2001). 'Civic Virtue and Religious Reason: and Islamic Counterpublic,' in *Cultural Anthropology,* Volume 16, no. 1, 3-34.

Hoexter, M. (2003). 'Charity, the Poor and Distribution of Alms in Ottoman Algiers', in *Poverty and Charity in Middle Eastern Contexts,* in M. Bonner, M. Ener and A. Singer (eds), Albany: State University of New York Press, 145-162.

Kepel, G. (2003). *Jihad, the Trail of Political Islam*, London and New York: I.B. Tauris.

Kuran, T. (2003) 'Islamic Redistribution Through Zakah,' in M. Bonner, M. Ener and A. Singer (eds), *Poverty and Charity in Middle Eastern Contexts*, Albany, State University of New York Press, 275-293.

Mahmood, S. (2005). *Politics of Piety, the Islamic Revival and the Feminist Subject*, Princeton, US and Oxford, UK: Princeton University Press.

Petersen, M.J. and Sparre, S. L. (2007). *Islam and Civil Society, Case Studies from Jordan and Egypt*, Danish Institute for International Studies Report no. 13, Copenhagen: Danish Institute for International Studies.

Petersen, M.J. and Sparre, S. L. (s.d.). 'We think that this job pleases Allah: Islamic Charity, Social Order and the Construction of Modern Muslim Selfhoods in Jordan' (unpublished document).

Roy, O. (2003). *De globalisering van de islam* (original title: *L'islam mondialisé*, translated into Dutch by Walter van der Star), Amsterdam: Van Gennep.

Salvatore, A. (2009). 'Tradition and Modernity within Islamic Civilisation and the West,' in A.S. Muhammad Masud and M. van Bruinessen (eds), *Islam and Modernity, Key Issues and Debates*, Edinburgh: Edinburgh University Press, 3-35.

Shteiwi, M. (2001). *Voluntarism and Volunteers in the Arab World, Case Studies,* no location mentioned: The Arab Network for NGOs.

Starett, G. (1995). 'The Hexis of Interpretation: Islam and the Body in the Egyptian Popular School,' in *American Ethnologist*, Volume 22, no.4, 953-969.

Wiktorowicz, Q. and Farouki, S. T. (2000) in: 'Islamic NGOS and Muslim Politics: a case from Jordan' in *Third World Quarterly*, Volume 21, no. 4, 691-692.

Zubaida, S. (s.d). *Civil Society, Community and Democracy in the Middle East* (article, unpublished version).

Fighting Poverty with *Kimse Yok Mu*

Thomas Michel, S.J.

The enemies of human societies

Almost a hundred years ago, the prominent Turkish thinker Said Nursi analysed the situation of Muslims in the modern world and came to the conclusion that, at the deepest level, the real enemies of Muslims were not one or another group of Christians, nor even one or another civilization of non-believers. In fact, the true enemies of humankind were not human at all. Rather, Nursi personified humankind's enemies as *Lord Ignorance, Sir Poverty, and Mister Disunity.*[1] These three destructive forces in human society – ignorance, poverty, and disunity – threaten not only Muslims but the followers of all religions; they are thus common enemies that must be faced together.

Although Said Nursi died in 1960, his writings, in the form of a 6600-page commentary on the Qur'an named the *Risale-i Nur* (Message of Light), continue to influence millions of Muslims, especially in Turkey. One of those whose thinking was stimulated by the writings of Nursi was Fethullah Gülen. Gülen came to know the writings of Nursi in 1958 when he was still in his teens, and he acknowledges that he reaped much benefit from studying the *Risale-i Nur.*

In fact, Gülen has sometimes been accused in Turkey of being a "Nurcu," that is, a follower of Said Nursi. Gülen does not deny that he learned much from reading Nursi, just as he profited from reading many other Muslim thinkers, but he rejects being categorized as being a disciple of Nursi in any sectarian sense.[2] While admitting the influence of Nursi on his own thinking, Gülen added his own emphases, interpretations, and directions to the original teaching of the *Risale-i Nur*.

Turkish scholars suggest various ways of relating the thought and social programme of Gülen to that of Nursi before him. According to Hakan Yavuz, Gülen was one of those who "reimagined" Nursi[3]; alluding to Gülen's appropriation of Nursi's ideas, Ihsan Yilmaz speaks of "economic, political, and educational transformations,"[4] and Mustafa Akyol refers to "new approaches of his [Gülen's] own."[5] According to Zeki Saritoprak, Gülen is simply "putting Nursi's theories into practice."[6]

One striking difference of emphasis between the directives given by the two men is where Nursi stressed *study*, Gülen puts the accent on *service*. There is no contradiction here, but the focus shifts from an inner, spiritual transformation brought about by the study of the *Risale-i Nur* to a transformation of society made possible through the efforts of a community of committed, generous agents of change.

Fighting humankind's true enemies

In this light, one can understand Gülen taking seriously the triple challenge posed by Nursi early in the 20th Century and his concern to mobilize his followers to combat ignorance, poverty, and disunity. In the early years of the movement, in the 1980s, the emphasis was placed on the battle against ignorance. Much has been written about the pedagogical theory and the accomplishments of more than 1000 so-called "Gülen inspired schools", and the dozen or so universities founded and run by members of the "Hizmet"[7] movement. These schools, as well as the other educational efforts of the community, such as the *Zaman* newspaper, the *Samanyolu* television network and the more than 35 professional and popular journals which they produce, are all evidence of the community's commitment to struggle against the pervasive phenomenon of ignorance.

Later on, in the 1990s, a second emphasis came to the fore with the establishment of Dialogue Centres and Institutes in many parts of the world. The "flagship" dialogue institute set up by the community was the "Writers and Journalists' Foundation," inaugurated in Istanbul in 1994. This foundation, which has promoted interreligious encounters such as the international Abrahamic seminars in Harran/Urfa (2000) and Mardin (2004), which brought together Jewish, Christian, and Muslim scholars to explore together monotheism's Abrahamic roots, as well as the civil "Abant Platform" encounters to discuss issues of concern in Turkish society, became the model for local and national dialogue initiatives in many countries.

Much notice has been given in recent years to the many Dialogue Centres and Institutes around the world that are inspired and maintained by the Gülen community. There is no catalogue listing these local centres, which may exceed 200 in the United States alone. These dialogue institutes are a direct attempt to fight disunity by breaking down the barriers of misunderstanding, suspicion, and half-truths that so often characterize interreligious relations.

Following upon their commitment in the 1980s to combat ignorance through education, and that in the 1990s to combat disunity through dialogue, the first decade of the new century has seen the creation of a movement to combat the third great enemy, poverty, through benevolent works of mercy. Compared to the well-documented reporting on the schools and dialogue centres run by members of the Gülen community, relatively little has been written about the struggle against poverty, perhaps the most pervasive of the enemies of modern societies identified by Said Nursi. In this chapter, I will try to outline the efforts of the Gülen community to combat poverty through aid and relief efforts and their founding of *Kimse Yok Mu* as an institutionalization of this concern.[8]

Origins of Kimse Yok Mu

Kimse Yok Mu is a fast-growing organization that has its origins in 2002 in a television programme of the same name on Samanyolu TV. The television programme was aimed at conscientizing the audience to the plight of "unfortunate, needy, unhappy, and hopeless people." The title of the programme, *Kimse Yok Mu*, is a Turkish phrase which means basically, "Doesn't anybody care?" or "Isn't there anyone out there who cares?" The television programme was a success, which led to the founding of the organization that has now become the main channel of aid and relief for the Gülen community.

The organization's original focus was more on relief than on poverty alleviation. They directed their attention towards supplying emergency relief and assistance to the victims of natural disasters as well as towards the victims of endemic poverty. At first, the focus of their activities was mainly directed towards the victims of poverty in Turkey, and from that experience they later moved to respond to international calls for help. The magnitude of the problem was daunting for a new organization addressing the issue of poverty. As Mehmet

Z. Özkara, Chairman of the Kimse Yok Mu Executive Committee, noted, "After we had started such social solidarity and aid activity, we saw that the dimensions of poverty in our country were beyond our imagination."

Kimse Yok Mu projects in Turkey

Nevertheless, various programmes were set up which were aimed at alleviating poverty. Kimse Yok Mu started small and gradually became more ambitious in its efforts to fight poverty.

The "Sister Family Project" seeks to "twin" middle- and upper-income families with poorer families to help the needy families confront their economic crises, support the education of children, and reach a dignified standard of living. What is interesting about this project, which has found hundreds of sister families for those in need, is the emphasis on the personal interaction of family life. The family twinning is an effort to avoid the "faceless charity" which can fail to maintain the self-respect of the recipients of aid projects.

A second project initiated by Kimse Yok Mu is that of food aid. In June, 2004, the Istanbul Food Campaign provided various staple foods for over 600 families that had applied to the association. In the same month, over 200 packages of foodstuffs were distributed to the victims of an earthquake in Doğubeyazıt on the slopes of Mt. Ararat in eastern Anatolia. In the following year, a greater number of food packages were distributed to families in Karlıova in Bingöl province, also in eastern Anatolia, after an earthquake in the midwinter of 2005. In 2006, after severe flooding struck cities in south-east Turkey such as Batman, Urfa, Mardin, Iskenderun and Diyarbakir, the equivalent of almost 2 million Euros of foodstuffs were distributed to the victims.

In August 2006, a forest fire destroyed half the village of Yaylatepe in the Cankiri district of Central Anatolia. Kimse Yok Mu helped rebuild homes and the mosque and distributed refrigerators, home furnishings, blankets, food and clothing to families who had taken refuge in tents. In May 2010 heavy rains caused flooding in the region of Ağrı in Eastern Anatolia; Kimse Yok Mu responded with blankets and clothing for over 70 families.

In addition to the emergency relief extended to victims of natural disasters, Kimse Yok Mu set up Ramadan tents in various neighborhoods of Istanbul and other big cities of Turkey which provided an open invitation every evening during the month of Ramadan to anyone who wanted to break their fast with an evening meal. The tents were located in those parts of the city where impoverished families and individuals could have easy access. Once again, as with the Sister Family programme, a formula was found by which the needy and the comfortably placed would be brought together in human interaction, in this case the sharing of food at an *iftar* dinner, rather than relying on impersonal hand-outs.

During the month of Ramadan in 2006, Kimse Yok Mu took the idea of Ramadan tents to an international level, and the tents were set up not only in seven cities in Turkey but also in the Philippines, Indonesia, Pakistan, Lebanon and Ethiopia. By 2007, the number of tents increased rapidly, reaching 22 cities in Turkey and another ten countries (Mongolia, Pakistan, Sri Lanka, Indonesia, Lebanon, Sudan, Afghanistan, Kenya, Ethiopia and the Philippines). In the city of Denizli alone, over 4,000 people were fed daily during the month of Ramadan. In Ramadan 2009, in Turkey about 270,000 meals were distributed throughout the month at centres and mosques, and another 335,000 people were fed with hot meals in their homes. Elsewhere, 100,000 people took part in daily *iftars* or received gift food packages. By Ramadan 2010, 28 local branches had been set up in Turkey to organize and distribute food to the needy.

The Kimse Yok Mu programmes have an educational dimension. By means of the aid projects, in which the general population is encouraged to participate, Kimse Yok Mu tries to educate people that they have a religious, moral, and national duty to help the victims of poverty and misfortune. In recognizing Kimse Yok Mu's efforts to feed the hungry during Ramadan, Prime Minster Erdoğan of Turkey noted, "I thank [you] for the activities you accomplished as Kimse Yok Mu Association. May God be pleased." It should be noted that although the Charter of Kimse Yok Mu permits cooperation with governmental, non-governmental and private agencies, the association is explicitly forbidden to interfere in politics.[9]

The assistance extended to the needy is not limited to providing food. In 2005, pyjamas were distributed to patients in the Bakırkoy Mental Hospital in Istanbul, and stoves and fuel oil were provided for the needy during the winters of 2004 and 2005. Over 1,000 students in various regions of Turkey were helped with books and other educational supplies during the school year of 2006. In September, 2004, the association participated in a literacy programme and cooperated with an agency created to find employment for street children. Visits to homes for the elderly, clothing drives, and assistance to the physically handicapped are among the projects undertaken by the 22 local branches of the association.

International aid projects

Although the Kimse Yok Mu Association began by striving to address the question of poverty in Turkey, its efforts quickly moved into the field of international aid and relief. After the underwater earthquake and resulting tsunami in the Indian Ocean that on 26 December 2006 devastated parts of Indonesia, Sri Lanka, India, and Thailand, and produced a death toll of over 128,000 people in Indonesia alone, Kimse Yok Mu was one of a host of international agencies that provided emergency relief and engaged in the effort to reconstruct the region. Kimse Yok Mu undertook a campaign to raise funds for the affected regions and delivered clothing, food, and medicine to those who had taken refuge in camps, and provided chemicals to purify drinking water. The association funded repairs to houses and schools and reactivated a school destroyed by the tsunami.

After the devastating earthquake in Kashmir, Pakistan, Kimse Yok Mu erected three tent cities for the victims. The association rented a cargo plane to provide instant emergency relief and also took responsibility for supplying the food and clothing needs for 5,000 refugees for a period of six months. 29 tractor-trailers with emergency aid, including the meat of over 400 steers, were dispatched from Turkey to Pakistan. The association built and furnished ten prefabricated schools, each with a capacity of 350 students, and handed these schools over to Pakistan's Ministry of Education to administer.

After the Israeli invasion of Lebanon in July, 2006, Kimse Yok Mu responded with humanitarian aid for victims of the war, mainly women and children. Thirteen tractor-trailers filled with flour and dry food were sent overland from Turkey and delivered to the Jordanian Embassy to Palestine. The aid was distributed by the Palestine Red Crescent Society. Another three tractor-trailers with flour and dry food were sent directly to Lebanon, and a second convoy of ten tractor trailers filled with food followed shortly thereafter.

In 2007, Kimse Yok Mu began its aid programmes in Africa. Beginning with Ethiopia and Kenya, the association now assists people in Niger, Uganda, Central Africa, Cameroon, Senegal, Guinea, Congo, Burkina Faso, Chad, Togo, Ghana, Liberia, Madagascar, Benin, Mauritania and, since March 2006, the organization has conducted a special campaign for Darfur in the Sudan. In 2009-2010, 23 deep wells were dug in Niger to assist in meeting the recurrent water shortages in the country.

In Asia, the association has projects, in addition to those mentioned above, in Bangladesh and the Philippines. In Bangladesh, the association dispatched rescue and relief teams after the 2007 hurricane.

More recently, the Kimse Yok Mu organization has responded to tragedies in Myanmar and China. Already in May, 2008, the first team of volunteers and aid supplies from Kimse Yok Mu arrived in Myanmar and was given permission to distribute emergency assistance – vegetables, rice, drinking water, and disinfectant materials – to victims of the cyclone. It was teachers in the schools run by members of the Hizmet community associated with the followers of Fethullah Gülen who were already in Myanmar that were able to coordinate the humanitarian relief efforts. Shortly after the volunteer effort in Myanmar, Kimse Yok Mu announced a second campaign to collect funds for victims of the earthquake in China. On 21 May 2008, the association announced the new campaign, which was personally inaugurated with a $15,000 contribution by Fethullah Gülen.

The most recent involvement of Kimse Yok Mu in Asia came as a response to the ethnic violence that occurred in Kırgızstan in 2010. At the request of the government of Kırgızstan and the United Nations, Kimse Yok Mu distributed care packages to more than 2,300 families in the conflict-ridden Osh and Jalalabad regions of the country. The organization is sending overland ten supply trucks with food, clothes and housing supplies for the victims of the conflict.

Perhaps the greatest tragedy of recent times was the massive earthquake that struck the Caribbean island of Haiti in January, 2010. In the early days after the tragedy hit, Kimse Yok Mu sent search and rescue teams to the island, and when the full complement of aid workers arrived, the organization was daily feeding 2,500 earthquake victims. The organization now has obtained land in Haiti on which it has established a temporary tent city for the homeless and has plans to build a school and hospital.

Looking toward the future

By 2007, aid programmes administered by Kimse Yok Mu had reached 37 cities in Turkey and 42 countries around the world. Although the majority of these were in the Middle East, Asia, and Africa, Kimse Yok Mu has also carried out aid and relief programmes in six European countries, Haiti in the Caribbean and Peru in South America. The organization has achieved much in the relatively short time since it was founded in 2002. I know of few organizations that have grown so quickly or accomplished so much in such a short time.

The association has already gained a niche in international aid circles. For example, publications of works on humanitarian aid published by Kimse Yok Mu were on display at the London Book Fair held in London in April, 2009. The association is not afraid to try innovative methods to pursue its ends. A campaign to gather funds among Turkish youths for victims of violence in Darfur was carried out by encouraging young people to make a 5 TL contribution (approximately US $2.75) by sending an SMS message through Turkey's major mobile phone operators.

As the organization looks to the future, the association is already speaking of instituting a volunteer corps of aid workers tentatively named "Kimse Yok Mu Volunteers" who will carry on aid activities in Turkey and other countries. One wonders whether, as the association continues to grow and develop, like many other agencies, it will eventually spend a greater part of its time and efforts addressing the systemic causes of poverty, and relatively less on emergency responses of immediate relief assistance to those in need.

Kimse Yok Mu is an initiative inspired by the highest ideals of Islamic teaching and life. The model of the assistance given by Muslims from the Madina region (*Ansar*) to the Emigrants from Mecca (*Muhajirun*) during the lifetime of the prophet Muhammad roots the ideals of the association in the experience of the earliest generations of Muslims. The Islamic Feasts have become occasions for concrete expressions of concern for the poor. Ramadan is a focal moment for drawing the attention of Muslims to the poor. "Sacrifice 2007" sought to use the occasion of Id al-Adha, the Feast of the Sacrifice, to distribute meat to the needy in many countries. The initiative involved 1,500 volunteers who slaughtered and distributed meat to the poor, Muslim and non-Muslim, in 42 countries. By Id al-Adha in 2008, over one and a half million people in more than 50 countries were recipients of meat packages donated and distributed by Kimse Yok Mu.[10]

Although Kimse Yok Mu finds its spiritual motivation in the teachings of Islam, the aid offered to the needy is not limited to Muslims. Emergency relief efforts in Myanmar, China, Haiti, Peru, and Sri Lanka, and the distribution of meat packages on the occasion of Id al-Adha with no distinction as regards the religion of the recipients show that the association's concern is not limited to the needy within the Islamic *umma*.

Christians, Jews, and others will recognize many of the programmes of Kimse Yok Mu as being similar – in some cases, identical – to those carried out by other philanthropic agencies of religious or secular inspiration, including other Muslim agencies such as Islamic Relief. The websites of Kimse Yok Mu and Catholic Relief Services, for example, show such close similarities that the two associations could seem to be sister organizations. This convergence should not surprise anyone, for the common inspiration of one God who cares deeply about the plight of the poor is a common element of the Jewish, Christian, and Muslim traditions. Kimse Yok Mu can be seen as the latest and very welcome expression of the followers of Abrahamic faith to put that commitment into concrete practice.

Kimse Yok Mu today

The needs of our world keep changing, and the priorities for the most effective use of the limited capabilities of aid organizations keep changing as well. Organizations like Kimse Yok Mu are learning from their experience how better to integrate their efforts at fighting poverty with their educational efforts and those aimed at building greater unity and understanding among peoples.

At the present time Kimse Yok Mu have seven international campaigns in progress.

1. **The Syrian Refugees Campaign.** The one closest to home involves emergency care for tens of thousands of Syrians who have fled their homes due to the fighting between the rebels and the Syrian regime of Bashar Al-Assad. In general, those refugees who have fled to Turkey are adequately cared for by the efforts of the Turkish government, hence Kimse Yok Mu's attention is mainly focused on serving those who have fled to Lebanon and Jordan. The great majority of refugees in these countries are women whose needs run to foodstuffs, child and infant necessities, blankets, and cleaning supplies. Kimse Yok Mu has provided 5.5 tons of relief supplies, including portable toilets, bathrooms, garbage containers, and kitchen facilities, to over 14,000 refugees from Syria in Lebanon and Jordan. They serve a hot meal to 1,000 people every day, and in September, 2012, the organization opened a healthcare centre with a staff that includes two full-time Syrian doctors, two nurses, and two pharmacists on duty. Approximately 150 refugees are treated daily in the polyclinic and small-scale surgical operations are performed.

   The slogan for the Syrian Refugees Campaign is: "It doesn't suit you when you are full and your neighbor is hungry." Metin Çetiner, vice-president of Kimse Yok Mu, described the situation of the refugees as follows: "People suffer at an extreme level. The needs of people for shelter and goods have increased with decreasing weather temperatures in the region. They need many supplies, especially household tools, kitchen utensils, stationery for children, winter clothes and blankets. People suffer a great deal with the approaching winter."

2. **The Rohingya Refugee Campaign.** A human tragedy on an even greater scale is the plight of the Rohingya refugees who have fled from Myanmar and settled in makeshift camps on the Myanmar-Bangladesh border. Their numbers are said to be in the hundreds of thousands. Over 90,000 of these Muslim refugees are being served by Kimse Yok Mu's Rohingya Campaign. Having earned the trust of the Myanmar government through its relief efforts for the victims of the 2008 cyclone, Kimse Yok Mu is permitted to provide foodstuffs and medical supplies to the unaccredited border camps which are reluctantly tolerated by the two countries.

3. **East Africa Campaigns.** A third project of Kimse Yok Mu covers four countries of East Africa: Somalia, Uganda, Kenya, and Ethiopia and focuses on emergency assistance to those faced with hunger and thirst. The hardest hit of these countries by decades of civil unrest was Somalia. In August, 2011, 160 tons of food were sent to Somalia in container ships from the Turkish port of Mersin. During Ramadan of that year, 12,000 Somali families were given two hot meals a day at five centres and baby formula was distributed to 4,000 infants. By September of that year, the number of those receiving daily hot meals had increased to 90,000 in six camps.

Medical teams set up clinics to treat children's malnutrition and infectious diseases and the Banadir Maternity Hospital in Mogadishu was completely restored, with both operating theatres and outpatient services being brought up to modern standards. Medical aid offered by Kimse Yok Mu doctors has been treating broken bones, bomb explosion injuries, orthopedic and kidney operations, gynecological treatments and pre- and post-natal care. Since August, 2011, approximately 70,000 patients have been treated. Malaria tests and anti-malarial medicines are being widely distributed and a campaign of sterile circumcision procedures is being carried out.

The lack of clean water has been a critical problem in the camps, which are often located in arid regions. To provide clean drinking water, a reservoir and two large springs have been drilled at Mogadishu with a daily flow of 22 tons of water. To combat the numerous cases of enteritis caused by dirty water, Kimse Yok Mu is bringing clean water to all the camps, building toilets and baths, and delivering detergent, liquid soap, and toilet paper to the camp residents.

While the need is not so dire in other East African countries, aid programmes are also being carried out in Kenya, Ethiopia, and Uganda. In Kenya, thousands of care packages have been distributed to meet emergency needs, but more permanent solutions are beginning to take priority. Plans are in process for Kimse Yok Mu to dig more water wells, organize courses in landscaping, farming, and bee-keeping, build orphanages, and upgrade medical facilities.

Similar projects of relief and development are being carried out in Ethiopia and Uganda. The author of this chapter has personally visited two medical clinics in Uganda run by volunteer medical staff from Turkey and can testify to the effective humanitarian service provided in these Kimse Yok Mu projects. In Jinja, Uganda, the present clinic will give way soon to a new hospital/medical centre complex. Construction of the new complex is already underway.

4. **Ikbaliye village in Pakistan.** As mentioned above, Kimse Yok Mu erected three tent cities to house the victims of the 2010 earthquake in Pakistan. The organization has now committed itself to transforming the temporary emergency housing erected after the quake into a permanent housing complex with homes, deep water wells, primary and high schools, shops, a playground and a health care centre for the earthquake victims. These plans are taking shape in the new Ikbaliye village which is already under construction; the cost of the whole project is expected to come to six million US dollars.

5. **Other campaigns.** The Water Wells Project, mentioned above, is using high-tech digging technologies to bring clean drinking water to residents of Niger and Palestine. It is estimated that each well serve approximately 3,000 people with the clean water so essential to health.

Finally, Kimse Yok Mu has two orphanage campaigns, one in Palestine and the other in Sudan. It is estimated that there are 20,000 orphaned children in Palestine's Gaza Strip. Kimse Yok Mu has set up a "Scholarship for Orphaned Palestinian Children Project," which seeks donors in Turkey and elsewhere to sponsor an orphan's living expenses and tuition for a year's education.

Similarly, Sudan's Darfur region has approximately 7,000 orphans, many of whom lost their families in the armed conflict between the Sudanese government forces and the Darfur rebels. The children reside in primitive *halves* where food and other basic necessities are rare. As it does in the case of the Palestinian orphans, Kimse Yok Mu seeks sponsors in Turkey to adopt the living and educational expenses of these children.

This overview of the work of Kimse Yok Mu shows the concrete ways in which the organization is seeking to live out its mission. This vision is expressed in the Kimse Yok Mu Mission Statement itself:

- To build a more comfortable, serene and peaceful world while fighting poverty and attempting to eliminate social inequalities;

- To encourage society to be more understanding and engaging with the notion of 'Humanitarian Aid';
- To protect innocent people in war-torn areas;
- And to accept and help people from all races, ages, religions, and social statuses in order to spread kindness around the world and to create and follow social support models.[11]

Notes

1   Said Nursi, *Münâzarat*, p. 433, cited in Şükran Vahide, *Bediuzzaman Said Nursi*, Istanbul, 1992, p. 95.

2   Emily Lynne Webb, *Fethullah Gülen: Is There More to Him Than Meets the Eye?*, Patterson, NJ: n.d., p. 96. Cited in Thomas Michel, "Fethullah Gülen as Educator," in *Turkish Islam and the Secular State*, Syracuse: Syracuse UP, 2003, p. 81.

3   M. Hakan Yavuz, "Islam in the Public Square: The Case of the Nur Movement," *Turkish Islam and the Secular State* (ed. By M. Hakan Yavuz and John L. Esposito) Syracuse: Syracuse U.P.

4   Ihsan Yilmaz, "Changing Turkish-Muslim Discourses on Modernity, West and Dialogue," paper delivered at the International Association of Middle East Studies (IAMES), Berlin, 5-7 October 2000, footnote 33.

5   Mustafa Akyol, "What Made the Gülen Movement Possible?" *Muslim World in Transition: Contributions of the Gülen Movement*, London: Leeds Metropolitan UP, 2007, p. 28.

6   Zeki Saritoprak, "Fethullah Gülen and His Theology of Social Responsibility," *Mastering Knowledge in Modern Times: Fethullah Gülen as an Islamic Scholar*, New York: Blue Dome Press, 2011, p. 91.

7   Those influenced by the teachings of Gülen prefer to refer to their community collectively as the *Hizmet* or the "Service" community, rather than the "followers of Gülen," which could imply a personality cult.

8   The official title in English is "Kimse Yok Mu Aid and Solidarity Association." The association website can be found at http://www.kimseyokmu.org.tr/en/

9   "Charter of Kimse Yok Mu Solidarity and Aid Association," art. 3.

10 "Eid Helps Boost Unity in Turkey," *Today's Zaman*, 1 July 2008.

11 Kimse Yok Mu, "Our Mission and Vision," http://global.kimseyokmu.org.tr/?p=content &cl=hakkimizda&i=1589

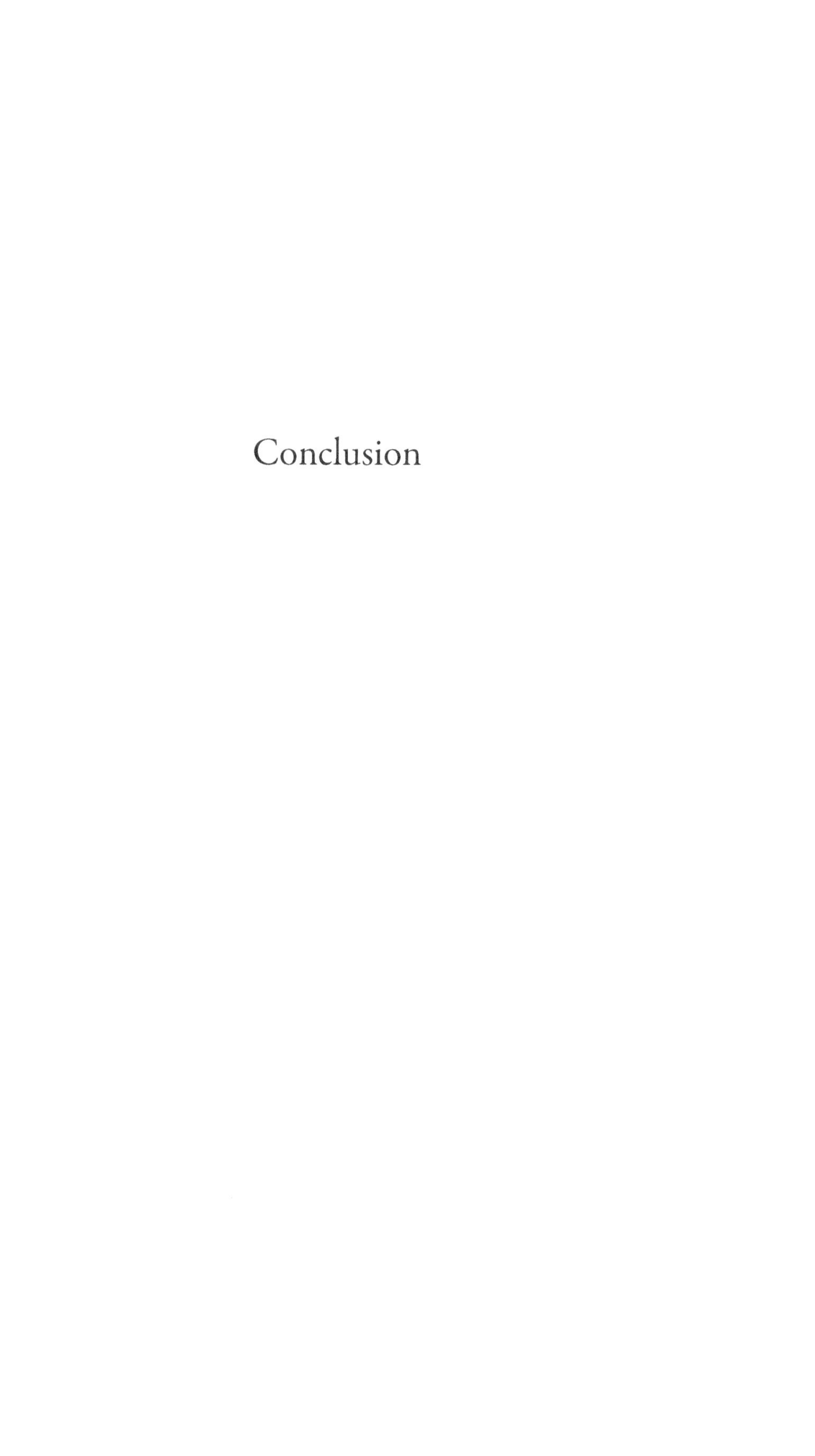

Conclusion

Translocality and Hybridization in Current Modern Islamic Activism

Erkan Toğuşlu and Johan Leman

In this book, Muslim activism is examined along three dimensions and relations: intellectual thought, political activism and social work. Contemporary Muslim activism offers some elements and fault lines for the development of civil society, new political thought, liberalization and human rights. Each of these areas and dimensions appears among Muslim activists and presents a variety and multiplicity of engagements with traditional and modern types of Islamic notions. This dynamism provides a general acceptance of civil initiatives, a kind of pluralism in politics and Islamic thought, a shift to humanitarian discourse. However, these are some impetus to see the changes and shifts in Islamic activism which does not represent the Muslims in a general sense.

Islamic activism is dealing with the question of modernity. One of the questions about modernity is whether it is a single tradition, structural and institutional setting, attitude, an integrated social-practical norm which generates a kind of experience linked to a geographical area. What are the criteria for being called modern? Who defines the modern condition? If there are varieties of modernity, what differentiates them from each other? When we are talking about modernity, we are discussing a specific zone, a part of Europe. We are not interested in the history of the non-Western world. The assumption is that all political-social and economic change should follow the historical experience of the West.[1] Muslim societies engage with modernity in its various forms through humanitarian work, immigration, international students, media and transnational Muslim communities. The modernity question in the Muslim world is interrelated with the Muslim subjectivity associated with several socio-cultural transformations, and opens new avenues to negotiate with some notions of human rights, democracy, civil society and gender relations.

Since the events of September 11 2001 and the Arab Spring, one of the arguments has been that Muslims need to reform Islam and secularize the state and politics to bring about democracy. This assumption is widely circulated in public debates to note that Islam should be reshaped by a normative secularity imposed from state power to develop a moderate-liberal Islam that can be open and tolerant to Western life and civilization (Esposito and Burgat 2003; An-Naim 1990). It is not simply a matter of state neutrality, but secularism reveals the disciplinary and civilizational aspects (Mahmood 2006: 330).

The concept of travelling and mobility introduced by Mandaville is explicitly connected with understanding how a transnational activism is formulated and re-activated in Muslim networks. We cannot avoid returning to the classical political thinkers and the tune of political thinking to see what happens when an idea moves across borders and beyond states.

Translocal Islamic activism: a new patriotism without nationality

A change in social-political morphology in Muslim societies and communities has extended the transnational ties and relations in different areas such as Islamic knowledge, Muslim consciousness, cultural reproduction, and organizational networks. Applying transnational studies to understand the transformation of Islamic activities broadens the definition of contemporary Islamic activism and Islamic identity (Toğuşlu, Leman and Sezgin 2014). For Mandaville, a political sociology of Islam is lacking in the literature (Mandaville 2001). Migration, entrepreneurs, diaspora communities, charity organizations offer global sociocultural transformations about transnational Islamic activism (Vertovec 2002; Bruneau 2010; Osella and Osella 2009). Mandaville suggests that international studies can use some connections with especially anthropological scopes (Mandaville 2001). Within the scope of transnational and translocal Islamic activities, one can address three issues: the specification and location of agency; the relationship between transnational processes and states; and the interaction between global, transnational, national, and local social fields (Glick Schiller 1997: 156).

Let us start first with the interaction between local, national and global social fields. Globalization has a strong impact on the transportation and the settlement of the religious replacement, not only in geographical terms, but in different spaces and cultures. Telecommunications, film, TV and the Internet have contributed to the creation of the translocal spaces and replacements of the religious. Globalization studies have called attention to recent reconfigurations of space and polity and the growth of global cities (Featherstone 1990; Sassen 1991). In contrast, scholars of transnational migration have been concerned with the actual social interactions that migrants maintain and construct across borders (Basch, Glick Schiller and Blanc 1993). Transnational migration provides some tools to differentiate the translocalization processes of the Islamic networks, organizations and ties (Mandaville 2001; Saint-Blancat 2002).

Transnational ties and organizations change and transform the relations between people and spaces "by creating social fields" and connecting one to certain places, country, homeland and hostland. In this regard, the transnational movements and organizations are frequently mentioned as observing the religious-humanitarian shift which necessitates a new map defining Islamic activities. The spread of civil society and initiatives does not target just specific religious-ethnic communities. The emergence of new humanitarian discourse in NGOs run by Muslims is pluralized by different people and religious-humanitarian groups.

Muslim activists create new localities, using the term of Appadurai (1996). New translocalities[2] emerge in these activities undertaken by Muslim organizations. They navigate between different cities. They are connecting with each other as nodes via e-mail and virtual offices. Media emerge in different ways to rehearse connections and raise consciousness and memory. In these areas, being translocal describes the effects of being between two or more than two geographical situations, locations and feelings. Muslim actors cannot be described in a given borderland (Grinell 2010). The classical division of borders, where the identity is created, changed and transformed, is unstable and insignificant for social movements defining in a given transborder challenge about belonging to a certain ethnic-religious or political community. Being in a translocal situation changes the way of life, constructing of identity of Islamic movements and activities.

The rise of consciousness marked by multiple appurtenances and belongings is strengthened by transnational Islamic ties and networks which offer new places to improve the translocality of Muslim identities. The coexistence (pacific-active) of several ties and networks of Muslim communities maintains the hybrid elements of Muslim subjectivities which are fragmented and reproduced in new circumstances. The multi-locality and connection with other people from other places who share the same roots and routes maintain the new Muslim subjectivities according to their practices and knowledge. The new subjectivities are formed in the global arena through educational institutions, charity and politics. Mandaville calls this process the re-imagination of the *umma* (Mandaville 2001); it requires formal and informal networks to share a collective imaginary, solidarity and coherence. The memories and a common link shared by Muslims are fragile and fragmented. In this transnational arena, this collective memory can be observed and reshaped by Islamic activities which construct a community identity on a daily basis. A socio-religious reproduction is realized within the transnational framework in terms of knowledge, politics and social work. Facets of Muslim identity are selected, syncretized and elaborated while Muslims engage with civil society, politics and religion.

The numbers of transnational entrepreneurs and corporations (including professionals, NGOs) have increased rapidly. They work globally and interest local charity initiatives. The nexus between social and economic actors determines the influence of transnational and global to see how transnationalism and globalization influence this pluralization within the faith based social movements. This local-global interest is a key to understanding the socio-economic transformation of Muslim actors in the globalization process.

This new dialectic of global and local questions cannot be analysed in a national context. The obvious and conventional forms of such activity are international NGOs (Dijkzeul 2008). Their number has been rapidly increasing. The NGOs create alternative spaces to claim rights and seek to change political debates; they work in the areas of environment, human rights, development and economic goals. These areas in which NGOs have been involving themselves are trans-boundary in character. Some NGOs are interested more in political activities, and actively participate in political engagement within a local-national and global context. In this vein, diasporic Muslim communities, such as Palestinians-Somalians etc., are not only the objects of social help; these refugees become a kind of political aim and patronage in these NGOs. However, some critics points out the essentialist, semi-nationalist and subversively religious dominant character of these organizations and movements in migrant situations in the US and Europe (Katharyne Mitchell 1997, cited by Vertovec 1999: 454).

This new patronage can be analysed in terms of "new patriotism" to portray the new transnational presence in the social and political realm, oscillating between settlement in a new homeland and diasporic nationalism linked with their homelands (Appadurai 1996: 158-177). Vertovec labelled this kind of political activism a "politics of homeland" expanded in multiple ways (Vertovec 1999: 455). The translocal and transnational Islamic charity organizations are the sites of this new patriotism without nationality.

Translocal Islamic aid without borders

The role of NGOs in humanitarian relief activities has increased in recent years. These humanitarian relief organizations are located in majority or minority Muslim societies. The style and characteristics of these NGOs vary from one to another. The objectives, methods and the settlement of the NGOs are the key impetus for noting such variation among these transnational NGOs. They embody different trajectories, discourses and conflicts. Being secular and religious, humanitarian and Islamic are key elements for understanding the character of these NGOs (Clark 2003).

The increasing number of NGOs in the international arena pushes scholars to study transnational Islamic humanitarian organizations the activities of which cross borders and challenge the nation state. They work closely with local people, having a good reputation in the local context. The neo-liberal economies provide certain good opportunities to these increasing NGOs to establish powerful relations across countries, peoples and organizations. In this way, the humanitarian NGOs spark the interest of scholars (Dijkzeul 2008).

The examples discussed in this book indicate several typologies of NGOs run by Muslims. Singer distinguishes three groups of Islamic NGOs according to their works: *da'wa* (preaching-missionary) oriented; *jihad* (military) oriented and *ighata* (relief) oriented. However, this distinction remains very residual and does not carefully discern the practical and ethnographic scope of these NGOs. In the broader sense, all of these activities, including humanitarian ones, can be regarded and considered as *jihad*-oriented, but not in terms of the military. This religious motivation acknowledges a collective-individual spiritual struggle against their self, for this reason it is not considered as a military *jihad*. They donate money from their incomes in pursuit of their religious belief and spiritual reason. Moreover, the organizational level can hide deep motivations and understanding as regards charitable activities, so that the charity is very flexible. It is shaped by political, economic and spiritual circumstances. All of these activities are classified under the faith-based initiatives that refer to new ways of collaboration between states, governments and civil organizations. Briefly, we note that some organizations are political (ideological reasons, focusing only specific geographies); others are very developmentalist (business and micro finance); finally the third case is socio-humanitarian (the scope is very large and diffuse).

One of the features of Islamic activism is related to the flow of migrants, objects, symbols, ideas and images that are important elements in more closely examining transnational Islamic activities. We need to look at the ways in which the texts, discourses and symbols are reproduced and circulated among Muslims. The focus on these elements in the translocal and transnational process helps us to locate Muslim activists in globalization. As globalization studies the extent of a political-economic-cultural structure, one of the aims of the book is to analyse the interaction between states, governments and agents depending on Islamic activism (Glick Schiller 1997:156). In the case of transnationalism, the interaction is "between two or more social subjects from two or more state-nations when at least one of these subjects is not an agent of a government or intergovernmental organization" (Mato 1997: 171). This distinction allows us to see Islamic agency, local subjectivities and identifications as a result of involvement in Islamic activism. One of the central terms used in transnational processes is a borderland. Being at borders does not necessarily mean an escape from disciplining regimes of the state and authority. "The very existence of border cultures or border crossings has sometimes been equated with the demise of nation-states" (Glick Schiller 1997: 159). The movement of people and ideas across borders depends also on power relations and the positioning of the actors in the transnational process. Translocal peoples live differently in these regimes of authority crossing borders and this interaction with regimes of authority influences also the identity of Islamic aid and NGOs.

Traditional, modern and reformist Islamic identity

At the level of political Islam, there are indeed some political activists and thinkers who reject the idea of an Islamic state; even these are minority groups in majority Muslim population countries. They are not so close to ideas such as the separation of religion and politics, acceptance of democratic rules, constitutional government. But, they do not totally reject these ideas, and some of them find some points of reconciliation between Islamic principles, Islamic law and democracy, and human rights (Mayer 1999; Nasr 2005). The new faces of Muslim scholars emphasize some specific questions of coexistence, pluralism, interfaith dialogue and environment crises (Safi 2003; Toguslu 2008). They turn away from strict and traditionalist approaches that are very exclusive. Some use modern historical and epistemological discourses to give new interpretations (Filali-Ansary 2003; Arkoun 2005; An-Naim 1990); others use Islamic traditional sources to renew them (Gülen 2005; Ramadan 2004). Their influence on and contributions to Muslims differ. Their language attempts to renew traditional Islamic notions. This modernizing form of Islamic thought nourishes the new modes of Islamic activities and creates new opportunities to change the traditional framework of Islamist movements. The many different views on engaging in politics, developing social work to which Islam relates, enable us also to evaluate the evolution of Muslim intellectuals' and scholars' discourses. Whether Islam can provide some tools for social cohesion, coexist with democratic systems and develop a particular 'secular' model for Muslims becomes a crucial question, especially after the 9/11 events. The answers differ according to particular views, practices and contexts of Muslim societies. The recent history of revolutions in the Middle East and North Africa reveals this variation and differentiation among Muslim activists, thinkers, organizations and NGOs. In this variation, the role of Muslim intellectuals and scholars is relatively important in suggesting the new orientations including radical-modern and traditional ways. In the early 19th century, Muslim thinkers such as Jamal ad-Din al-Afghani (1839-1897) and Muhammad Abduh (1849-1905) were known as important reformists. This generation of reformers attempted to reconstruct the traditional settings. Armando Salvatore analyses how the reformist discourse emerges in the public sphere by highlighting different political, social and public reasons (2009). This reformist movement gave rise to other political movements and thinkers. Hassan al-Banna (1906-1949) who was influenced by both these thinkers, reacts against Western political and cultural domination, using modern rational Islamic references. In his formulation of renewing Islam, he develops an Islamic activism which is also against the traditional *ulama* role. In the course of history, another Islamist thinker Sayyid Qutb (1906-1966), who led the Muslim Brotherhood in the 1950s, was theorizing on the radical turn of Islamism among the Muslim Brotherhood. This idea is strongly held by Islamists who politicized Islam.

Al-Mawdudi (1903-1979) also significantly contributed to the shape and content of political Islam by his writings and activism. He took part in the foundation of the *Jamaat-Islami* movement. He was the pioneer of pan-Islamism and defended the *umma* as opposed to the nation state model. He became an advocate of the political ideologues of Islamism (Kepel 2002; 2004).

Al-Banna, Qutb, and al-Mawdudi had great influence, inspiring the leaders of political Islam and in particular the Islamic revolution in Iran. The intellectual source of the Iranian revolution was provided by Ali Shariati (1933-1977). He was strongly influenced by leftist thinkers when he studied philosophy in France. His ideas ground on reconciliation between Marxist leftist philosophy and Islam, which emphasizes the liberation idea that is very familiar with the idea of western thinkers on colonialism. Shariati mixed Islamist political ideology with Marxist connotations and references to encounters with the static Shiite *ulama* in Iran. We discussed some key thinkers, whose efforts were primarily directed towards the creation of an Islamic society and state, opposing the authority of the classical *ulama* and traditional Islamic settings. In the 19th century the authority of classical *ulama* was weakened and destabilized by the new practices and forms of knowledge. Muhammad Qasim Zaman talks about the struggle between the *ulama* and the modern Islamist thinkers (Zaman 2009). In the postcolonial era, the traditional *ulama* gave way to the increasing power of Muslim nationalists and Islamists. The ambiguity between *ulama* and modern Muslim scholars is expressed in various debates around the question of gender, politics and secularism. The component of the Islamic political activism included apparently the capture of state-oriented political power. The Islamic state apparatus, for them, provided the application of the *Sharia*.

The legacy of this political thought has mainly served as a repertory of action for political purposes in Muslim politics; however, a practical and discursive change has occurred in Muslim views, which fosters more inclusive and non-politically oriented Islamic thinking. Many Muslim scholars (*ulama*) are also concerned with the new issues, especially related social-economic ones, using Islamic traditional resources to answer questions. While the first Muslim thinkers and scholars use political Islamic logic, the new pioneers of Muslim scholars develop their thinking on the question of renewing Islamic settings and traditional Islamic knowledge without islamizing the state; they follow principles and methods to modernize-reform-revitalize Islam. Reformative action takes ground on the level of the rejection of the classical Islamic *ulama* tendency and pure secular discourse (Esposito 1998: see chapter Revival and Reform; Kurzman 1998). They use new Islamic public reasoning for their arguments. The enemy is not outside, but the backwardness of Muslims should be found inside because most Muslims do not have a clear and correct understanding of Islam. Intellectual, political and cultural change is needed for a revival of Muslims, according to these new Muslim scholars (see chapters in this book). Bayat remarks that Islamist movements have become post-islamist where there emerged a new intellectual positioning and reflection (Bayat 2005). They are concerned with rationality, modern knowledge and contemporary social issues. Being aware of the current issues in Islam let them rethink and reformulate the message of Islam in the spirit of the traditional sources (Voll and Esposito 2001). Zaman draws a distinction between modernists and Islamists in their attitudes to the Islamic tradition (Zaman 2007:9). He gave the examples of Moroccan Muhammad Abid al-Jabiri, the Egyptian Hasan Hanafi and the Syrian Muhammad Shahrur to discuss how the modernist discourse keeps alive the Arab-Islamic heritage. They attempt to discover the resources to respond to the socio-political malaise of the modern Arab world. By employing modern elements and sources in their writings they have been in a situation of contextualizing Islam. Contextuality approaches may differ one from another. Textuality and hermeneutics are also other methodological approaches used by new Muslim scholars. Some of the Muslim scholars such as Egyptian writer and intellectual Taha Husayn (1889-1973), a reformist intellectual Amin al-Khuli (d.1967), Nasr Abu Zayd accepted the Qur'an as a 'text' and applied it to historical-literal categories to make clear what the Qur'an says. These writers and intellectuals stress the role of the interpreter (Taji-Farouki 2004). It can be seen as a kind of secular view on the Qur'an by assuming that only the literary method and historiography of the text covers the meaning of the revelation. As a result of this approach, the text of the Qur'an is not considered ultimately a sacred text. This approach questions the status of the Qur'an as being an ultimate book in science, history and modern social-political problems.

The Quran in this sense can be understood as an object of aesthetic, literature, history rather than accepted as an ultimate unique source which guides Muslims. Quranic verses should be studied in the lens of socio-political human conditions. The writing of some contemporary Muslim thinkers exemplifies this hermeneutic look at the Quran. This claim finds echoes and functions with secular normativity (Mahmood 2006; Asad 2003). There is a convergence between the secular Muslim reformation idea and the liberal secular normativity that requires a particular scriptural hermeneutic understanding of religious texts. This normative secularity forces one to produce a particular kind of religion and truth which is compatible with rationality and free will (Mahmood 2006: 344). According to Mahmood, this hermeneutical project

"...is aimed at creating the conditions for the emergence of a normative religious subject who understands religion – its scriptures and its ritual forms – as a congeries of symbols to be flexibly interpreted in a manner consonant with the imperatives of secular liberal political rule. This insistence on a particularly singular relationship between subject and text is essential to what might be called *secularity*..." (Mahmood 2006: 344).

In this sense, the rituals and practices are always literalist-salafi expressions which pose a threat to the liberal western understanding of democracy (Parekh 2006). In spite of these various ways of approaching the traditional resources including modernist, reformist and traditionalist approaches, the challenging question remains: what are the boundaries of the Islamic knowledge?

In Muslim-minority countries, public intellectuals and authorities have sought to develop appropriately domesticated versions of Islam in accordance with local norms and values (see Leman 2000 for e.g. Belgium) – the vicissitudes of which John R. Bowen explored elsewhere for France (2009). The examples dealt with extensively in Bowen's study are the existence and situational manifestation of multiple levels of belonging in the Muslim community, and the idea that Muslim authority is created across boundaries. Literate young Muslims construct their religious affiliations and understanding of Islam in trans-local spaces which explore a number of issues in the study of transnational public space, such as the use of Islamic texts and discourses. In this case, the authority of discourse and Islamic text is based on highly politicized arenas such as the question of the headscarf. We can give the example of *Union des organisations islamiques de France* (UOIF) that regroups many Muslim associations in France, a Muslim intellectual Tariq Ramadan, Yusuf al-Qaradawi, the TV channel Al-Jazira. This is a transnational space in which Muslims involve themselves and try to tackle their daily questions to reformulate Islamic issues (Bowen 2004). The new patterns influence a shift not only about discourses on Islam; at the same time the daily practices lead to a new configuration of Islamic practices.

Notes

1 Post-colonial theories which emphasize the question of the non-Western historical experience of rationality and modernity come to mind. For post-colonial thinkers, liberal modern thoughts do not pay attention to the idea of polity and community which can be found also in the history of different cultures. In this vein, have Islamist and Muslim politics a distinctive kind of polity, or is it simply a translation of modernity projects into Islamic terms?

2 The term translocality, in the words of the anthropologist Appadurai (1996) specifies a geographical creation of migrant workers who have their settlement in two countries. This settlement changes their habits, everyday life experience and tradition.

References

An-Na'im, A. (1990). *Towards an Islamic Reformation. Civil Liberties, Human Rights, and International Law*, Caïro: The American University in Caïro Press.

Arkoun, M. (2005). *Humanisme et islam. Combats et propositions*, Paris, Vrin.

Asad, T. (2003). *Formations of the Secular: Christianity, Islam, Modernity*, Stanford: Stanford University Press.

Appadurai, A. (1996). *Modernity at Large, Cultural Dimensions of Globalization*, Minneapolis, University of Minnesota Press.

Basch, L., Glick-Schiller, N. and Szanton Blanc, C. (1993). *Nations Unbound: Transnational Projects, Postcolonial Predicaments, and Deterritorialized Nation-States*, Routledge.

Bayat, A. (2005). 'What is Post-Islamism?', *ISIM Review*, 16, Autumn 2005.

Bowen, John R. (2004). 'Beyond migration: Islam as a transnational public space', *Journal of Ethnic and Migration Studies*, 30(5):879–894.

Bowen, John R. (2009). *Can Islam be French? Pluralism and Pragmatism in a Secularist State*, Princeton: Princeton UniversityPress.

Bruneau, M. (2010). 'Diasporas, transnational spaces and communities', in *Diaspora and Transnationalism: Concepts, Theories and Methods*, R. Bauböck and T. Faist (eds), Amsterdam University, Amsterdam, 35-50.

Esposito, J. (1998). *Islam and Politics*, Syracuse: Syracuse University Press.

Esposito, J. and Burgat, F. (eds) (2003). *Modernizing Islam. Religion in the Public Sphere in the Middle East and Europe*, London: Hurst.

Featherstone, M. (1990). 'Global Culture: an Introduction' in M. Featherstone (ed.) *Global Culture: Nationalism, Globalization and Modernity*, London, Sage.

Filali-Ansary, A. (2003). 'What is liberal Islam? The sources of enlightened Muslim thought', *Journal of Democracy*, 14, 2, 19-33.

Glick-Schiller, N. (1997). 'The Situation of Transnational Studies', *Identities*, Vol. 4, No. 2: 155–66.

Göle, N. (2002). 'Islam in Public: New Visibilities and New Imaginaries', in *Public Culture*, v. 14, n.1: 173-190.

Kepel, G. (2002). *Jihad. The Trail of Political Islam*, London: Tauris.

Kepel, G. (2004). *The War for Muslim Minds: Islam and the West*, Cambridge, MA: Harvard University Press.

Kurzman, C. (1998). *Liberal Islam, A Source Book*, Oxford: Oxford University Press.

Lapidus, I. (2002). *A History of Islamic Societies*, Cambridge: Cambridge University Press.

Leman, J. (2000). 'Minority Leadership, Science, Symbols and the Media: The Belgian Islam Debate and its Relevance for Other Countries in Europe', Journal of International Migration and Integration, vol. 1, 3: 351-372.

Mahmood, S. (2006). 'Secularism, Hermeneutics, and Empire: The Politics of Islamic Reformation', *Public Culture*, 18.2: 323-47.

Mandaville, P. (2001). *Transnational Muslim Politics. Reimagining the Umma*, London: Routledge.

Mato, D. (1997). 'On Global and Local Agents and the Social Making of Transnational Identities and Related Agendas in 'Latin' America', *Identities*, n. 4(2).

Mawdudi, A. (1980). *The Islamic Law and Constitution*, Lahore: Islamic Publications.

Mayer, A. (1999). *Islam and Human Rights. Tradition and Politics*, Colorado: WestviewPress.

Nasr, V. (2005). 'The Rise of 'Muslim Democracy'', Journal of Democracy, 16, 1, 13-27.

Parekh, B. (2006). 'Europe, liberalism and the 'Muslim question', in *Multiculturalism, Muslims and Citizenship, A European Approach*, T. Modood, A. Triandafyllidou and R. Zapata-Barrero (eds.), Routledge, London, 179-203.

Al-Qaradawi, Y. (s.d.) *The Status of Women in Islam*, Caïro: Islamic inc. Publishing& Distribution.

Ramadan, T. (2004). *Western Muslims and the Future of Islam*, New York: Oxford University Press.

Osella, F. and Osella, C. (eds) (2009). 'Muslim entrepreneurs in public life between India and the Gulf: Making good and doing good', *Journal of the Royal Anthropological Institute* 15: 202–221.

Safi, O. (eds) (2003). *Progressive Muslims. On Justice, Gender, and Pluralism*, Oxford: Oneworld Publications.

Saint-Blancat, C. (2002). 'Islam in diaspora: Between reterritorialization and extraterritoriality', *International Journal of Urban and Regional Research* 26(1):138-151.

Salvatore, A. (2009). 'The Reform Project in the Emerging Public Sphere,' in *Islam and Modernity: key issues and debates,* S. Masud and M. van Bruinessen (eds), Edinburg: Edinburg University Press.

Sassen, S. (1991). *The Global City: New York, London, Tokyo,* Princeton University Press.

Scott, J. C. (1990). *Domination and the Arts of Resistance. Hidden Transcripts,* New Haven, CT: Yale University Press.

Taji-Farouki, S. (eds) (2004) *Modern Muslim Intellectuals and the Qur'an,* Oxford University

Vertovec, S., (1999). 'Conceiving and researching transnationalism', *Ethnic and Racial Studies,* 22-2: 447-62.

Vertovec, S. (2002). 'Diaspora, transnationalism and Islam: Sites of Change and Modes of Research', in S. Allievi, and J. Nielsen (eds), *Muslim networks and transnational communities in and across Europe.* Leiden: Brill, 312-326.

Voll J. and Esposito, John L. (2001). *Makers of Contemporary Islam,* New York City: Oxford University Press.

About the Authors

Jonathan Benthall is an Honorary Research Fellow in the Department of Anthropology, University College London. He was formerly Director of the Royal Anthropological Institute, Founder Editor of *Anthropology Today*, and Chair of the International NGO Training and Research Centre, Oxford. His published books include *Disasters, Relief and the Media* (1993, new edition 2010*)*, *The Charitable Crescent: Politics of aid in the Muslim World* (2003, with Jérôme Bellion-Jourdan, new edition 2009), and *Returning to Religion: Why a secular age is haunted by faith* (2008). In 2014, he published (with Robert Lacey as co-editor) *Gulf Charities and Islamic Philanthropy in the 'Age of Terror' and Beyond*. Between 2005 and 2013 he was an advisor to the Islamic Charities Project (formerly Montreux Initiative) sponsored by the Swiss Federal Department of Foreign Affairs.
e-mail: **jonathanbenthall@hotmail.com**

Eric Geoffroy is an expert in the Islamic religion and professor of Islamic Studies in the Department of Arabic and Islamic Studies at the University of Strasbourg. He also teaches at the Open University of Catalogna (Barcelona). He is a specialist in the study of Sufism and sanctity in Islam. His research extends to comparison of mysticism and to issues on spirituality in the contemporary world. Eric Geoffroy has published nine books, and about 20 articles in the Encyclopaedia of Islam. One of his books has been translated into English by World Wisdom (USA): *Introduction to Sufism: The Inner Path of Islam* (2010). This book won the USA Best Book Award in the "Islam/Sufism" category. Otherwise, Eric has collaborated on the English titles: *Sufism – Love & Wisdom* (World Wisdom, 2006) and *Universal Dimensions of Islam* (World Wisdom, 2011).
e-mail: **e.geoffroy7@free.fr**

Egbert Harmsen has a multidisciplinary background in Middle Eastern and Islamic Studies, with a particular stress on cultural anthropology. Since 2010, he has been an Assistant Professor Middle Eastern Studies at Leiden University, teaching mainly anthropological subjects with a special focus on Islamic thought and activism. His PhD-thesis dealt with patronage and empowerment in discourse and practice of Islamic voluntary welfare associations in Jordan, from a civil society

perspective. He has done research on Islam in the West as well, in particular, as the aspects of conversion to Islam and the role of sharia. He has also experience with sociolegal aid to asylum-seekers, refugees, other migrants and war victims in the Netherlands. The Palestinians, Jordan, (Islamic) social movements, social welfare and development and Muslim migrants are central to his academic interest.
e-mail: harmsen67@hotmail.com

Johan Leman is an MA in philosophy, theology (O.T. exegesis), oriental philology and history, and social and cultural anthropology from the KU Leuven. He is emeritus professor of social and cultural anthropology, and the Gülen Chair for intercultural studies (see gcis-kuleuven), KU Leuven. He was formerly chief of cabinet of the Royal Commissioner for Migrant Policy in Belgium (1989-1993), former director of the federal Centre for equal opportunities and the fight against racism in Belgium (1993-2003), former co-ordinator of IMMRC at Social Sciences in KU Leuven. He is currently president of Foyer, an integration centre in Brussels (www.foyer.be). For a selection of research and publications, see www.johanleman.be.
e-mail: johan.leman@soc.kuleuven.be

Thierry Limpens (b. 1971) is finishing a PhD in political sciences at Ghent University (Belgium) and preparing a PhD in social and cultural anthropology at the Catholic University of Leuven (Belgium). Of the latter university he is a double Master in religious sciences and theological ethics. His research has been on Islam and Christianity in relation to politics in Northern Nigeria. He lived in that region between 2005 and 2007 and has set up a local school project. His current field work is focused on the influence of Tariq Ramadan on emancipating Moroccan Muslim women in Brussels, Belgium. Several of his international conference contributions are in preparation for publication. Thierry Limpens is former director of the Brussels Avicenna school and ex-secretary of the al-Khalil mosque.
e-mail: thierry.limpens@soc.kuleuven.be

Roel Meijer (PhD) teaches history of the Middle East at Radboud University in Nijmegen and is the head of the Arabic section of the Middle East desk at the International Institute of Social History in Amsterdam (IISH). His main interest is in Islamist movements. He was postdoctorate fellow at the ISIM in Leiden

from 2004 to 2008, doing comparative research on Islamist movements in Iraq, Saudi Arabia and Egypt. He wrote his PhD on intellectuals and Nasser, *The Quest for Modernity: Secular Liberal and Left-wing Political Thought in Egypt, 1945-1958* (2002), is editor of four anthologies: *Cosmopolitanism, Identity and Authenticity in the Middle East* (1999), *Alienation or Integration of Arab Youth: Arab Youth between the Family, the State and the Street* (2000), *Irak in chaos. Botsende meningen over een humanitaire ramp* (2007, together with Pim van Harten), and *Global Islam: Islam's New Religious Movement*, London/New York: Hurst & Co./Columbia University Press.
e-mail: Roel-Meijer@planet.nl

Thomas Michel is professor at Georgetown University, Washington D.C. After studying Arabic and Islamic studies in Egypt and Lebanon, he completed his studies and received a doctorate in Islamic theology at the University of Chicago in the U.S.A. His doctoral thesis was directed by Professor Fazlur Rahman and entitled "Ibn Taymiyya's Al-Jawab al-Sahih: A Muslim Theologian's Critique of Christianity." In 1978, after a year teaching at Columbia University in New York, he returned to Indonesia where he taught Islamic studies at the Catholic Faculty of Theology in Sanata Dharma University and Christian theology at Islamic theological institutes. He now teaches at the School of Foreign Service of Georgetown University in Doha, Qatar.
e-mail: tfm9@georgetown.edu

Emilio Platti: after his Dominican formation at the St. Thomas Institute in Leuven, he devoted himself to theology and Oriental studies at the KU Leuven. In 1972, he joined the IDEO where he prepared his PhD in literature under the supervision of Fr. Anawati (Cairo) and Pr. Van Roey (Leuven). This PhD would later give rise to the publication of many works about the Jacobite theologian and philosopher Yahyâ Ibn 'Adî and about the Arab Christian medieval heritage. From 1980 to 2010, he taught at the KULeuven, the UCL (Louvain-la-Neuve), US Thomas (Manila) and at the Catholic Institute of Paris. His teachings are mainly geared towards the relationships between Christianism and Islam. He has published several books among which *Islam, étrange?* and *Islam, Friend or Foe?* have been edited and translated into many languages.
e-mail: emilio.platti@theo.kuleuven.be

Erkan Toğuşlu is Assistant Professor in Gülen Chair for Intercultural Studies and Interculturalism, Migration and Minorities Research Center at KU Leuven University. He received his MA and PhD in sociology from Ecole des Hautes Etudes en Sciences Sociales (EHESS) in Paris. His research focuses on transnational Muslim networks in Europe, the emergence of Islamic intellectuals, interfaith dialogue, the debate on public-private Islam, the nexus immigration and religion. He is the author of: *New Multicultural Identities in Europe*, (Leuven University Press, 2014, co-edited with J. Leman and I. M. Sezgin); *Société civil, démocratie et islam: perspectives du mouvement Gülen*, (Paris: L'Harmattan, 2013); and *European Public Sphere, Islam and Islamic authority: Tariq Ramadan and Fethullah Gülen*, in: Weller P., Yilmaz I. (eds.), *European Muslims, Civility and Public Life. Perspectives On and From the Gülen Movement*, (Continuum, 2012). **e-mail: Erkan.toguslu@soc.kuleuven.be**

Ihsan Yilmaz is Associate Professor of Political Science at Fatih University, Istanbul, Turkey where he is also the Director of the PhD Programme in Political Science and International Relations. He received his BA in Political Science and International Relations from the Bosporus University in 1994 and completed his PhD at the Faculty of Law and Social Sciences, School of Oriental and African Studies (SOAS), University of London in 1999. He then worked at the University of Oxford as a Fellow between 1999 and 2001 and taught Turkish government and politics, legal sociology, comparative law and Islamic law at SOAS, University of London between 2001 and 2008. He is the author of *Muslim Laws, Politics and Society in Modern Nation States: Dynamic Legal Pluralisms in England, Turkey and Pakistan* (Aldershot, Ashgate, 2005). He is the editor of *Turkish Journal of Politics* (TJP). He is a regular columnist of *Today's Zaman*, an English language daily published in Turkey. His current research interests are Islam-constitutional law-human rights; and Federal Shariat Court of Pakistan. **e-mail: ihsanyilmaz@yahoo.com; iyilmaz@fatih.edu.tr**